THE
HISTORY and CONSTITUTIONS

OF THE

Moſt ancient and honourable Fraternity

OF

Free and Accepted MASONS:

CONTAINING

An ACCOUNT of MASONRY. I. From the Creation, throughout the known Earth, till true Architecture was demoliſhed by the *Goths*, and at laſt revived in *Italy*. II. From *Julius Cæſar* to the firſt Arrival of the *Saxons* in *Britain*. III. From the Union of the Crowns of *England* and *Scotland*, in the Perſon of King *James* the Firſt, to the preſent Time.

To WHICH ARE ADDED

I. A Liſt of the GRAND MASTERS or Patrons of the Free Maſons in *England*, from the coming in of the *Anglo Saxons* to theſe Times, who are mentioned in this Work.

II. The old Charges of the Maſons, collected from their earlieſt Records, at the Command of his Grace the Duke of *Montague*.

III. The Manner of conſtituting a Lodge.

IV. The general Regulations of the free and accepted Maſons, both ancient and modern, in diſtinct Columns.

V. The Conſtitution of the Committee of their Charity.

VI. A Liſt of the Lodges in and about *London* and *Weſtminſter*; with the Deputations of ſeveral grand Maſters for the forming of Lodges in *Wales*, the remote Parts of *England*, and ſo reign Realms.

VII. The Songs ſung at the Lodges.

VIII. A Defence of Maſonry, occaſioned by a Pamphlet called *Maſonry Diſſected*: With Brother *Euclid*'s Letter to the Author againſt unjuſt Cavils.

By *JAMES ANDERSON* D. D.

LONDON: Printed; and ſold by J. ROBINSON, at the *Golden-Lion* in *Ludgate-ſtreet*.

In the vulgar Year of MASONRY 5746

INTRODUCTION.

HE first "Book of Constitutions" for the premier Grand Lodge was published in 1723, and was by the Rev. James Anderson. As Dr. J. T. Desaguliers wrote the Dedication, his name has been quoted as the Editor, but in error, for in the list of twenty Masters (with their Wardens) who united with the Grand Master and Grand Officers in their approbation of the volume, the 17th Lodge has conspicuously displayed, "JAMES ANDERSON, A.M., The Author of this Book."

The Society then was called the "Right Worshipful FRATER-NITY of Accepted Free MASONS," but towards the end of the book the more lengthy and appropriate title is noted of "The Right Worshipful and most ancient *Fraternity* of *Free* and *Accepted Masons*." Another change is observable in the second edition of 1738 by James Anderson, D.D., the words "Antient and Honourable" being introduced.

The original Regulations, numbered I. to XXXIX. were "Compiled first by Mr. George Payne, *Anno* 1720, when he was Grand Master," but were "digested" and arranged by the "*Author* of this Book, for the Use of the Lodges in and about *London* and *Westminster*."[1] From 1724, Lodges were constituted in the Provinces, and from 1728-9 also abroad, so that the Laws soon needed considerable revision and additions. Accordingly, at the Grand Lodge on February 24th, 1735,

> "Bro. Dr. Anderson, formerly Grand Warden, represented
> that he had spent some thoughts upon some alterations
> and additions that might fittly be made to the
> Constitutions, the first Edition being all sold off.
> *Resolved.* That a Committee be appointed * * * * *
> to revise and compare the same," etc.[2]

The "*New* Book of *Constitutions*" was approved by the Grand Lodge, and the members "order'd the Author Brother *Anderson* to print the same," on January 25th, 1738. In the work Dr. Anderson is supposed to have reprinted the "Old REGULATIONS," and added "the New REGULATIONS in a distinct opposite Column," but even a cursory examination of the former, side by side, with the first edition of 1723, will reveal the fact that the reproduction was not only carelessly done, but in several instances distinct departures from the original text are to be detected, so much so as to considerably lessen the value of the reprint. The unwarrantable alterations are just those which tend to introduce Masonic terms, *as of* 1723, which were then unfamiliar or unknown, such as "Master Mason" instead of "Fellow Craft;" hence due care must be exercised in accepting any part of the reproduction of these Rules as being in exact accord with the originals.

There is thus no lack of confirmation of the statement in Scott's "Pocket Companion," (1754, etc.), that the "Constitutions of 1738 appeared in a very mangled condition." But whatever may be its merits or demerits, according as we look at the volume leniently or critically, the fact remains that to it, and to it alone, we are indebted for a history of the Grand Lodge of England from its inauguration in 1717 to 1723, when the official Records begin, and from that period for an able extract of the Proceedings; hence the work has been described as the "*basis of Masonic History*" by Professor Robison, and its author is termed by the Rev. A. F. A. Woodford "*the Father of English Masonic History*," both titles being fairly earned in respect to the sketch of the premier Grand Lodge.

The importance of the work, united with its admitted scarcity, sufficiently justify the Committee in selecting it as one of the series of Reprints which are a special feature of the

---

[1] Constitutions 1723, p. 58. (*Lodge Catalogue* No. 1074.)
[2] Bro. Gould's "History of Freemasonry," chapter xii. (*Catalogue* No. 242, etc.)

" Quatuor Coronati " Lodge, and contribute considerably to its usefulness as a Masonic organization.

The major portion of the Historical Chapters " from the Creation " to the " Grand Mastership of Sir Christopher Wren," had better be left in the hands of those brethren who care to test the statement of the compiler that " most of the Facts are generally well known in *Sacred*, *Civil*, and *Ecclesiastical* Histories," and likewise that the omission of any " necessary vouchers " is supplied by an " *exact Chronology*."

As to these points, as Dr. Anderson observes, " It is good to know what not to say ;" but unfortunately his practice was quite the reverse of the advice he gave, " from his *Study* in 𝕰𝖝𝖊𝖙𝖊𝖗 𝕮𝖔𝖚𝖗𝖙, *Strand*, 4th November, 1738," on completing the Address " to the Reader."

The extracts from the " Old Charges " of the mainly operative *régime* in the two editions of the " Constitutions " call for a few words of explanation. The first excerpt, relative to St. Alban, p. 57 edit. 1738, was not in the original issue, and seems to have been taken from " A Book of the Antient Constitutions of the Free and Accepted Masons," engraved and published by B. Cole, 1728-9, and also in 1731. Very few of the Scrolls have the wages noted at so low a rate as " *two shillings a week and three pence to their chear*," and it is probable that only one or two of these, which agree with Cole and Anderson, were known to the latter Brother. Not one, however, of all the versions of the " Old Charges, etc.," traced and collated of late years and numbering over fifty (ranging from the 14th to the present century), confirm the pernicious interpolation of that modern title, " *Grand Master*," made by Dr. Anderson, who was lamentably prone to modernize the phraseology of ancient documents, and alter them to suit his whims, whenever he had occasion to cite their testimony.

The second extract (page 63) is somewhat after the style of the 1723 edition, only that now Edwin is described as the " King's Brother," according to the " Inigo Jones' " and " Cole's " texts ; whereas formerly that Prince was termed the " King's youngest son," thus favouring the reading of " Roberts' MS.," 1722, " Briscoe's MS.," 1724-5, and most other texts, manuscript and printed. Possibly Anderson preferred to follow the lead of Dr. Plot in his " History of Staffordshire," 1686, which work may not have been known to him in the year 1723. In this garbled extract the " General Lodge " of 1723 is altered to " Grand Lodge," and the year 926 is added. The " Inigo Jones MS." has 932 ; no more evidence existing for the one than the other, as the MSS. generally are silent as to the date.

The third quotation (page 71) immediately follows the foregoing citation, in the 1723 edition ; nothing being said about " *the glorious Reign of* KING EDWARD III." The fourth and two succeeding paragraphs in the 2nd edition occur in a foot note in the senior publication, with the intimation that they were taken from " another transcript more ancient."

The document thus noted was probably one of the " old Copies of the *Gothic Constitutions* produced and collated " in 1718[1] ; possibly the " Matthew Cooke MS.,"[2] which in 1728 was copied by Grand Secretary Cowper, who styled it " a very ancient Record of Masonry."[3] This handsome transcript, known as " Woodford's MS.," is now the property of our Lodge, No. 2076.[4] On June 24th, 1721, Dr. Stukeley states in his Diary, " Grand Master Pain [Payne] produced an old MS. of the Constitutions," and exhibited it to the members of Grand Lodge. Dr. Stukeley copied the opening sentences, which are still preserved, and from these we know that it was the " Cooke MS.," or a similar text.[5] The most important extract from the " Old Charges " occurs at page 101, but is not in the 1723 edition. The first typographical reproduction of these Regulations was by Roberts in 1722, in which rare pamphlet they are entitled,

> " Additional Orders and Constitutions made and agreed
> upon at a General Assembly held at   . . . . . .
> on the Eighth Day of December, 1663."

I daresay Roberts supplied the above title, but in what may fairly be classed as the original text, viz., the " Harleian MS., No. 1942 " (British Museum) these Rules are simply termed " The New Articles,"[6] and are peculiar to that Codex. Dr. Anderson apparently was not satisfied with the date selected, so changed it to " St. John's Day, 27th Dec., 1663," in order to give it a Masonic flavour ! This, however, is far from being the most serious of

---

[1] *Constitutions*, 1738, p. 110.   [2] Vol 2 " Quatuor Coronatorum Antigrapha."
[3] Hughan's " Old Charges of British Freemasons," 1872, p. 4. (*Catalogue* No. 239.)
[4] No. 253 in *Catalogue*.   [5] Bro. T. B. Whytehead, " Freemason," 31st July, 1880.
[6] O.C. p. 56, and Q.C. Antigrapha, Vol. 2.

the alterations and departures from the " Harleian MS."[1] or of the " Roberts' " pamphlet. Clause 1 has added, "*unless in a regular Lodge*," and in the 5th " *Master* " is transformed into " *Grand Master*," whilst the 7th is omitted !

Into the larger question of the actual age of the " Harleian MS., No. 1942," or of the " Inigo Jones MS.," I must not now enter, save to state that the latter part of the 17th century appears to me a very safe estimate. The period of fifty years earlier has been assigned to the former by a very eminent paleographist, but Dr. Begemann favours a much later date for both these MSS. At present, however, I can only refer my readers to the arguments of that industrious Masonic student,[2] and to a careful consideration of the texts of both documents.

Dr. Anderson undoubtedly consulted several copies of the " Old Charges " whilst preparing the 2nd edition of his " Book of Constitutions." These or similar versions are still preserved, and are well known to Masonic experts. To them may possibly be added the " Aberdeen MS." of A.D. 1670 (the unusual reference to " Ninus," page 16, agreeing with that document), and also the missing York MS. of A.D. 1630.[3]

The author did not think enough of the Abraham-Euclid legend to cite it (both of these old worthies, however, are incidentally alluded to), though common to all the regular MSS. except the " Lansdowne " and " Antiquity." The order of the " Seven Liberal Sciences " accords with nearly all the complete Masonic MSS. known, and so does the paragraph concerning CHARLES MARTEL and his Teacher *Mimus Græcus* (with variations), the few exceptions as to the latter legend (" Inigo Jones " family or group) scarcely requiring particularization.

Happily, in due time, the whole of the valuable copies of the " Old Charges " of English and Scottish Freemasons (which communicate light and information during centuries when the minutes of Lodges are silent), will be reproduced, with scrupulous exactitude, by the " Quatuor Coronati " Lodge, and then intelligent and earnest Craftsmen throughout the " wide, wide world " will be able to study those ancient documents for themselves, both in relation to this work of 1738, and to the much more important and extensive question of the usages and customs of the Freemasons during the past five centuries and still earlier times. We are already being prepared to welcome such extensive publications and reproductions by the scholarly labours of Bro. R. F. Gould in relation to the " Regius MS."[4] (the venerable senior of the series), and the able services of Bro. G. W. Speth in relation to the second oldest document, the " Matthew Cooke MS."[5]

" The Charges of a Free-Mason," which introduce the " General Regulations " of 1723, are mainly to be found in the 2nd edition of 1738, but again the insatiable desire of Anderson to modernize and alter is conspicuously manifest. Strictly speaking, the second issue is not the same as that " Ordered to be printed in the first Edition of the Book of Constitutions on 25 March 1722," though the compiler says otherwise. The first charge, concerning " God and Religion," is an old favourite, and substantially remains to this day, save in the vexatious alterations in the 1738 edition. No better exposition, in brief, of the true basis of the Fraternity, or description of its aims and tendency, has ever been written.

Of course, these Charges, which preface the Laws from 1723 onwards, were not actually " collected by the Author from the old Records of the Free and Accepted Masons," but were the composition of Dr. Anderson, who thus produced, in modern verbiage, a more or less accurate digest of the Laws that formerly governed the Lodges.

The Dedication to H.R.H. the Prince of Wales, " A *Master* MASON, and *Master* of a LODGE," was by order of the Grand Master and the Grand Lodge. The Author had the honour of an introduction to the Prince early in 1739, and in the name of the Fraternity presented a copy of the new Book of Constitutions to His Royal Highness, which was graciously accepted.

It is remarkable that " the geniuses to whom the world is indebted for the memorable invention of Modern Masonry " *in* 1717, according to Bro. Thomas Grinsell (*cited by Bro. Laurence Dermott* in the " Ahiman Rezon," 1778, etc., and declared to be " a man of great veracity ") were the brethren who were present at the palace of Kew, and formed the

---

[1] Vide Reproduction of the Harleian MS., No. 1942, Vol. 2 " Quatuor Coronatorum Antigrapha."
[2] " Freemason," July 9th and 16th, 1887. Transactions, Vol. 1.
[3] Hargroves " History of York," Vol. 2, 1818, pp. 475-480.
[4] Commentary, Vol. 1, " Masonic Reprints."
[5] Introduction to the " Matthew Cooke MS." etc., Vol. 2, M.R.

" occasional Lodge" for the initiation of H.R.H. Frederic, Prince of Wales, *on 5th Nov.,* 1737 ! From 1778 to 1881 no one seems to have detected the anachronism, but in the latter year Bro. Gould ably exposed the treacherous memory of Dermott's friend and completely shattered the pretentious declaration.[1]

When and where Dr. Anderson was born we know not, and we are in like ignorance as to his initiation. Bro. Gould thinks he may have first " seen the light " at Aberdeen, and there is much to favour that supposition, though no actual facts. Anderson certainly was familiar with Scottish phraseology, and in all probability the visit of Dr. Desaguliers, F.R.S. to Edinburgh in 1721 for scientific purposes contributed also to the same result. Of " the creationist school of Masonic Historians he is the *facile princeps*,"[2] but those who would discard his labours on that account would commit a grave error, as it is not difficult to distinguish between his facts and his fancies, and the value of the former to a great extent counterbalances the frequency of the latter.

The Rev. James Anderson was the minister of the Scottish Presbyterian Church, Swallow Street, Piccadilly, and known to fame as the author of the " Royal Genealogies," 1732 (2nd edition, 1736). He was Master of a Lodge as early as 1722, was appointed J.G.W. by the Duke of Wharton, G.M., on 17th January, 1723, and was a member of the Lodge known as " Original No. 4 " (*now* No. 4), with his friends Grand Masters Payne and Desaguliers. As the author of the Constitutions 1723-38, and for his devotion to the Fraternity his name will be gratefully remembered so long as Freemasonry exists. Dr. Anderson's last appearance in Grand Lodge was on April 6th, 1738, when he acted as J.G.W., and his death occurred on May 28th, 1739. He was described in the latter year as " a gentleman of uncommon abilities and most facetious conversation."[3] Dr. Desaguliers was equally devoted to the Craft, his last attendance in Grand Lodge being on Feb. 8th, 1742, his death occurring just two years later (Feb. 29th). The third of the zealous trio, George Payne, was present in Grand Lodge so late as November 29th, 1754, and was appointed on the Committee for the revision of the Constitutions 1738, (April, 1754), preparatory to the publication of the 3rd edition of 1756. He died soon afterwards, viz., on Jan. 23rd, 1757.

Bro. Gould's noble *History* should be consulted as to the period 1717-38, particularly in relation to these three respected Masonic veterans, for, much as I should wish, any attempt to dwell on that interesting subject must resolutely be deferred.

It only remains for me now to say a few brief words on the bibliographical aspect of the question. First of all, the edition of the " Book of Constitutions " for 1723 claims attention.[4] It became the model or standard of all the Laws of the Craft promulgated by other Grand Lodges, was reprinted in Philadelphia, U.S.A., so soon as 1734, by Bro. Benjamin Franklin, and also reproduced in other Regulations abroad, being accepted almost as veritable " Old Landmarks." An excellent reprint of this very scarce book is to be found in Bro. Kenning's " Archæological Library," Vol. I., which includes a reproduction of one of the " Phillipps' MSS." of the 17th century.[5] Another capital reissue of the work forms one of Bro. Spencer's " Old Constitutions,"[6] 1871, which also contains the " Roberts' MS." of 1722, " Spencer's " 1726 *circa* (" Cole's " text), and the Laws of the Grand Lodge of Ireland for 1730.

The 2nd edition of 1738 *has never been reprinted in this country*, and the reproduction by Bro. Hyneman in America was poorly and imperfectly done, so that virtually this is the first of the kind worthy of the name. It is in *exact facsimile*, by Charles Praetorius, Clareville Grove, Hereford Sq., S.W. The process is so perfect that had it been printed on paper of the period it would almost pass as the original work.

As a few were left on hands of the publishers in either 1742 or 1746, but most likely the latter year (" Year of Masonry, 5746 "), a new title page was inserted in lieu of the one of 1738, of rather an elaborate character, which by my desire Bro. Speth has had reproduced, and which faces p. v., supplied from Bro. John Lane's copy, who fraternally placed it at the Editor's disposal. Save in this respect, through possibly a change of publishers, the 1738 and 1746 are one and the same work, the latter being the rarer of the two. I have only succeeded in tracing twenty-six of the original issue, and nineteen of the one with the new title page, making forty-five in all, (about one-third " large paper " and two-thirds " small paper,") of which eleven of each have been reported as having Frontispieces the same

[1] " Freemason," Feb. 12th and April 9th, 1831.   [2] Gould, Vol. 1 p. 105.
[3] " Scot's Magazine," 1739, Vol. 1, p. 236.
[4] One of the original edition, with Frontispiece, is in the Library of the " Quatuor Coronati " Lodge (*Catalogue* No. 1074).   [5] Cat. No. 1085.   [6] Cat. No. 944.

as those of 1723, only without the lettering at foot.[1] These are located in England and the United States, so that probably there are a few more in existence elsewhere.

Bro. John E. Le Feuvre (who has a complete set of the Constitutions 1723-1888),[2] kindly lent his copy of A.D. 1738, having the Frontispiece, for reproduction in our series of Reprints, and I feel assured this tangible proof of his interest in the spread of Masonic literature will be warmly appreciated by all the members of the "Inner" and "Outer" Circles of the "Quatuor Coronati" Lodge.

From internal evidence, I do not think this edition was out of the hands of the printers until early in 1739.[3]

Bro. W. H. Rylands has directed my attention to the leaf pp. 129-30, which was substituted for one cancelled in consequence of its errors. I had not noticed it, neither has anyone else to my knowledge. In his copy, curiously enough, he found, attached to the cover, the central part of the confiscated leaf, which shows some of the errors, such as "STEPHEN," instead of "FRANCIS, Duke of *Lorrain*," and also some other mistakes.

Bro. Rylands tells me that in the "History of the Works of the Learned for the year 1739," (issued in November) vol. II., pp. 317-352, is a long series of extracts from this Book of Constitutions, but not a review proper. It is headed "An incorrect Sketch of this Article was communicated to us by Dr. Anderson himself, a little before his Decease."

The "Defence of Masonry," in answer to Prichard's "Masonry Dissected," is supposed to have been originally published in 1730, but no copy of that date is known. The edition reprinted in the first volume of the "Quatuor Coronatorum Antigrapha" was taken from the "Pocket Companion" of 1738, which was doubtless printed and circulated in the year named, and consequently prior to the publication of the "Constitutions" of 1738. As to its authorship, which is uncertain, I must again forbear extending the limits of this introduction, but evidently Dr. Anderson did not write it, though he has been credited with so doing. Neither do we know who wrote Euclid's letter.

The 3rd edition of the "Book of Constitutions" edited by the Rev. John Entick, was published in 1756, and the 4th in 1767, both having a frontispiece by B. Cole, the Arms of the Grand Lodge forming a special feature of the design. In 1776 an Appendix was issued, written by Bro. William Preston, but now rarely met with. An unauthorized edition was published in 1769 (8vo.) by G. Kearsly, London, and, with another title page and plates, by Thomas Wilkinson, Dublin, in the same year.

The 5th edition is a volume of noble proportions, and though published in 1784, the plate by Bros. Bartolozzi, Cipriani, etc., does not appear to have been ready before 1786. It was edited by Bro. John Noorthouck, and is the last that contains either the long Historical Introduction, or the Transactions of the Grand Lodge and other particulars.[4]

The 6th edition of 1815[5] was the first after the "Union" of December 27th, 1813, and with the 7th of 1819 (corrected sheets) and 8th of 1827 were entitled "Second Part," the first portion containing the Historical Summary, being deferred, but ultimately was dropt, so that the 9th edition of 1841 began the regular series, since continued, with the plates of jewels, etc. The year 1819 saw the last of the quarto series. The 10th, 11th, and 12th editions were published in 1847, 1853, and 1855, respectively, the last mentioned being also issued in 32mo., termed "a Pocket Edition,"—but is very rare now.

The 13th of 1858, and 14th of 1861 are still often to be met with, the junior of the two commencing their sale at the reduced price of 1/6 each. The 15th, of 1863, is now difficult to procure, especially in the larger size, though 2000 were published in 8vo. and 4000 in 32mo. Two editions in 32mo., of 1865 and 1866, (16th and 17th) are very scarce, particularly the former, only two having been traced quite recently. In 1867 the 18th, and in 1871 the 19th appeared, followed in 1873 by the 20th. An entirely new issue began in 1884, being the 21st; the "Book of Constitutions" having been thoroughly revised and re-arranged, after considerable labour was bestowed on its compilation by the Board of General Purposes, and a draft of the proposed revision was circulated by order of the Grand

---

[1] *Vide* letter by Bro. Le Feuvre, "Freemason," Oct. 9th, 1886.
[2] Exhibited at the Plymouth Masonic Exhibition, June 27th, 1887 (*Catalogue* No. 109).
[3] See Bro. Lane's "Handy Book to the Lists of Lodges, 1723-1814" (pp. 35-8) as to this point, and also concerning the Roll of Lodges given by Dr. Anderson, pp. 185-196. (*Catalogue* No. 901).
[4] I gave a brief sketch of the "Constitutions 1723-1888" in the "Freemason," Sept. 15th, 1888, and at more length in a series of articles in that paper for 1886. (*Catalogue* No. 582).
[5] Reprinted in Hughan's "Memorials of the Union," (1872).

Lodge, June 7th, 1882.   Meetings of that Body were held on June 29th and August 8th, 1883, and on 5th December following the revision was settled to the complete satisfaction of the many concerned.   Although 10,000 were printed of the 8vo. and 20,000 of the 32mo. sizes, another edition was soon demanded, and was issued A.D. 1888, in 32mo., (slips were inserted in those that remained of the 8vo. edition) thus making twenty-two editions in all from 1723 to 1888.   I have already alluded to a complete set being owned by Bro. Le Feuvre ; another was also exhibited by Bro. George Taylor at the Masonic Exhibition, Shanklin, September 1886.[1]   I am not aware that any other brethren have been so fortunate.

It may be as well to state that the Regulations published for the " Ancient " Grand Lodge or " Atholl Masons," and known as the " Ahiman Rezon," were eight in number, viz., I. 1756 ; II. 1764 ; III. 1778 ; IV. 1787 ; V. 1800 ; VI. 1801 ; VII. 1807 ; VIII. 1813 ; the last two having Lists of Lodges.

W. J. HUGHAN.

---

[1] *Lodge Catalogue* No. 324

THE
NEW BOOK

OF

CONSTITUTIONS

OF THE

Antient and *Honourable* Fraternity

OF

FREE and Accepted MASONS.

CONTAINING

Their *History, Charges, Regulations,* &c.

COLLECTED and DIGESTED

By Order of the GRAND LODGE from their old *Records,*
faithful *Traditions* and *Lodge-Books,*

For the Use of the LODGES.

By JAMES ANDERSON D. D.

LONDON:
Printed for Brothers CÆSAR WARD and RICHARD CHANDLER,
Bookfellers, at the *Ship* without *Temple-Bar* ; and fold at their
Shops in *Coney-Street,* YORK, and at SCARBOROUGH-SPAW.
M DCC XXXVIII.
In the *Vulgar* Year of 𝕸𝖆𝖋𝖔𝖓𝖗𝖞 5738.

J. Pine sculp.

TO THE

Most *High*, *Puissant* and most *Illustrious* PRINCE

FRIDERICK LEWIS,

Prince *Royal* of GREAT-BRITAIN,

Prince and Stewart of SCOTLAND,

PRINCE of *WALES*,

Electoral Prince of Brunswick-Luneburg,

Duke of *Cornwall*, *Rothsay*, and *Edinburgh*,

Marquis of the *Isle of Ely*,

Earl of *Chester* and *Flint*, *Eltham* and *Carrick*,

Viscount *Launceston*,

Lord of the *Isles*, *Kyle* and *Cunningham*,

Baron of *Snaudon* and *Renfrew*,

Knight of the most noble Order of the Garter,

Fellow of the *Royal* Society,

A *Master* MASON, and *Master* of a LODGE.

GREAT SIR,

GREAT SIR,

HE *Marquis* of CAERNARVON our Right Worſhipful GRAND MASTER, with his 𝕯𝖊𝖕𝖚𝖙𝖞 and 𝖜𝖆𝖗𝖉𝖊𝖓𝖘, and the *Fraternity*, have ordered me their Author humbly to dedicate, in their Name, this their Book of 𝕮𝖔𝖓𝖘𝖙𝖎𝖙𝖚𝖙𝖎𝖔𝖓𝖘 to Your ROYAL HIGHNESS.

It was peruſed and approved by the former and preſent *Grand* Officers, and was order'd to be publiſh'd by our late *Grand Maſter* the Earl of DARNLEY with his 𝕯𝖊𝖕𝖚𝖙𝖞 and 𝖂𝖆𝖗𝖉𝖊𝖓𝖘, and by the GRAND LODGE in his *Maſterſhip.*

Your ROYAL HIGHNESS well knows, that our *Fraternity* has been often patronized by *Royal* Perſons in former Ages; whereby *Architecture* early obtain'd the Title of the 𝕽𝖔𝖞𝖆𝖑 𝕬𝖗𝖙: And the *Free-Maſons* have always endeavour'd to deſerve that Patronage by their Loyalty.

For

For we meddle not with Affairs of State in our *Lodges*, nor with any Thing that may give Umbrage to Civil *Magistrates*, that may break the Harmony of our own *Communications*, or that may weaken the *Cement* of the LODGE.

And whatever are our different Opinions in other Things (leaving all Men to Liberty of Confcience) as *Masons* we harmoniously agree in the noble *Science* and the *Royal Art*, in the *Social* Virtues, in being *True* and *Faithful*, and in avoiding what may give Offence to any Powers round the Globe, under whom we can peaceably affemble in *Ample Form*; as now we happily do in thefe Iflands under Your *Royal Father*, and our Sovereign *Lord*

King GEORGE II.

The *Fraternity* being All duly fenfible of the very great Honour done them by your becoming their ROYAL *Brother* and *Patron*, have commanded me thus to fignify their Gratitude, their brotherly Love to your *Royal* Perfon, and

their

DEDICATION.

their humble Duty to Your *Royal* PRINCESS, wishing her to be the happy Mother of many *Sons*, whose Descendants shall also prove the Patrons of the *Fraternity* in all future Ages.

In this the *Free* and *Accepted* 𝕸𝖆𝖘𝖔𝖓𝖘 are unanimous, and none can more heartily wish it, than in all Humility,

GREAT SIR,

Your ROYAL HIGHNESS's.

True and *Faithful*

James Anderson.

The *Author* to the *Reader*.

THE FREE-MASONS had always a Book in *Manuscript* call'd the *Book* of **Constitutions,** (of which they have several very antient Copies remaining) containing not only their *Charges* and *Regulations*, but also the History of *Architecture* from the Beginning of Time; in order to shew the Antiquity and Excellency of the *Craft* or *Art*, and how it gradually arose upon its solid Foundation the noble *Science* of GEOMETRY, by the Encouragement of *Royal*, *Noble* and *Learned* Patrons in every Age and in all polite Nations.

But they had no *Book* of **Constitutions** in Print, till his *Grace* the present Duke of MONTAGU, when *Grand Master*, order'd me to peruse the old *Manuscripts*, and digest the **Constitutions** with a just *Chronology*.

This *new* Book is above twice as large, having many proper Additions, especially the principal Transactions of the *Grand Lodge* ever since.

The History is now in three Parts, and each Part in seven Chapters, *viz.*

PART I.

The *History* of MASONRY from the *Creation* throughout the known Earth, till good old *Architecture*, demolish'd by the **Goths**, was revived in *Italy*.

Part

NEXT,

NEXT,

Moft regular Societies have had, and will have, their own *Secrets*; and, to be fure, the *Free-Mafons* always had theirs, which they never divulged in *Manufcript*; and therefore cannot be expected in *Print*: Only, an expert Brother, by the true Light, can readily find many ufeful Hints in almoft every Page of this Book, which *Cowans,* and Others not Initiated, cannot difcern.

It had been tedious, and of no great Ufe, to have pointed at all the *Authors* confulted and collated in compiling the *Hiftory* of this Book; efpecially as moft of the Facts are generally well known in *Sacred, Civil* and *Ecclefiaftical* Hiftories: Only fome Authors are quoted as more neceffary Vouchers. But the Omiffion is well enough fupply'd by an exact *Chronology,* viz.

The

The *Hebrew* CHRONOLOGY before the *Christian Era*, according to Ufher, Spanheim, Prideaux, and other such accurate *Chronologers*. And after the *Christian Era* begins, the *History* is here deduced according to the Vulgar *Anno Domini*, or the Year of the *Christian Era*; as on the Margin of Page 2.

Some few *Genealogies* are put in the Margin (not to hinder the Reader) that are needful for the Connection of the History. But in PART II. and III. they shew more distinctly how the *Craft* has been well encouraged in the several Periods and Successions of the *Saxon*, *Danish*, *Norman*, *Plantagenet*, *Welch* and *Scots* Kings of *England*, down to the present ROYAL *Family*.

But the *History* here chiefly concerns MASONRY, without meddling with other Transactions, more than what only serves to connect the *History* of MASONRY, the strict Subject of this Book. It is good to know WHAT NOT TO SAY! Candid *Reader*, farewell.

From my *Study* in
Exeter=Court, *Strand*.
4 Nov. 1738.

James Anderson.

The SANCTION.

WHEREAS on 25 *Nov.* 1723. the *Grand Lodge* in *ample* Form refolved, *That no Alterations fhall be made in their printed Book of* CONSTITUTIONS *without Leave of the Grand Lodge* :

And *whereas* fome have written and printed Books and Pamphlets relating to the Fraternity without Leave of the Grand Lodge; fome of which have been condemn'd as pyratical and ftupid by the *Grand Lodge* in *Ample* Form on 24 *Feb.* 173¾. when the Brethren were warned *not to ufe them nor encourage them to be fold* :

And *whereas* on 25 *January* 173⅞. the laft *Grand Mafter* the Earl of DARNLEY, with his *Deputy* and *Wardens*, and the *Grand Lodge*, after due Approbation, order'd our Brother *Anderfon*, the Author, to print and publifh this our *new Book* of CONSTITUTIONS, which they recommended as *the only Book for the Ufe of the* Lodges, as appears by their APPROBATION, Page 199.

Therefore we. alfo, the *prefent* GRAND MASTER, Deputy and Wardens, do hereby RECOMMEND this our *new printed Book* as the *only Book of* CONSTITUTIONS, to the *Free* and *Accepted* MASONS; and difclaiming all other Books, that have not the Sanction of the *Grand Lodge*, we warn all the Brethren againft being employ'd or concern'd in writing and fpreading, printing and publifhing *any other Books* relating to *Mafons* or *Mafonry*, and againft ufing *any other Book* in any *Lodge* as a *Lodge-Book*, as they fhall be anfwerable to the Grand Lodge.

CAERNARVON, Grand Mafter,
JOHN WARD, *Deputy* Grand Mafter,
GEORGE GRAHAM, ⎱ Grand
ANDREW ROBINSON, ⎰ Wardens.

John Rebis,
Secretary.

Frater J.ᵉ Thornhill Eq. inv.   I. Pine Sculp.

The Right Honourable
the Marquis of Carnarvon
Gentleman of the Bed-Chamber to His
Royal Highnefs the Prince of Wales
and Kᵗ. of the most Honᵇˡᵉ Order of the Bath.

A.D.1738.   Grand Master.   A.L.5738.

THE
CONSTITUTIONS

OF THE

Right Worshipful FRATERNITY

OF THE

Free and Accepted MASONS.

Collected from their old *Records* and faithful *Traditions.*

TO BE READ

At the Admiffion of a NEW BROTHER, when the *Mafter* or *Warden* fhall begin, or order fome other Brother to read, as follows.

PART I.

The Hiftory of Mafonry *from the* Creation *throughout the known* Earth ; *till true old* Architecture *was demolifh'd by the* 𝔊𝔬𝔱𝔥𝔰 *and at laft Revived in* Italy.

CHAPTER I.

From the Creation *to* 𝔊𝔯𝔞𝔫𝔡 𝔐𝔞𝔰𝔱𝔢𝔯 NIMROD.

THE ALMIGHTY Architect and *Grand-Mafter* of the Univerfe having created all Things very Good and according to *Geometry*, laft of all formed ADAM after his own Image, ingraving on his Heart the faid noble Science; which *Adam* foon difcover'd by furveying his Earthly Paradife and the Fabrication of the *Arbour* or Silvan Lodgment that God had prepared

B
for

for him, a well proportion'd and convenient Place of Shelter from Heat, and of Retirement, Reſt, and Repaſt after his wholeſome Labour in cultivating his Garden of Delights, and the firſt *Temple* or Place of Worſhip, agreeable to his original, perfect and innocent State.   *A. M.* or Year of the World   1 ⎫
         * *B. C.* or before the Chriſtian Era 4003 ⎭

But tho' by Sin *Adam* fell from his original happy State, and was expell'd from his lovely *Arbour* and Earthly *Paradiſe* into the wide World, he ſtill retain'd great Knowledge, eſpecially in GEOMETRY; and its Principles remaining in the Hearts of his Offspring, have in Proceſs of Time been drawn forth in a convenient Method of Propoſitions, according to the Laws of Proportion taken from *Mechaniſm*: and as the *Mechanical* Arts gave occaſion to the Learned to reduce the Elements of *Geometry* into Method; ſo this noble *Science*, thus reduced and methodized, is now the Foundation of all thoſe Arts (eſpecially of *Architecture*) and the Rule by which they are conducted and finiſh'd.

ADAM, when expell'd, reſided in the moſt convenient natural Abodes of the Land of *Eden*, where He could be beſt ſhelter'd

---

* The firſt *Chriſtians* computed their Times as the Nations did among whom They lived till *A. D.* 532. when

Dionyſius Exiguus, a Roman *Abbot*, taught them firſt to compute from the Birth of *Chriſt*: but He loſt 4 Years or began the *Chriſtian* Era 4 Years later than juſt. Therefore, tho' according to the *Hebrew* Chronology of the old Teſtament and other good Vouchers, CHRIST was truly born in ſome Month of the Year of the World or *A. M.* 4000. yet theſe 4 Years added make ———————— 4004 ⎫
Not *before the Birth of Chriſt*, but *before the Chriſtian Era*, viz. ———— 1737 ⎭
For the true *Anno Domini* or Year after *Chriſt*'s Birth is ———— 1740 .

But the MASONS being uſed to compute by
the Vulgar *Anno* Domini or Chriſtian *Era*   1737 | and ſo theſe Letters *A. M.*
and adding to it not 4004 as it ought, but | ſignify *Anno Mundi* or Year
the ſtrict Years before *Chriſt*'s Birth, *viz.*   4000 | of the World: and here
————— | *B. C.* is not *Before Chriſt*
They uſually call this the *Year* of MASONRY 5737 | but *Before the Chriſtian*
Inſtead of the accurate Year ———— 5740 | *Era*.
and we muſt keep to the Vulgar Computation. |

    The *A. M.* or *Anno Mundi* is the ſame follow'd by *Uſher* and *Prideaux*, &c.

from

from Colds and Heats, from Winds, Rains and Tempefts and from Wild Beafts; till his Sons grew up to form a *Lodge*, whom he taught *Geometry* and the great Ufe of it in *Architecture*, without which the Children of Men muft have liv'd like *Brutes*, in Woods, Dens and Caves, &c. or at beft in poor Huts of Mud or Arbours made of Branches of Trees, &c.

Thus K A I N, when expell'd * with his Family *A.M.* 130. and Adherents from *Adam*'s Altars, built forthwith a ftrong City, and call'd it D E D I C A T E or C O N S E C R A T E, after the Name of his eldeft Son *Enoch*; whofe Race follow'd the Example, improving the Arts and Sciences of their Patriarch: for T U B A L K A I N wrought in *Metals*, J U B A L elevated *Mufick*, and J A B A L extended his *Tents*.

Nor was his Brother S E T H lefs inftructed, the Patriarch of the other half of Mankind, who tranfmitted *Geometry* and *Mafonry* to his late Pofterity, who were the better skill'd by *Adam*'s living among them till he died. *A. M.* 930.

A D A M was fucceeded in the Grand Direction of the *Craft* by S E T H, E N O S H, K A I N A N, M A H A L A L E E L and J A R E D, whofe Son *Godly* E N O C H died not, but was tranflated alive, Soul and Body, into Heaven, aged 365 Years *.   He was * *A. M.* 987 expert and bright both in the *Science* and the *Art*, and being a Prophet, He foretold the Deftruction of the Earth for Sin, firft by *Water*, and afterwards by *Fire*: therefore E N O C H erected *Two* large P I L L A R S *, the one of Stone and the other of *Brick*, whereon he engraved the Abridgment of the Arts and Sciences, particularly *Geometry* and *Mafonry*.

* Some call them S E T H's *Pillars*, but the old *Mafons* always call'd them E N O C H's *Pillars*, and firmly believ'd this Tradition: nay *Jofephus* (Lib. i. cap. 2.) affirms the *Stone-Pillar* ftill remain'd in *Syria* to his Time.

J A R E D liv'd after his Son *Enoch* Years 435. and died aged 962 *A. M.*——1422. the oldeft Man except his Grandfon M E T H U S E L A H the Son of *Enoch*, who fucceeded *Jared*; but *Methufelah* ruled not long: for the Immoral Corruption univerfally prevailing,

M E T H U S E L A H, with his Son L A M E C H and Grandfon N O A H,
retired

retired from the corrupt World, and in their own peculiar Family preserved the good old Religion of the promised *Messiah* pure, and also the *Royal Art*, till the *Flood*: for LAMECH died only five Years before the *Flood*, and METHUSELAH died a few Days before It, aged 969 Years: and so He could well communicate the Traditions of his learned Progenitors to *Noah*'s 3 Sons; for JAPHET liv'd with him 100 Years, SHEM 98, and HAM 96.

At last, when the World's Destruction drew nigh, God commanded NOAH to build the *great* ARK or floating Castle, and his 3 Sons assisted like a *Deputy* and two *Wardens*: That Edifice though of Wood only, was fabricated by *Geometry* as nicely as any Stone Building (like true *Ship-Building* to this Day) a curious and large Piece of *Architecture*, and finish'd when *Noah* enter'd into his 600 Year; aboard which he and his 3 Sons and their 4 Wives passed, and having received the Cargo of Animals by God's Direction, they were saved in the Ark, while the rest perish'd in the *Flood* *   * *B. M.* —— 1656.
for their Immorality and Unbelief.   *A. C.* —— 2348.

And so from these MASONS, or four *Grand Officers*, the whole present Race of Mankind are descended.

After the *Flood*, NOAH and his 3 Sons, having preserved the Knowledge of the Arts and Sciences, communicated It to their growing Off-spring, who were all *of one Language and Speech*. *And it came to pass,* * *as they journeyd from the* East (the Plains of Mount *Ararat*,   * *Gen.* XI. 1, 2. where the *Ark* rested) towards the *West*, they found *a Plain in the Land of* SHINAR, *and dwelt there* together, as NOACHIDÆ *, or Sons of *Noah*: and when *Peleg* was born there to   * The first Name of *Heber*, after the Flood 101 Years, Father *Noah* partition'd the *Earth*, ordering   *Masons*, according to some old Traditions. them to disperse and take Possession; but from a Fear of the ill Consequences of Separation, they resolved to keep together.

CHAP.

CHAP. II.

From NIMROD *to* Grand-Master SOLOMON.

NIMROD the Son of *Cuſh*, the Eldeſt Son of *Ham*, was at the Head of thoſe that would not diſperſe; or if th ey muſt ſeparate, They reſolved to tranſmit their Memorial illuſtrious to all future Ages; and ſo employed themſelves under

NIMROD ſignifies a *Rebel*, the name that the *Iſraelites* gave him; but his Friends call'd him Belus LORD.

Grand Maſter NIMROD, in the large and fertile Vale of Shinar along the Banks of the *Tygris*, in building a great and ſtately *Tower* and *City*, the largeſt Work that ever the World ſaw (deſcribed by various Authors) and ſoon fil.'d the Vale with ſplendid Edifices; but They over-built it, and knew not when to deſiſt 'till their Vanity provoked their Maker to confound their *Grand Deſign*, by confounding their *Lip* or Speech. Hence the City was called Babel *Confuſion*.

Thus they were ſorced to diſperſe about 53 Years after they began to build, or after the Flood 154 Years, * when

* *A. M.* 1810.
B. C. 2194.

The General MIGRATION from Shinar commenced.

They went off at various Times, and travell'd North, South, *Eaſt* and *Weſt*, with their mighty Skill, and found the good Uſe of it in ſettling their Colonies.

But NIMROD went forth no farther than into the Land of *Aſſyria*, and founded the *firſt* Great *Empire* at his Capital Niniveh, where he long reign'd; and under him flouriſh'd many learned Mathematicians, whoſe Succeſſors were, long afterwards, called *Chaldees* and *Magians*: and though many of them turned Image-Worſhippers, yet even that Idolatry occaſion'd an Improvement in the *Arts* of Deſigning: * for NINUS King of *Nineveh* or *Aſſyria*, ordered his beſt Artiſts to frame the *Statue* of Baal, that was worſhipped in a gorgeous *Temple*.

viz. * *Architecture, Sculpture, Statuary, Plaſtering and Painting.*

From

From SHINAR, the *Science* and the *Art* were carried to the diftant Parts of the Earth, notwithftandihg the *Confufion* of *Dialects* : That indeed gave Rife to the *Mafons* Faculty and univerfal Practice of converfing without fpeaking, and of knowing each other by *Signs* and *Tokens* (* which they fettled upon the *Difperfion* or Migration, in cafe any of them fhould meet in diftant Parts, who had been before in

Shinar) but It hinder'd not the Propagation of *Mafonry*, which was cultivated by all the firft Nations ; till the Negligence of their Chiefs, and their horrid Wars, made them turn ignorant, and lofe their original Skill in Arts and Sciences.

Thus the *Earth* was again planted and replenifh'd with MA-SONS from the Vale of SHINAR, whofe various Improvements we fhall trace.

MITZRAIM or *Menes*, the fecond Son of HAM, led his Colony from *Shinar* to EGYPT (which is *Mitzraim* in *Hebrew*, a dual Word, fignifying both *Egypts*, Upper and Lower) after the *Flood* 160 Years, and after the *Confufion* fix Years, *A. M.* 1816. where they preferved their original Skill, and much cultivated the *Art :* for antient Hiftory informs us * of the early fine Tafte of the *Egyptians*,   * *Diod. Sicul.* lib. 1. their many magnificent Edifices and great Cities, as *Memphis*, *Heliopolis*, *Thebes* with 100 Gates, &c. befides their *Palaces* and *Sepulchres*, their *Obelisks* and *Statues*, the Coloffal *Statue* of SPHINX, whofe Head was 120 Foot round, and their famous 𝔓𝔶𝔯𝔞𝔪𝔦𝔡𝔰, the greateft * being reckoned the firft or earlieft of the feven *Wonders* of *Art* after the general *Migration*.

The *Egyptiaus* excell'd all Nations alfo in their amafing LABY-RINTHS, One of them cover'd the Ground of a whole Province, containing many fine Palaces and

* Some fay it was built of Marble Stones brought from the Quarries of *Arabia* ; for there is no Veftige of a Quarry near it. Others call them artificial Stones made on the Spot, moft of them 30 Foot long. The *Pile* at Bottom was 700 Foot fquare, and 481 Foot high ; but Others make it much higher : And in rearing it 360,000 *Mafons* were employ'd for 20 Years, as if all the People had join'd in the GRAND DESIGN.

100 *Temples*, difpofed in its feveral Quarters and Divifions, adorned with Columns of the beft *Porphyre*, and the accurate *Statues* of their Gods and Princes; which *Labyrinth* the *Greeks*, long afterwards, endeavour'd to imitate, but never arrived at Its *Extenfion* and *Sublime*.

The Succeffors of 𝕸𝖎𝖙𝖟𝖗𝖆𝖎𝖒 (who ftiled themfelves the *Sons of antient Kings*) encouraged the *Royal Art* down to the laft of the Race, the learned King AMASIS. See Chap. IV.

But Hiftory fails us in the South and Weft of *Africa*. Nor have we any juft Accounts of the fair and gallant Pofterity of *Noah*'s eldeft Son *JAPHET*, that firft replenifh'd vaft *old Scythia*, from *Norway* Eaftward to *America*; nor of the 𝕵𝖆𝖕𝖍𝖊𝖙𝖎𝖙𝖊𝖘 in *Greece* and *Italy*, *Germany*, *Gaul* and *Britain*, &c. 'till their original Skill was loft: But, no doubt, they were good Architects at their firft *Migration* from *Shinar*.

SHEM, the fecond Son of *Noah*, remain'd at UR of the *Chaldees* in *Shinar*, with his Father and great Grandfon HEBER, where they liv'd private and died in Peace; but *Shem*'s Off-fpring travell'd into the South and Eaft of Great *Afia*, viz. ELAM, ASHUR, ARPHAXAD, LUD and ARAM, with SALA the Father of *Heber*; and their Off-fpring propagatd the *Science* and the *Art* as far as CHINA and 𝕵𝖆𝖕𝖆𝖓: while NOAH, SHEM and HEBER diverted themfelves at *Ur*, in Mathematical Studies, teaching *Peleg* the Father of *Rehu*, Father of *Serug*, Father of *Nachor*, Father of *Terah*, Father of ABRAM, a learned Race of Mathematicians and Geometricians *.

* The old *Conftitutions* affirm this ftrongly, and expatiate on ABRAM's great Skill in *Geometry*, and of his teaching it to many Scholars, tho' all the Sons of the *Free-born* only.

Thus ABRAM, born two Years after the Death of *Noah*, * had learned well the *Science* and the *Art*, before the GOD of GLORY call'd him

* A. M. 2008.

to travel from *Ur* of the *Chaldees*, and to live a Peregrin, not in *Stone* and *Brick*, but in 𝕿𝖊𝖓𝖙𝖘 erected alfo by *Geometry*. So travelling with his Family and Flocks through *Mefopotamia*, he pitched

at

at *Charran**, where old TERAH in 5 Years died and then ABRAM aged 75 Years, travell'd into the Land of the *Canaanites** : but a Famine soon forced him down to *Egypt* ; and returning next Year, he began to communicate his great Skill to the Chiefs of the *Canaanites*, for which they honour'd him as a Prince.

    * A. M. 2078.*

    * A. M. 2083.*
    B. C. 1921.

    ABRAM tranfmitted his *Geometry* to all his Off-fpring ; *Ifaac* did the fame to his two Sons, and JACOB well inftructed his Family ; while his Son JOSEPH was 𝕲𝖗𝖆𝖓𝖉-𝕸𝖆𝖘𝖙𝖊𝖗 of the *Egyptian* Mafons, and employ'd them in building many Granaries and Store-Cities throughout the Land of *Egypt* before the *Defcent* of *Jacob* and his Family.

    Indeed this *peculiar Nation* were chiefly converfant in *Tents* and *Flocks* and military Skill, for about 350 Years after *Abram* came to *Canaan*, till their Perfecution began in *Egypt*, about 80 Years before the *Exodus* of *Mofes* : But then the 𝕰𝖌𝖞𝖕𝖙𝖎𝖆𝖓𝖘 having fpoil'd and enflaved the *Hebrews*, train'd them up in *Mafonry* of 𝕾𝖙𝖔𝖓𝖊 and 𝕭𝖗𝖎𝖈𝖐, and made them build two ftrong and ftately Cities for the Royal Treafures, *Pithom* and *Raamfes*. Thus the divine Wifdom appeared in permitting them to be thus employ'd, before they poffefs'd the promis'd Land then abounding with fine *Architecture*.

    At length, after *Abram* left *Charran* 430 Years, MOSES marched out of *Egypt* at the Head of 600,000 *Hebrew* Males, marfhall'd in due Form ; for whofe fake God divided the *Red Sea*, to let them pafs through, and drowned *Pharaoh* and the *Egyptians* that purfu'd them.

    A. M. ——2513.
    B. C. ——1491.

    While marching through *Arabia* to *Canaan*, 𝕲𝖔𝖉 was pleafed to infpire their 𝕲𝖗𝖆𝖓𝖉 𝕸𝖆𝖘𝖙𝖊𝖗 *MOSES*, *Joshuah* his Deputy, and *Aholiab* and *Bezaleel* } 𝕲𝖗𝖆𝖓𝖉 Wardens. } with Wifdom of Heart ; and fo next Year they raifed the curious TABERNACLE or *Tent* (where the divine 𝕾𝖍𝖊𝖈𝖍𝖎𝖓𝖆𝖍 refided

    Exod XXXII. 6.

refided, and the holy *Ark* or *Cheft*, the Symbole of God's Prefence) which, though not of *Stone* or *Brick*, was framed by *Geometry*, a moft beautiful Piece of true fymmetrical Architecture,
according to the Pattern that GOD difcover'd to *Mofes* on Mount
Sinai, and it was afterwards the Model of SOLOMON's Temple.

MOSES being well skill'd in all the *Egyptian* Learning, and alfo
divinely infpired, excell'd all *Grand Mafters* before him, and
ordered the more skillful to meet him, as in a *Grand Lodge*, near
the Tabernacle in the *Paffover*-Week, and gave them wife *Charges,
Regulations*, &c. though we wifh they had been more diftinctly
tranfmitted by Oral Tradition. But of this enough.

When MOSES King of *Jeffurun* died *A. M.* 2553.

JOSHUAH fucceeded in the Direction, with *Kaleb* as Deputy,
and *Eleazar* with his Son *Phineas* as *Grand Wardens* He
marfhall'd his *Ifraelites*, and led them over the *Jordan* (which
God made dry for their March) into the promis'd Land : and
Jofhuah foon found the *Canaanites* had fo regularly fortified their
great Cities and Paffes, that without the fpecial Intervention of
EL SHADDAI, in behalf of his *Peculiar*, They were impregnable
and invincible.

JOSHUAH having finifh'd his Wars in 6 Years, *A. M.* 2559.
fixed the Tabernacle at *Shiloh* in *Ephraim*, ordering the *Chiefs*
of *Ifrael* not only to ferve JEHOVAH their God, and to cultivate
the Land, but alfo to carry on the *Grand Defign* of Architecture
in the beft Mofaic Stile.

Indeed the *Ifraelites*, refined in Cities and Manfions, having
many expert Artifts in every *Tribe* that met in *Lodges* or Societies
for that Purpofe, except when for their Sins they came under
Servitude ; but their occafional Princes, call'd *Judges* and *Sa-
viours*, revived the *Mofaic Stile* along with Liberty and the
Mofaic Conftitution ; and only came fhort of the *Phenicians* and *Canaanites* in facred Architecture of *Stone* ; for the *Phenicians* had
many Temples for their many Gods : and yet the one *Temple* or
Tabernacle of the one true God at *Shiloh*, exceeded them all in
Wifdom and *Beauty*, though not in *Strength* and *Dimenfions*.

C   Mean

Mean while, in *Leſſer Aſia*, about 10 Years before the *Exodus* of *Moſes*, TROY was founded and ſtood ſublime till deſtroy'd by the emulous *Greeks*, about the 12th Year of *Tola* Judge of *Iſrael*. *A. M.* 2819.

And ſoon after the *Exodus*, the famous *Temple* of JUPITER HAMMON in *Libian Africa* was erected, that ſtood till demoliſh'd by the firſt Chriſtians in thoſe Parts.

The SIDONIANS alſo, expert Artiſts, firſt built *Tyre*, and a Colony of *Tyrians* firſt built CARTHAGE ; while the *Greeks* were obſcure, and the *Romans* exiſted not yet.

But the *Phenicians* improved in their *ſacred* Architecture ; for we read of the *Temple* of Dagon in *Gaza*, very magnificent and capacious of 3000 People under its *Roof*, that was artfully ſupported only by *Two Columns*, not too big to be graſped in the Arms of SAMSON, who tugg'd them down ; and the large *Roof*, like a Burſt of Thunder, fell upon the Lords and Ladies, the Prieſts and People of the *Philiſtins* ; nay *Samſon* was alſo intangled in the ſame Death that he drew upon his Enemies for the Loſs of Liberty and Eyes. After the *Exodus* of *Moſes* 379. Before the *Temple* of *Solomon* 101 *.

ABIBALUS, King of *Tyre*, beautified that City ; and ſo did his Son King HIRAM who built 3 ſtately *Temples* to Jupiter, Hercules, and Aſtarte, the *Tyrian* Gods, and aſſiſted *David* King of *Iſrael* in erecting his *Palace of Cedar*.

Many Monuments of the primitive Architecture are obſcured with Fables ; for the true old Hiſtories are loſt, or worn out by the Teeth of Time, and alſo the *oral* Tradition is darkened by the Blending of the Nations.

---

* The *Tradition* of old Maſons is, that a learned *Phenician* called SANCONIATHON was the Architect, or *Grand Maſter*, of this curious *Temple :* And that SAMSON had been too credulous and effeminate in revealing his Secrets to his Wife, who betray'd him into the Hands of the *Philiſtins* ; for which he is not numbered among the antient *Maſons*. But no more of this.

CHAP.

CHAP. III.

From SOLOMON to Grand Master CYRUS.

BUT the moſt magnificent Structures of *Gaza*, *Gath* and *Aſkelon*, *Jebuſi* and *Hebron*, *Tyre* and *Sidon*, *Egypt* and *Aſſyria*, &c. were not comparable to the *Eternal*'s 𝕮𝖊𝖒𝖕𝖑𝖊 at *Jeruſalem*, built by that wiſeſt mere Man and moſt glorious King of *Iſrael*, SOLOMON, (the Son of *David*, who was denied that Honour for being a Man of Blood) the Prince of Peace and Architecture, the GRAND MASTER MASON of his Day, who performed all by divine Direction, and without the Noiſe of Tools ; all the Stones, Timbers and Foundings being brought ready cut, fram'd and poliſh'd to *Jeruſalem*.

It was founded in the 4th Year of SOLOMON, on the ſecond Day of the ſecond Month of the Year after the *Exodus* —— 480 and SOLOMON employ'd about it, tho' not all *A. M.* 2993. upon it, the following Number of Operators, viz. *B. C.* 1011.

1. 𝕳𝖆𝖗𝖔𝖉𝖎𝖒, Rulers or *Provoſts*, call'd alſo See 1 *Kings* V. 16. 18. 𝕸𝖊𝖓𝖆𝖙𝖟𝖈𝖍𝖎𝖒, *Overſeers* and Comforters 2 *Chron.* II. 18. of the People in Working, that were expert *Maſter Maſons*, in Number ———————— 3600

2. 𝕲𝖍𝖎𝖇𝖑𝖎𝖒, *Stone-Cutters* and *Sculptors*, and 𝕴𝖈𝖍 𝕮𝖍𝖔𝖙𝖟𝖊𝖇, *Men of Hewing*, and 𝕭𝖔𝖓𝖆𝖎, *Setters*, Layers or Builders, or bright *Fellow-Crafts*, in Number ———— 80000

3. The Levy of Aſſiſtants, under the noble ADONIRAM — 30000 who was the *Junior* 𝕲𝖗𝖆𝖓𝖉-𝖂𝖆𝖗𝖉𝖊𝖓.

In all *Free-Maſons* ——————— 113600

Beſides the *Labourers* called, 𝕴𝖈𝖍 𝕾𝖆𝖇𝖇𝖆𝖑, or *Men of Burden*, who were of the Remains of the old *Canaanites*, and 70000 being *Bondmen*, are not to be reckoned among *Maſons*,

In all — 183,600

SOLOMON

SOLOMON had the *Labourers* of his own; but was much obliged to HIRAM King of *Tyre*, for many of the 𝔊𝔥𝔦𝔟𝔩𝔦𝔪 and 𝔅𝔬𝔫𝔞𝔦, who lent him his beſt Artiſts, and ſent him the Firs and Cedars of *Lebanon*: But above all, he ſent his Name ſake * HIRAM ABBIF, the moſt accompliſh'd Deſigner and Operator upon Earth, who in *Solomon*'s Abſence fill'd the Chair as *Deputy* 𝔊𝔯𝔞𝔫𝔡 𝔐𝔞𝔰𝔱𝔢𝔯, and in his Preſence was the *Senior* 𝔊𝔯𝔞𝔫𝔡 𝔚𝔞𝔯𝔡𝔢𝔫, or principal Surveyor and *Maſter* of *Work*.

SOLOMON

---

* In 2 *Chron.* II. 13. HIRAM King of *Tyre* (called there HURAM) in his Letter to King SOLOMON, ſays, *I have ſent a Cunning Man* le Huram Abbi; which is not to be tranſlated, like the Vulgate *Greek* and *Latin*, HURAM *my Father*; for his Deſcription verſe 14 refutes it; and the Words import only HURAM *of my Father's*, or the Chief *Maſter Maſon* of my Father ABIBALUS. Yet ſome think that King HIRAM might call the Architect HIRAM his Father, as learned and wiſe Men were wont to be call'd by Royal Patrons in old Times: Thus JOSEPH was call'd ABRECH, or the King's Father; and this ſame HIRAM the Architect is called SOLOMON's Father, 2 *Chron.* iv. 6.

𝔊𝔫𝔞𝔰𝔞𝔥 ℭ𝔥𝔲𝔯𝔞𝔪 𝔄𝔟𝔟𝔦𝔣 𝔩𝔞 𝔐𝔢𝔩𝔢𝔠𝔥 𝔖𝔥𝔢𝔩𝔬𝔪𝔬𝔥

Did HIRAM *his Father make to King* SOLOMON.

But the Difficulty is over at once by allowing the Word ABBIF to be the Sur-name of HIRAM the *Artiſt*, call'd above *Hiram Abbi*, and here call'd *Huram Abbif*, as in the *Lodge* he is called HIRAM ABBIF, to diſtinguiſh him from King HIRAM: For this Reading makes the Senſe plain and compleat, *viz.* that HIRAM King of *Tyre*, ſent to King SOLOMON the cunning Workman call'd HIRAM ABBIF.

He is deſcribed in two Places, 1 *Kings* vii. 13, 14, 15. and 2 *Chron* ii. 13, 14. In the firſt he is call'd *a Widow's Son of the Tribe of* Naphtali, and in the other he is called *the Son of a Woman of the Daughters of* Dan; but in both, that his Father was *a Man of* Tyre: That is, ſhe was of the Daughters of the City *Dan*, in the Tribe of *Naphtali*, and is call'd *a Widow of* Naphtali, as her Huſband was a *Naphtalite*; for he is not call'd a *Tyrian* by Deſcent, but a Man of *Tyre* by Habitation, as *Obed Edom* the *Levite* is call'd a *Gittite*, and the Apoſtle *Paul* *a Man of* Tarſus.

But

SOLOMON partition'd the *Fellow Crafts* into certain *Lodges*, with a *Master* and *Wardens* in each; that they might receive Commands in a regular Manner, might take Care of their Tools and Jewels, might be regularly paid every Week, and be duly fed and clothed, *&c.* and the *Fellow Crafts* took Care of their Succession by educating 𝕰𝖓𝖙𝖊𝖗'𝖉 𝕻𝖗𝖊𝖓𝖙𝖎𝖈𝖊𝖘.

According to the Traditions of old Masons, who talk much of these Things.

Thus a solid Foundation was laid of perfect *Harmony* among the Brotherhood, the *Lodge* was strongly cemented with Love and Friendship, every Brother was duly taught Secrecy and Prudence, Morality and good Fellowship, each knew his peculiar Business, and the *Grand Design* was vigorously pursued at a prodigious Expence.

For besides King DAVID's vast Preparations, his richer Son SOLOMON, and all the wealthy *Israelites*, nay even the Princes of the neighbouring *Gentiles*, largely contributed towards It, in Gold, Silver and rich Jewels, that amounted to a Sum almost incredible : but was all needful ;

For the *Wall* round It was in Compass 7700 Foot, the Materials were the best that the Earth produced, and no Structure was ever like it for exactly proportion'd and beautiful Dimensions, from the most magnificent PORTICO on the *East*, to the glorious and reverend 𝕾𝖆𝖓𝖈𝖙𝖚𝖒 𝕾𝖆𝖓𝖈𝖙𝖔𝖗𝖚𝖒 on the *West*, with numerous Apartments, pleasant and convenient Chambers and Lodgings for the Kings and Princes, the *Sanhedrin*, the Priests and Levites
of

But tho' HIRAM ABBIF had been a *Tyrian* by Blood, that derogates not from his vast Capacity ; for the *Tyrians* now were the best Artificers, by the Encouragement of King HIRAM : and those *Texts* testify that God had endued this HIRAM ABBIF with Wisdom, Understanding, and mechanical Cunning to perform every Thing that SOLOMON required, not only in building the TEMPLE with all its costly Magnificence ; but also in founding, fashioning and framing all the holy *Utensils* thereof, according to *Geometry*, and to *find out every Device that shall be put to him !* and the Scripture assures us that He fully maintain'd his Character in far larger Works than those of *Aholiab* and *Bezaleel*, for which he will be honoured in the *Lodges* till the End of Time.

of *Israel*, and the outer *Court* of the *Gentiles* too, It being an *House of Prayer for all Nations*, and capable of receiving in all its Courts and Apartments together about 300000 People.

It was adorned with 1453 *Columns* of *Parian Marble* twisted, or sculptured or fluted, with twice as many *Pillasters*, both having exquisite *Capitels* or Chapiters of several different noble *Orders*, and about 2246 Windows, besides those in the curious Pavement ; and it was lined with massy Gold, set with innumerable Diamonds and other precious Stones, in the most harmonious, beautiful and costly *Decoration :* tho' much more might be said, if it had not been so often delineated, particularly by *Villalpandus*.

So that its Prospect highly transcended all that we are now capable to imagine, and has been ever esteemed the finest Piece of *Masonry* upon Earth, before or since, the 2d and *Chief* of the 7 *Wonders of Art*, since the general *Migration* from *Shinar*.

It was finish'd in the short Space of 7 Years and 6 Months, to the Amazement of all the World ; when the *Cape-Stone* was celebrated by the *Fraternity* with great Joy. But their Joy was soon inter-rupted by the sudden Death of their dear Master HIRAM ABBIF, whom they decently interr'd in the *Lodge* near the *Temple* accord-ing to antient Usage.

A. M. 3000.
B. C. 1004.

After HIRAM ABBIF was mourn'd for, the **Tabernacle** of MOSES and its holy Reliques being lodged in the **Temple**, SOLOMON in a General Assembly dedicated or consecrated It by solemn Prayer and costly Sacrifices past Number, with the finest Music, vocal and instrumental, praising JEHOVAH, upon fixing the *Holy* ARK in its proper Place between the *Cherubims* ; when JEHOVAH fill'd his own **Temple** with a *Cloud of Glory !*

But leaving what must not, and indeed what cannot be committed to Writing, we may certainly affirm, that however ambitious and emulous the *Gentiles* were in improving the *Royal Art*, it was never perfected till the building of this **gorgeous** *House* of GOD fit for the special Refulgence of his Glory upon Earth, where he

dwelt

dwelt between the *Cherubims* on the *Mercy Seat* above the *Ark*, and from thence gave his People frequent oraculous Responses. This glorious Edifice attracted soon the inquisitive Connoisseurs of all Nations to travel, and spend some Time at *Jerusalem*, to survey its peculiar Excellencies, as much as was allow'd to the *Gentiles*; and they soon discover'd that all the World, with their joint Skill, came far short of the *Israelites* in the *Wisdom*, *Strength* and *Beauty* of Architecture; when the *wise* King SOLOMON was 𝕲𝖗𝖆𝖓𝖉 𝕸𝖆𝖘𝖙𝖊𝖗 of all *Masons* at *Jerusalem*, and the *learned* King HIRAM * was *Grand Master* at *Tyre*, and inspired HIRAM ABBIF, had been *Master* of *Work*; when true compleat *Masonry* was under the immediate Care and Direction of Heaven; when the NOBLE and the *Wise* thought it their Honour to be the Associates of the ingenious Craftsmen in their well form'd *Lodges*; and so the 𝕿𝖊𝖒𝖕𝖑𝖊 of JEHOVAH, the one true God, became the just Wonder of all *Travellers*, by which, as by the most perfect Pattern, they resolved to correct the *Architecture* of their own Countries upon their Return.

* The *Tradition* is, that King HIRAM had been *Grand Master* of all *Masons*; but when the TEMPLE was finish'd, HIRAM came to survey It before its Consecration, and to commune with SOLOMON about *Wisdom* and *Art*; and finding the Great *Architect* of the Universe, had inspired SOLOMON above all mortal Men, HIRAM very readily yeelded the Pre-eminence to SOLOMON JEDIDIAH, the *Beloved of God*.

SOLOMON next employ'd the *Fraternity* in carrying on his other Works, viz. — His two PALACES at *Jerusalem* for himself and his Queen.—— The stately HALL of Judicature with his *Ivory Throne* and *Golden Lyons*.--- MILLO, or the *Royal Exchange*, made by filling up the Great Gulph, between Mount *Moriah* and Mount *Zion*, with strong Arches, upon which many beautiful *Piazzas* were erected with lofty *Collonading* on each Side, and between the Columns a spacious *Walk* from *Zion Castle* to the *Temple*, where Men of Business met.——— The HOUSE of the *Forrest* of *Lebanon* built upon 4 Rows of *Cedar-Pillars*, his Summer-House to retire from the Heat of Business, with a *Watch-Tower* that looked to the Road to *Damascus*. Several *Cities* on the Road between *Jerusalem* and *Lebanon*. Many Store-houses *West* of
the

the *Jordan* and several Store Cities *East* of that River well forti-
tify'd,——and the City 𝕿𝖆𝖉𝖒𝖔𝖗 (call'd afterwards by the *Greeks
Palmyra)* with a splendid Palace in it, the glorious Ruins of
which are seen by Travellers to this Day.

All these and many more costly Buildings were finish'd in the
short Space of 13 Years after the *Temple*, by the Care of 550
𝕳𝖆𝖗𝖔𝖉𝖎𝖒 and 𝕸𝖊𝖓𝖆𝖙𝖟𝖈𝖍𝖎𝖒 : for *Masonry* was carried on throughout all his Dominions, and many particular *Lodges* were constituted under *Grand Master* Solomon, who annually assembled the
𝕲𝖗𝖆𝖓𝖉 𝕷𝖔𝖉𝖌𝖊 at *Jerusalem* for transmitting their Affairs to Posterity : tho' still the Loss of good Hiram Abbif was lamented.

Indeed this wise *Grand Master* Solomon shew'd the Imperfection of *human* Nature, even at its Hight of Excellency, by
loving too much many *strange Women*, who turn'd him from
the true Religion : But our Business with him is only as a Mason ;
for even during his Idolatry he built some curious *Temples* to
𝕮𝖍𝖊𝖒𝖔𝖘𝖍, 𝕸𝖔𝖑𝖊𝖈𝖍 and 𝕬𝖘𝖍𝖙𝖆𝖗𝖔𝖙𝖍, the Gods of his Concubines,
till about 3 Years before he died, when he composed his peni-
tential Song, the *Ecclesiastes* ; and fixed the true Motto on all
earthly Glory, *viz.* Vanity of Vanities, all is Vanity
without the Fear *of* God *and the keeping of his Commands, which
is the whole Duty of Man!* and died aged 58
Years.

Many of Solomon's *Masons* before he   A. M. —— 3029.
died began to travel, and carry'd with   A. C. —— 975.
'em the *High Taste* of Architecture, with the Secrets of the Fraternity, into *Syria, Lesser Asia, Mesopotamia, Scythia, Assyria,
Chaldæa, Media, Bactria, India, Persia, Arabia, Egypt,* and
other Parts of great Asia and Africa ; also into Europe, no
doubt, tho' we have no History to assure us yet of the Transactions of *Greece* and *Italy :* But the Tradition is that they travell'd to Hercules Pillars on the *West*, and to China on
the *East :* And the old *Constitutions* affirm, that one call'd Ninus,
who had been at the building of *Solomon's Temple*, brought the
refined Knowledge of the Science and the *Art* into *Germany* and
Gaul.

In

In many Places being highly efteem'd, they obtain'd fpecial Privileges ; and becaufe they taught their *liberal Art* only to the *Freeborn*, They were call'd F REE M ASONS ; conftituting *Lodges* in the Places where they built ftately Piles, by the Encouragement of the Great and Wealthy, who foon requefted to be accepted as Members of the *Lodge* and *Brothers* of the *Craft* ; till by Merit thofe *Free* and *accepted Mafons* came to be *Mafters* and *Wardens*.

Nay Kings, Princes and Potentates became 𝕲𝖗𝖆𝖓𝖉 𝕸𝖆𝖘𝖙𝖊𝖗𝖘, each in his own Dominion, in Imitation of King *Solomon*, whofe Memory, *as a Mafon*, has been duly worfhipp'd, and will be, till *Architecture* fhall be confumed in the general Conflagration ; for he never can be rivall'd but by one equally infpired from above.

After SOLOMON's Death, the Partition of his Empire into the Kingdoms of *Ifrael* and *Judah*, did not demolifh the *Lodges* : For in *Ifrael*, King J EROBOAM erected the curious *Statues* of the two 𝕲𝖔𝖑𝖉𝖊𝖓 𝕮𝖆𝖑𝖛𝖊𝖘 at *Dan* and *Bethel*, with 𝕿𝖊𝖒𝖕𝖑𝖊𝖘 for their Worfhip ; King *Baafha* built *Tirzah* for his Palace, and King *Omri* built *Samaria* for his Capital ; where his Son King A CHAB built a large and fumptuous 𝕿𝖊𝖒𝖕𝖑𝖊 for his *Idol* 𝕭𝖆𝖆𝖑 (afterwards deftroy'd by King *Jehu*) and a *Palace of Ivory*, befides many Caftles and fenced Cities.

But SOLOMON's Royal Race, the Kings of *Judah*, fucceeded him alfo in the G RAND M ASTER's *Chair*, or deputed the High Prieft to preferve the *Royal Art*. Their Care of the Temple with the many Buildings they raifed, and ftrong Forts, are mention'd in holy Writ down to J OSIAH the laft good King of *Judah*.

SOLOMON's 𝕿𝖗𝖆𝖛𝖊𝖑𝖑𝖊𝖗𝖘 improved the *Gentiles* beyond Expreffion. Thus the *Syrians* adorned their *Damafcus* with a lofty *Temple* and a Royal *Palace*. Thofe of *Leffer Afia* became excellent *Mafons*, particularly at *Sardis* in *Lydia*, and along the Sea Coafts in the mercantil Cities, as at 𝕰𝖕𝖍𝖊𝖘𝖚𝖘.

There the old *Temple* of 𝕯𝖎𝖆𝖓𝖆, built by fome *Japhetites* about the Days of *Mofes*, being burnt down about 34 Years after *Solomon*'s Death, the Kings of *Leffer Afia* refounded and adorn'd it with 127 *Columns* of the beft Marble, each 60 Foot

D   high,

high, and 36 of them were of the moſt noble *Sculpture*, by the Direction of 𝔇𝔯𝔢𝔰𝔭𝔥𝔬𝔫 and 𝔄𝔯𝔠𝔥𝔦𝔭𝔥𝔯𝔬𝔴, the Diſciples of *Solomon's* Travellers; but it was not finiſhed till after 220 Years in the 7th Year of *Hezekiab* King of *Judab*. *A. M.* 3283.

This Temple was in Length 425 Foot, and in Breadth 220 Foot with a duly proportion'd Height, ſo magnificent, ſo admirable a Fabrick, that it became the 3d of the 7 *Wonders of Art*, the charming Miſtreſs of *Leſſer Aſia*, which even *Xerxes*, the avowed Enemy of *Image Worſhip*, left ſtanding, while he burnt all the other *Temples* in his Way to *Greece*.

But at laſt, it was burnt down by a vile Fellow, only for the Luſt of being talkt of in after Ages (whoſe Name therefore ſhall not be mention'd here) on the Birth Day of *Alexander the Great*, after it had ſtood 365 Years, about *A. M.* 3680. when jocoſe People ſaid, *The Goddeſs was ſo deeply engaged at the Birth of her Hero in* Pella *of* Macedonia *that ſhe had no Leiſure to ſave her* Temple *at* EPHESUS. It was rebuilt by the Architect *Denocrates* at the Expence of the neighbouring Princes and States.

The ASSYRIANS, ever ſince NIMROD and NINUS, had cultivated the Royal *Art*, eſpecially at their *Great* NINIVEH, down to King PUL (to whom *Jonah* preached) and his Son *Sardan Pul* or SARDANAPALUS, call'd alſo *Tonos Concoleros*, who was beſieged by his Brother *Tiglath Pul Eſer* and his General *Nabonaſſar*, till he burnt himſelf with his Concubines and Treaſure in old *Nimrod's* Palace in the 12th Year of *Jotham* King of *Judab*, *A. M.* ----3257. when the Empire was partition'd between TIGLATH PUL ESER who ſucceeded at *NINIVEH*, and NABONASSAR who got *CHALDÆA*. *See the Margin of next Page.*

NABONASSAR, called alſo *Beleſis* or *Baladan*, an excellent Aſtronomer and Architect, built his new Metropolis upon the Ruins of a Part of old *Nimrod's* Works near the Great *old Tower* of *Babel* then ſtanding, and call'd It BABYLON, founded in the firſt Year of the *Nabonaſſarian Era*. *A. M.* 3257.

For this City BABYLON is not mentioned by any Author before *Iſaiah*, who mentions both Its Riſe and Its Ruin *Cb* XXIII. 13.

NABONASSAR reign'd 14 Years, ſucceeded by See *Marſham's* Canon. Sec. 17

4 Kings,

4 Kings, who reign'd 12 Years, till his Son was of Age, *viz.*

MERODACH BALADAN, or *Mardoch Empadus*, who reign'd 12 Years: and after him 5 more Kings, tho' not of his Issue, who reign'd 21 Years. Then follow'd an *Interregnum* of 8 Years, ending *An. Nabon.* 67.

The

ASSYRIA *A. M.* 3257. *Sardanapalus* being dead

1. TIGLATH PUL ESER, called also *Arbaces* and NINUS *junior*, succeeded at *Niniveh*, and died *A. M.* 3275

2 SALMAN ESER died 3289, and his Son 3 SENACHERIB died 3297

4 ESERHADDON succeeded his Father *Sennacherib*, and after he had reign'd at *Nineveh* 27 Years he took in BABYLON at the End of the *Interregnum* An Nabon 67. *A. M.* 3324 and so annexed *Chaldæa* again to *Assyria*. He died —— 3336

5 SAOSDUCHINUS, call'd in *Judith*, NABUCHODONOSOR, died 3635

6 CHINILADANUS slain by his General *Nabopolassar* 3378

7 *Saracus* slain by *Nabopolassnr* 3392

NABOPOLASSAR sometimes called NEBUCHADNEZZAR, I. then seized *Chaldæa* and reign'd in the Throne of old NABONASSAR at *Babylon*, years —— 14

till he destroy'd *Saracus*, A. M. 3392

1. NABOPOLASSAR willing to please his Allies the *Medes*, demolish'd the Great NINIVEH. Thus BABYLON was now the *Capital* of the *Assyrian* Empire. He died —— 3399

2. NEBUCHADNEZZAR who captivated the *Jews* and adorned *Babylon*, died 3442.

AMYTIS the other Daughter of *Astyages* King of *Media*.

3 EVILMERODACH slain A. M. —— 3444

N. N. Wife of 4 NERIGLISSAR who slew *Evil-Merodach*, and reigned 3 Years.

6 BELSHAZZAR succeeded *Laborosoarchod*, and was slain by CYRUS A. M. 3465

5 LABOROSOARCHOD 1 Year.

5 CYAXARES II. K. of *Media*, call'd in Scripture DARIUS *the Mede*, join'd his Nephew and Son-in-Law CYRUS in his Wars, reign'd at *Babylon* after *Belshazzar* 2 Years, died 3467

CASSENDANA the Heiress of *Media* and Wife of CYRUS.

CAMBYSES King of *Persia*, see Chapter IV

MEDIA.

The *Medes* revolting from *Senacherib* King of *Assyria* A.M. 3296 chose for their King 1 DEJOCES, who inlarged and adorned his Capital EKBATANA till slain in Battel by the *Assyrians* 3348

2 PHRAORTES died 3370

3 CYAXARES I. was the Patron of the Learned in the *East* and died 3410

4 ASTYAGES married ARIENA Sister of *Croesus* King of *Lydia*. He died 3445, leaving a Son and two Daughters *viz.*

MANDANE the eldest Daughter, Wife of CAMBYSES a *Persian* Prince, call'd by some King of *Persia*, the Father and Mother of

CYRUS the *Great*, began the *Persian* Monarchy 3468

The *Science* and the *Art* long flourish'd in Eastern *Asia* to the fartheft *East Indies*. But alfo before the Days of *Nebuchadnezzar* the *Great*, we find that old *Mafonry* took a Weftern Courfe: For the Difciples of *Solomon*'s Travellers, by the Encouragement of Princes and States *Weft* of the *Affyrian* Bounds, built, enlarged and adorn'd Cities paft Number, as appears from the Hiftory of their Foundations in many Books of *Chronology*. *

After godly JOSIAH King of *Judah* fighting for his fuperior *Nabopolaffar*, was flain in the Battel of *Hadad Rimmon* by *Pharoah Necho*, A. M. 3394. } all Things went wrong in *Judah*.
B. C. 610. }

For the Grand Monarch NEBUCHADNEZZAR, firft his Father's Partner having defeated *Necho*, made *Jofiah*'s Son *Jehoiakim* his Vaffal, and for his revolting He ruin'd him, and at length captivated all the remaining *Royal* Family of *Judah* with the Flower of the *Nobles*, efpecially of the more ingenious *Craftfmen*, laid wafte the whole Land of *Ifrael*, burnt and demolifht all the fine Edifices, and alfo the *glorious* and *Inimitable* 𝕿𝖊𝖒𝖕𝖑𝖊 of SOLOMON, after It was finifht and confecrated 416 Years,

A. M. 3416. } oh lamentable !
B. C. --- 588. }

Mean while, *Nebuchadnezzar* was carrying on his Grand Defign of inlarging and beautifying BABYLON, and employ'd the more Skillful Artifts of *Judah*. and of his other captivated Nations, to join his *Chaldees* in raifing the *Walls*, the *Palaces*, the *Hanging Gardens*, the amazing *Bridge*, the *Temples*, the long and broad Streets, the Squares, &c. of that proud *Metropolis*, accounted the 4th of the 7 *Wonders of Art*, defcribed at large in many Books, and therefore needlefs to be rehearfed particularly here.

---

* Such as *Borifthenes* and *Sinope* in PONTUS : *Nicomedia, Prufias* and *Chalcedon* in BITHYNIA : *Bizantium* (now *Conftantinople*) *Cyzicus* alfo and *Lampfacus* in the HELLESPONT : *Abdera* in THRACE : Many Cities in GREECE : *Tarentum, Regium, Rome, Ravenna, Crotona, Florence*, and many more in ITALY : *Granada, Malaga, Gades*, &c. in SPAIN : *Maffilia* and others on the Coaft of GAUL : while BRITAIN was unknown.

But

But for all his unfpeakable Advantages of Wealth and Power, and for all his vaft Ambition, he could not arrive at the *fublime* of the *Solomonian Stile*. 'Tis true, after his Wars, He was a mighty Encourager of Architecture, a fumptuous 𝕮𝖑𝖆𝖓𝖉 𝕸𝖆𝖋𝖙𝖊𝖗; and his Artifts difcover'd great Knowledge in raifing his *Golden Image* in the Vale of *Dura* 60 Cubits high and 6 broad, and alfo in all the beautiful Parts of his *Great* BABYLON : Yet It was never fully peopled ; for his Pride provoked God to afflict him with Brutal Madnefs for 7 Years, and when reftored, He liv'd about one Year only and died *A. M.* 3442, but 23 Years after, his Grandfon *Belfhazzar* was flain by CYRUS, who conquer'd that Empire and foon removed the Throne to SUSIANA in *Perfia*.

The MEDES and PERSIANS had much improved in the *Royal Art*, and had rivall'd the *Affyrians* and *Chaldeans* in *Mafonry* at 𝕰𝖐𝖇𝖆𝖙𝖆𝖓𝖆, 𝕾𝖚𝖋𝖎𝖆𝖓𝖆, 𝕻𝖊𝖗𝖋𝖊𝖕𝖔𝖑𝖎𝖘, and many more fine Cities, before They conquer'd 'em in War ; tho' They had nothing fo large as 𝕹𝖎𝖓𝖎𝖛𝖊𝖍 and 𝕭𝖆𝖇𝖞𝖑𝖔𝖓, nor fo accurate as the 𝕿𝖊𝖒𝖕𝖑𝖊 and the other Structures of SOLOMON.

The *Jewifh* Captives, after *Nebuchadnezzar's* Death, kept themfelves at Work in regular *Lodges*, till the fet Time of their Deliverance ; and were thus the more capable, at the *Reduction*, of Rebuilding the *Holy Temple* and *City* of *Salem* upon the old Foundations ; which was ordered by the *Decree* of CYRUS, according to God's Word that had foretold his Exaltation and that Decree, publifht *A. M.*————3468.⸱
⸱⸱⸱⸱⸱⸱⸱⸱⸱⸱⸱⸱⸱⸱⸱⸱*B. C.* ———— 536.⸱

CHAP.

CHAP IV

From CYRUS to Grand Master SELEUCUS Nicator.

1. CYRUS now King of Kings, having founded the *Persian* Monarchy made his famous *Decree* to rebuild the Temple of *Jerusalem* and constituted, for his *Provincial* Grand Master in *Judah*, ZERUBBABEL the lineal Heir of DAVID's Royal Race and Prince of the *Reduction*, with the High Priest Jeshuah his *Deputy*; who next Year founded the *second* TEMPLE. CYRUS built a great Palace near *Saras* in *Persia*, but before *Zerubbabel* had half finish'd, the good CYRUS died *A. M.* 3474.

$$\begin{cases} A.\ M. \text{ ---- } 3468. \\ B.\ C. \text{ ---- } 536. \end{cases}$$

2. CAMBYSES neglected the *Temple*, being wholly Intent upon the Conquest of *Egypt*, that had revolted under AMASYS, the last of *Mitzraim*'s Race, a learned *Grand Master*; for whom the *Fellow Crafts* cut out of a Rock an House all of *one Stone* 21 Cubits long, 12 broad and 8 deep, the Labour of 2000 *Masons* for 3 Years, and brought it safe to *Memphis*.

He had built many costly Structures, and contributed largely to the Rebuilding of Apollo's famous *Temple* at *Delphi* in *Greece*, and died much lamented just as *Cambyses* had reached to *Egypt*, *A. M.* 3478.

Cambyses conquer'd the Land, and destroy'd many *Temples*, *Palaces*, *Obelisks* and other glorious Monuments of the antient *Egyptian Masonry*, and died on his Way home, *A. M.* 3482.

3. The false *Smerdis*, the *Magian*, usurped during Part of this Year, call'd by *Ezrah* Artaxerxes, who stopt the building of the *Temple*.

4. DARIUS HYSTASPES, one of the 7 Princes that cut off *Smerdis*, succeeded, married *Artistona* the Daughter of CYRUS, and confirmed his *Decree*.

So

So that in his 6th Year, juft 20 Years after the Founding of the *Temple*, ZERUBBABEL finifh'd it * and celebrated the *Cape-Stone* ; and next Year Its Confecration or Dedication was folemnized.

$$\left\{ \begin{array}{l} * \; A. \; M. \; — \; 3489. \\ B \; C. \; — \; 515. \end{array} \right.$$

And tho' It came far fhort of SOLOMON's *Temple* in Extent and Decorations, nor had in it the *Cloud of Glory* or Divine Shechinah, and the holy Reliques of *Mofes* ; yet being rear'd in the *Solomonian Stile*, It was the fineft Building upon Earth.

In his Reign Zoroaftres flourifh'd, the *Archimagus* or *Grand Mafter* of the *Magians* (who worfhipped the *Sun* and the *Fire* made by his Rays) who became famous every where, call'd by the *Greeks*, *the Teacher of all human and divine Knowledge* ; and his Difciples were great Improvers of *Geometry* in the liberal Arts, erecting many *Palaces* and *Fire Temples* throughout the Empire, and long flourifh'd in Eaftern *Afia*, even till the *Mahometans* prevail'd. Yet a Remnant of 'em are fcatter'd in thofe Parts to this Day, who retain many of the old Ufages of the *Free Mafons*, for which They are here mention'd, and not for their Religious Rites that are not the Subject of this Book : For we leave every Brother to Liberty of Confcience ; but ftrictly charge him carefully to maintain the *Cement of the Lodge*, and the 3 Articles of NOAH.

Zoroaftres was flain by *Argafp* the *Scythian*, A. M. 3517. and *Hyftofpes* died 3518.

5. XERXES his Son fucceeded, who encouraged the *Magian Mafons*, and deftroy'd all the *Image-Temples* (except That of *Diana* at *Ephefus*) in his Way to *Greece*, with an Army of 5 Millions, and Ships paft Number : But the confederated *Greeks* fhamefully beat this common Enemy both at Sea and Land. A. M. 3525, at laft *Xerxes* was murder'd, *A. M.* 3539.

6. ARTAXERXES *Longimanus* his Son fucceeded, call'd *Abafhuerus* ; and he married the handfome *Jewefs* Queen *Hefter*. In his 3d Year he made a Feaft during 6 Months, for all his Princes and Servants, at his Palace of *Sufa* or *Sufiana* ; and the *Drinking*

was.

was according to the Law ; None was compell'd, for so the King had appointed to all the Officers of his House, that they should do according to every Man's Pleasure, Est. I. 5. &c.

He sent EZRAH the learned Scribe to succeed *Zerubbabel,* who built *Synagogues* in every City: And next NEHEMIAH who re-built the Walls of *Jerusalem,* and obliged the richer People to fill that City with fine Houses; whereby it recover'd its antient Splendor. When *Abashuerus* died *A. M.* 3580.

7. XERXES his Son by Queen HESTER succeeded, but reign'd only 45 Days, being murder'd by

8. SOGDIANUS the Bastard of *Abashuerus* who reign'd 6 Months till destroy'd by

9. DARIUS NOTHUS, another Bastard of that King who reign'd 19 Years

In his 15th Year *Nehemiah* made his last Reformation; and *Malachi* being dead, we read no more of the Prophets.

A. M. ——— 3595. }
B. C. ——— 409. }

This Year NOTHUS gave Leave to Sanballat to build the *Samaritan Temple* on Mount *Gerizzim,* like That of *Jerusalem,* and made his Son-in-Law *Manasseh* the High Priest of it; and It stood splendid till JOHN HYRCANUS, the *Asmonæan* King and *High Priest* demolisht it : when also he made the *Idumeans* or *Edomites* conform to the Law of *Moses.*

from the said *A. M.* 3595. }
during Years ——— 279. }

till——— *A. M.* 3874. }
B. C. --- 130. }

After *Nehemiah,* the High Priest of *Jerusalem* for the Time being, was the *Provincial Grand Master* of *Judæa,* first under the Kings of *Persia,* and afterwards under the *Grecian* Kings of *Egypt* and *Syria. Darius Nothus* died *A. M.* 3599.

10. ARTAXERXES *Mnemon* his Son succeeded 46 Years. He was a great Encourager of the *Craft,* especially after the Ascent of his Brother *Cyrus,* and the Retreat of *Xenophon* A. M. 3603.

In

In his 12th Year the brave CONON rebuilt the Walls of *Athens*, The King died, *A. M. 3645.*

11. DARIUS OCHUS his Son succeeded 21 Years.

In his 6th Year, *A. M. 3651.* MAUSOLUS King of *Caria*, in *Lesser Asia* died, and next Year his mournful Widow ARTEMISIA (also his Sister) founded for him a most splendid Sepulchral Monument at *Halicarnassus*, of the best Marble, (Hence all great Tombs are call'd Mausoleums) in Length from North to South 63 Cubits in Circuit, 411 Foot, and in Height 140 Foot, surrounded with 136 *Columns* of most *accurate Sculpture*, and the Fronts East and West had Arches 73 Foot wide, with a Pyramid on the side Wall, ending in a pointed Broch, on which was a Coach with 4 Horses of *one* Marble *Stone*. All was perform'd by the 4 best *Masons* of the Age, *viz. Scopas, Leochares, Timotheus* and *Briax.* It is reckoned the 5th of the 7 *Wonders of Art.*

Ochus was murder'd by his favourite Eunuch *Bagoas*, who set up,

12. ARSES his youngest Son, (the rest being murder'd) 3667. But *Bagoas* fearing ARSES, murder'd him in two Years, and set up one of the Royal Family, *viz.*

13. DARIUS CODOMANNUS, who began to reign 3669. *Bagoas* prepared a Dose of Poison for him, but *Darius* made him drink it himself. He reign'd 6 Years, till conquer'd by *Alexander the Great.*

At length the ROYAL ART flourish'd in *Greece.* Indeed we read of the old *Dedalus* and his Sons, the Imitators of the *Egyptians* and *Phenicians*, of the little Labyrinth in *Crete*, and the larger at *Lemnos*, of the Arts and Sciences early at *Athenes* and *Sicyon*, *Candia* and *Sicily* before the *Trojan War* ; of the *Temples* of *Jupiter Olympius, Esculapius, &c.* of the *Trojan Horse*, and other Things : But we are all in Darkness, Fable and Uncertainty till the *Olympiads.*

E

Now

Now the 35th Year of *Uzziah* King of *Judah* is the firſt Year of the firſt OLYMPIAD ⎰*A. M.* 3228.⎱ before the Founding when ſome of their bright ⎱*B. C.* 776.⎰ of *Rome* 28 Years. Men began to travel.

So that their moſt antient famous Buildings, as the Cittadel of *Athenes*, the Court of *Areopagus*, the *Parthenion* or *Temple* of 𝕸𝖎𝖓𝖊𝖗𝖛𝖆, the *Temples* of *Theſeus* and 𝕬𝖕𝖔𝖑𝖑𝖔, their *Porticos* and *Forums*, *Theatres* and *Gymnaſiums*, ſtately publick *Halls*, curious *Bridges*, regular *Fortifications*, ſtout *Ships* of War, and magnificent *Palaces*, with their beſt *Statues* and *Sculpture*, were All of 'em, either at firſt erected, or elſe rebuilt fine, even after the *Temple* of ZERUBBABEL ; for

THALES MILESIUS, their firſt Philoſopher, died eleven Years only before the *Decree* of *Cyrus* ; and the ſame Year 3457, PYTHAGORAS, his Scholar, travell'd into *Egypt* ; while PISISTRATUS, the Tyrant of *Athenes*, began to collect the *firſt Library* in *Greece*.

PYTHAGORAS liv'd 22 Years among the *Egyptian* Prieſts till ſent by *Cambyſes* to *Babylon* and *Perſia*, *A. M.* 3480, where he pickt up great Knowledge among the *Chaldæan Magians* and *Babyloniſh Jews* ; and return'd to *Greece* the Year that *Zerubbabel's* 𝕿𝖊𝖒𝖕𝖑𝖊 was finiſh'd *A. M.* 3489.

He became, not only the Head of a new Religion of Patch Work, but likewiſe of an *Academy* or *Lodge* of good *Geometricians*, to whom he communicated a Secret * viz. *That amazing Propoſition which* * *Euclid. lib.* 1. *Prop.* *is the Foundation of all Maſonry, of what-* XLVII. *ever Materials or Dimenſions*, call'd by *Maſons* his *HEUREKA* ; becauſe They think It was his own Invention.

But after *Pythagoras*, GEOMETRY was the darling Study of the *Greeks*, and their learned Men reduced the noble *Science* to the Uſe of the ingenious *Mechanicks* of all Sorts, that perform by *Geometry* as well as the Operators in *Stone* or *Brick*.

And

And as MASONRY kept pace with *Geometry*, so many *Lodges* appear'd, especially in the *Grecian* Republicks, where *Liberty*, *Trade* and *Learning* flourish'd; as at *Sicyon*, *Athenes*, *Corinth* and the Cities of *Ionia*, till They arrived at their beautiful DORIC, IONIC and CORINTHIAN *Orders* : And their Improvements were soon discover'd to the *Persians* with a Vengeance, when They defeated *Xerxes, A. M.* 3525.

GREECE now abounded with the best *Architects*, *Sculptors*, *Statuaries*, *Painters* and other fine *Designers*, most of 'em educated at the Academies of *Athenes* and *Sicyon*, who Instructed many Artists and *Fellow Crafts* to be the best Operators upon Earth : So that the Nations of *Asia* and *Africa*, who had taught the *Greeks*, were now taught by 'em.

The learned *Greeks* rightly judging, that the Rules of the beautiful Proportions in *Architecture* should be taken from the Proportions of the *Human Body*, their fine *Painters* and *Statuaries* were esteem'd *Architects*, and were then actually so (even as afterwards true *old Masonry* was revived in *Italy*
by the *Painters* *) nor could They have been   * See Chap. VII.
fine *Painters* without being *Architects*.

Therefore several of those in the *Margin below*, excellent *Painters* and *Philosophers*, are in the List of *antient Architects* : Nay They all openly taught *Geometry*, and many of 'em practis'd *Masonry* ; and being Gentlemen of good Repute, They were generally at the *Head* of the *Craft*, highly useful to the *Fellow Crafts*, by their Designs and fine Drawings, and bred them up

---

* No Country but *Greece* could now boast of such Men as *Mycon, Phidias, Demon, Androcides, Metor Anaxagoras, Dipænus* and *Scyllis, Glycon, Alcamenes, Praxitiles, Polycletus, Lysippus, Peneus, Euphranor, Perseus, Philostratus, Zeuxis, Appollodorus, Parhasius, Timanthes, Eupompus, Pamphilus, Apelles, Artemones, Socrates, Eudoxus, Metrodorus* (who wrote of *Masonry*) and the excellent *Theodorus Cyrenæus*, who amplify'd *Geometry*, and
publisht the *Art Analytic*, thn Master of the divine   * *Plato* died *A.M.* 3656. ⎫
PLATO *, from whose School came *Xenocrates* and   *B. C.*‒.348, ⎭
Aristotle the Preceptor of ALEXANDER *the Great.*

clever

clever Artifts : Only by a Law in *Greece*, no *Slave* was allowed to learn the 7 liberal Sciences, or thofe of the *Freeborn* * ; fo that in *Greece* alfo They were call'd FREE MASONS, and in their many *Lodges*, the Noble and Learned were accepted as Brothers, down to the Days of ALEXANDER *the Great* and afterwards for many Ages.

* According to the old *Conftitutions* Thefe are, 1. *Grammar.* 2 *Rhetoric.* 3. *Logic.* 4. *Arithmetic.* 5. GEOMETRY. 6. *Mufic.* 7. *Aftronomy.*

That warlike Prince began to reign in *Macedonia* a little before DARIUS *Codomannus* began in *Perfia*, and next Year ALEXANDER entering *Afia*, won the Battel of *Granicus* ; and next Year the Battel of *Iffus*, and next Year took in *Tyre* and *Gaza*, and over-ran *Egypt* ; and next Year won the Battel of *Arbela*, after which poor DARIUS, flying into *Bactria*, was murder'd by his General *Beffus*, after he had reign'd 6 Years. After *Cyrus* began 207 Years.

A. M. 3669. B. C. 335.

A. M. 3674. B.C.--- 330. when the *Perfian* Monarchy ended, and the *Grecian* commenced.

But tho' from Ambition ALEXANDER order'd Denotrates the *Architect* to found *Alexandria* in *Egypt*, yet he is not reckon'd a MASON ; becaufe at the Inftigation of a drunken Whore, in his Revels, he burnt the rich and fplendid Perfepolis, a City of *Palaces* in the beft Stile, *which no true Mafon would do, was he ever fo drunk.*

He found the Lofs of that fine City when He returned from *India*, but did not retrieve it : Nor did he encourage the noble Propofal of *Denocrates* to difpofe Mount *Athos* in the Form of the *King's Statue*, with a *City* in one Hand, and in the other Hand a large *Lake* to water the City : Only He deftroy'd no more Monuments of Art. Indeed he lov'd *Apelles* who drew his Picture, and *Lyfippus* who formed his Statue, and intended to encourage Arts and Sciences throughout the World ; but he was prevented by dying drunk at *Babylon*, 6 Years after CODOMANNUS. A. M. 3680. B. C---324.

ALEXANDER

ALEXANDER left his new *Grecian* Monarchy to be partition'd among his Generals, which may be said to commence 12 Years after his Death, when SELEUCUS *Nicator* took in BABYLON and began the *Seleucian Era.*

$$A.\ M.\ 3692.$$
$$B.\ C.----312.$$

CHAP. V.

From SELEUCUS *to Grand Mafter* AUGUSTUS CÆSAR.

SELEUCUS *Nicator* prov'd an excellent *Grand Mafter,* founded the Great *Seleucia* on the *Euphrates* for his *Deputy* in the *Eaft* ; and in the *Weft* He built his ftately Capital City the famous ANTIOCH in old *Syria*, with the Great Grove of *Daphne*, a facred *Afylum*, in the Middle of which He rear'd the *Temple* of APOLLO and DIANA (tho' It prov'd afterwards the *Temple* of 𝔙𝔢𝔫𝔲𝔰 and 𝔅𝔞𝔠𝔠𝔥𝔲𝔰) and alfo the lefter Cities of old *Syria*, as *Apamia, Berræa, Seleucia, Laodicea, Edeſſa, Pella, &c.* and having reigned 33 Years He died *A. M.* 3725.

ANTIOCHUS *Soter* fucceeded his Father, and died *A. M.* 3744.

ANTIOCHUS *Treos* fucceeded his Father, and died *A. M.* 3759. the Progenitor of a long *Royal* Race that were all fet afide by POMPEY. But in the 4th Year of *Theos*

ARSACES, a noble *Parthian*, revolted from the *Syro Grecian* Kings, and founded the famous Kingdom of *Parthia, Anno Eræ Seleuci* 57. in *A. M.*————3748.
Eaftern *Afia*, that in Time fet Bounds to *B. C.*————256.
the *Romans*.

Yet the *Arfacidæ*, and alfo the *Seleucidæ*, being chiefly converfant in War, we muft travel into *Egypt*, to find the beft *Free-Mafons*,

Masons, where the *Grecian* Architecture flourish'd under the *Ptolemaidæ*. For

PTOLEMY SOTER had set up   *A. M.* ——— 3700. ⎫
his Throne at *Alexandria*, which he much   *A. C.* ——— 304. ⎬
inlarged and beautify'd.

EUCLID the *Tyrian* came to *Ptolemy* in this first Year, who had collected in his Travels the scatter'd *Elements of Geometry*, and digested them into a Method that was never yet mended ; for which his Memory will be fragrant in the *Lodges* to the End of Time.

PTOLEMY, *Grand-Master*, * with EUCLID the *Geometrician* and STRATON the *Philosopher*, as *Grand-Wardens*, built his Palace at *Alexandria*, and the curious *Musæum* or College of the Learned, with

                             * According to the
                             Traditions and the old
                             Constitutions.

the Library of *Brucheum* near the Palace, that was fill'd with 400000 Books, or valuable Manuscripts, before It was burnt in the Wars of JULIUS CÆSAR. *Soter* died ——— *A. M.* 3719.

PTOLEMY PHILADELPHUS succeeded his Father in the Throne and *Solomon*'s Chair too : And in his 2d Year he carried on the Great *Tower* of Pharo, founded by his Father, * the 6th of the 7 *Wonders* of *Art*, built on an Island, as the Light House for the Harbour of *Alexandria*, (whence *Light Houses* in the *Mediterranean* are call'd *Faros*) a Piece of amazing Architecture, by the Care of his *Grand-Wardens* Deriphanes and his Son Sostratus, the Father built the *Heptastadium* for joining the Island to the Continent, while the Son rear'd the *Tower*.

---

* Some prefer to This the great *Obelisk* of Queen SEMIRAMIS 150 Foot high and 24 Foot square at Bottom, all of one intire Stone like a *Pyramid*, that was brought from *Armenia* to *Babylon* ; also an huge Rock cut into the Figure of *Semiramis*, with the smaller Rocks by it in the Shape of tributary Kings : If we may believe *Ctesias* against the Advice of *Berosus* and *Aristotle* : For she is not so antient as is generally thought, and seems to be only the Queen of NABONASSAR.

PHILADELPHUS founded the City *Myos Hormus* on the *Red Sea* for the *Eaſt India* Trade, built the *Temple* of the *Zephyrian* 𝔙𝔢𝔫𝔲𝔰 in *Crete*, *Ptolemais* in *Paleſtine*, and rebuilt old *Rabbah* of the *Ammonites*, calling it *Philadelphia*. Nay he was ſo accurate an Architect that for a long Time all fine *Maſonry* was call'd 𝔓𝔥𝔦𝔩𝔞𝔡𝔢𝔩𝔭𝔥𝔦𝔞𝔫, or after the *Stile* of *Philadelphus*. He died *A. M.* 3757.

PTOLEMY EUERGETES his Son ſucceeded the great Encourager of the *Craft*, with his *Grand-Wardens* his two learned Librarians, *viz.* 𝔈𝔯𝔞𝔱𝔬𝔰𝔱𝔥𝔢𝔫𝔢𝔰 of *Cyrene*, and 𝔄𝔭𝔬𝔩𝔩𝔬𝔫𝔦𝔲𝔰 of *Perga*. The Library of *Brucheum* being near full, He erected That of *Serapium*, which in Time contain'd 300000 *Manuſcripts*, to which CLEOPATRA added 200000 more from the Library of *Pergamus* given to her by *Mark Antony* ; but all were burnt in Ovens by the ignorant *Saracens* to bake Bread for their Army *, to the laſting and irreparable Da-   * *A. D.* 642. mage of the Learned.

EUERGETES was the laſt good *Grand Maſter* of *Egypt* ; and therefore we ſhall ſail over to the *Helleſpont* to view the glorious *Temple* of *Cyzicus*, with Threads of beaten Gold in the Joints of the Inſides of the Marble Stones, that caſt a fine Luſtre on all the *Statues* and *Images* : Beſides the curious *Eccho* of the 7 *Towers* at the *Thracian* Gate of *Cyzicus*, and a large *Bouleutorion* or *Town-Houſe*, without one Pin or Nail in the Carpenter's Work ; ſo that the Beams and Rafters could be taken off, and again put on, without Laces or Keys to bind 'em.

The RHODIANS alſo employ'd CARES (the Scholar of *Lyſippus*) the *Architect*, to erect the *great* COLOSSUS of *Rhodes*, the laſt of the 7 *Wonders of Art*, made of *Metal*, the greateſt *human Statue* under the SUN, to whom It was dedicated.

It was 70 Cubits high and duly proportion'd in every Part and Limb, ſtriding in the Harbour's Mouth, wide enough to receive between his Legs the largeſt Ship under ſail, and appearing at a Diſtance like an high Tower.

It

It began in the 4th Year of *Ptolemy Soter* A. M. 3704 ⟩
and finifh'd in Years 12 ⟨

A. M. 3716 ⟩
It ftood firm, Years —— 66 ⟨

and fell by an Earthquake 3782 ⟩
B. C. 222 ⟨
the laft Year of PTOLEMY *Euergetes.*

The great COLOSSUS lay in Ruins, Years —— 894
even till *A D.* —— 672
when *Mahowias* the 6. Caliph of the *Saracens* carried It off to *Egypt*, the Load of 900 Camels.

Tho' fome prefer to It the Statue of *Jupiter Olympius* fitting on a fine Throne in his old *Doric Temple* of *Achaia*, made of innumerable Pieces of *Porphyre*, *Gold* and *Ivory*, exceeding Grand and exactly proportion'd ; for tho' the *Temple* was in Height 68 Foot clear, *Jupiter* could not ftand upright. It was perform'd by the great *Phidias*, as was That of *Nemefis* at *Rhamnus*, 10 Cubits high, and That of *Minerva* at *Athens* 26 Cubits high.

While the *Greeks* were propagating the *Science* and the *Art* in the very beft Manner, founding new Cities, repairing old ones, and erecting *Statues* paft Numbers, the other *Africans* imitated the *Egyptians*, Southward in *Ethiopia* down to the *Cape of Good Hope* ; and alfo Weftward to the *Atlantic Shore* : tho' Hiftory fails, and no *Travellers* have yet difcover'd the valuable Remains of thofe many powerful Nations. Only we know that

The CARTHAGINIANS had formed a magnificent Republick long before the *Romans* ; had built fome Thoufands of ftately *Cities* and ftrong *Caftles*, and made their great Capital CARTHAGE the Terror of *Rome*, and her Rival for univerfal Empire. Great was their Skill in *Geometry* and *Mafonry* of all Sorts, in Marble *Temples*, golden *Statues*, ftately *Palaces*, regular *Forts*, and ftout *Ships* that fail'd in all the known Seas, and carried on the Chief Trade of the known World : Therefore the *Emulous Romans* long defign'd its Deftruction, having a prophetical Proverb, *Delenda eft Cathago* ! *Carthage muft be demolifh'd* ; which They accomplifh'd, as in the Sequel.

Thus

Thus HANNIBAL the Warlike, in his Retreat from *Carthage* to *Armenia*, shew'd his great Skill in drawing for King *Artaxes* the Plan of the City *Artaxata*, and survey'd the *Palace, Temples* and *Citadel* thereof.

The learned SICILIANS, descended from the *Greeks*, follow'd their Instructions in Architecture throughout the Island very early, at *Agrigentum, Messana, Gela, &c.* especially at *Syracusa*; for when It was besieged by the *Romans* It was 22 Miles round, and *Marcellus* could not storm it, because of the amazing Devices of the learned Geometrician, Architect, Mechanic and Ingenier, the Noble * ARCHIMEDES, till by mastering an ill-guarded Tower, the City was taken by Surprize on a Festival Day. But tho'

> * Call'd by the old Masons the Noble and Excellent *Grand Master* of *Syracuse*.

Marcellus gave a strict Charge to save ARCHIMEDES, a comman Soldier slew him, while, not minding the Uproar, the noble and learned Man was deeply engaged in mechanical Speculations and Schemes to repulse the *Romans* and save *Syracuse*. MARCELLUS shed Tears for him as a publick Loss to the Learned, and gave him an honourable Burial in the Year of *Rome* 537. —— A. M. 3792.⎱ while *Hannibal* distress'd
B. C.--- 212.⎰ *Italy*.

Many of the *Grecian, Carthaginian* and *Sicilian* MASONS had travell'd into the *North* and *West* of Europe, and propagated their useful Skill, particularly in *Italy, Spain,* the *Belearic* Islands, and the Coast of *Gaul*; but History fails, till the *Roman* Armies came there. Nor have we certain Accounts of the *Chinese* and other *East Indians*, till the *Europeans* navigated thither in these later Times; only the Wall of *China* makes a Figure in the *Map*, tho' we know not yet when It was built: Also their Great Cities and most splendid Palaces, as described by Travellers, evidently discover that those antient Nations had long cultivated Arts and Sciences, especially *Geometry* and *Masonry*.

Thus hitherto the MASONS, above all other *Artists*, have been the Favourites of the Eminent, who wisely join'd the *Lodges* for the better conducting of their various Undertakings in old

F   Architecture:

Architecture: And still great Men continued at the Head of the Craft; as will appear in the Sequel.

From *Sicily* we soon pass into ITALY, to view the first Improvements of the ROMANS, who for many Ages affected nothing but War, till by Degrees They learned the *Science* and the *Art* from their Neighbours. But

The HETRURIANS, or *Tuscans*, very early used their own natural TUSCAN ORDER, never used by the *Greeks*, and were the first in *Italy* that learned from the *Greeks* the DORIC, IONIC and CORINTHIAN *Orders*; till the *Royal Art* was there conspicuous under their King PORSENNA, who built a stately *Labyrinth*, not inferior to That of *Lemnos*, and the highest *Mausoleum* on Record.

PORSENNA died in the Year of *Rome* 303. *A. M.* 3558 the 19th Year of *Artaxerxes Longimanus*, while *B. C.* 446 the *Romans* were only engaged in subduing their Neighbours in *Italy*, and their *Taste* was yet but *low*; till

TURRENUS, the last King of the *Tuscans*, bequeathed his Kingdom to the *Romans*; in the 6th Year of *Philadelphus*, while *Pyrrhus* destress'd *Italy*. TURRENUS died *A. M.* —— 3725 The *Tuscans* had built many fine strong Places; and now their Disciples were invited to *Rome*, and taught the *Romans* the Royal *Art*, tho' still their Improvements were not considerable, till

MARCELLUS triumphed in the splendid Spoils of *Syracuse*, upon the Death of the *Great* ARCHIMEDES, as above.

MARCELLUS, the Patron of Arts and Sciences, employ'd his *Fellow-Crafts* to build at *Rome* his famous Cheatre, with a *Temple* to Uirtue, and another to Honour; yet the *High Taste* of the *Romans* was not general till

SCIPIO *Asiaticus* led 'em against *Antiochus Magnus* King of *Syria*, and took from him all the Country *West* of Mount *Taurus* —— *A. M.* 3814 In the Year of *Rome* 559 In the 15th Year of *Ptol. Epiphanes B. C.* 190 For then, with Astonishment, They beheld the unspeakable Beauties of the *Grecian* and *Asiatick* Architecture, standing in full Splendor, which They resolved to Imitate.

And

And fo They went on Improving, till

SCIPIO *Africanus* (who had always a fet of the Learned at tending him as their *Patron*) took in the great Rival of *Rome* the *glorious* CARTHAGE, which he demolifh'd againft his own Incli nation by Command of the Senate ; for

Delenda eft Carthago A. M. 3858 ⎫
The Account of its Deftruction   B.C.   146 ⎬ Year of *Rome* 603
  is lamentable   ——————— ⎭

while *Conful* MUMMIUS the fame Year fack'd *Corinth*, the wealthy Queen of *Greece*, who difcover'd his Ignorance, when he threatned thofe that carried home, from *Corinth*, the Inimitable Pictures of Hercules and Bacchus, that if they loft 'em, They muft make 'em good with new ones.

Both thefe Generals triumphed at *Rome* in the portable Monu ments of Art, brought from thofe Cities, that had been the moft opulent and glorious upon Earth. But now the ROMANS were fo wife as to bring home too the ableft Profeffors of *Science*, and Practitioners of *Art*. After which we read of feveral ftately Edifices at *Rome*, built in the fineft *Grecian Stile :* as the famous Palace of PAULUS EMILIUS of the beft *Phrygian* Marble ; the *Triumphal* Arch of MARIUS at *Orange* in *Gaul*, the Three fur- prizing *Theatres* of * SCAURUS at *Rome*, &c.

The mighty SYLLA brought the *Columns* of the *Temple* of Jupiter *Olympius* from *Greece*, to adorn the *Temple* of Jupiter *Capitolinus* at *Rome*, after the old one, built by *Tarquinius Superbus* was burnt ; in whofe Time *Jupiter* was only of *Clay*, but now of pure *Gold*.

LUCULLUS, the learned and brave, erected a fine *Library*, and a fplendid Houfe with Gardens, in the *Afiatick* Stile.

———————————————

† The one held 80000 People at the Shows or Plays. It had 3 Scenes or Lofts one above another, with 360 Columns: the firft Row of *Marble*, each 38 Foot high, the 2d Row was of *Chryftal*, and the 3d of *Gilded Wood :* between the Co lumns were 3000 *Statues* of Brafs.

The other two *Theatres* were of *Wood*, fuftained on great *Axles*, whereby They could be turn'd round, and joined in one great *Amphi-Theatre.*   Plin

POMPEY the Great, built a *Theatre* that held 40000 People at the Shows, near his fine Palace, and his *Temple* of 𝕍𝕚𝕔𝕥𝕠𝕣𝕪.

These and other great Men, during the *Roman* Republick, much encouraged *Architects* and *Masons* as their *Patrons*; and in their Absence, the *Consul Resident*, or the *High Priest* of *Rome*, or the *Arch Flamin*, or some other Great Man on the Spot, thought it his honour to be the *Patron* of Arts and Sciences (what we now call *Grand Master*) attended duly by the most ingenious of the Fraternity; till the *Republic* was near its Exit by the Competition of *Pompey* and *Cæsar* for Pre-eminence.

But POMPEY being routed at *Pharsalia*, and murder'd by the *Egyptians* in his Flight, the 𝕽epublic expired, and

JULIUS CÆSAR obtain'd the Pre-eminence —— *A. M.* 3956 ⎰

CÆSAR now perpetual *Dictator* ⎱ Year of *Rome* 701 *B.C.* 48 ⎰ and *Imperator*, a learned Geome- ⎱ Before the Birth of Christ 44 trician, Architect, Ingenier and Astronomer, being *High Priest*, reformed the *Roman* CALENDAR *B.C.* or before the Christian Era 45.

He and his Legions had built much in *Gaul*, and at *Rome* he rais'd his Great *Circus* or Square, a true *Oblong*, 3 Furlongs in Length, and one in Breadth, that held 260,000 People at the Shows: also his stately Palace, and lovely *Temple* of 𝕍enus, and ordered *Carthage* and *Corinth* to be rebuilt, about 100 Years after They were demolish'd.

See *Pliny*, who gives a full Account of these Things.

But CÆSAR, intending first to quell the *Parthians*; and then, as *Grand Master* of the *Roman Republic*, to encourage the *Science* and the *Art* beyond all before him in universal Peace, was basely murder'd by his ungrateful *Brutus* under *Pompey*'s Statue; upon which the Civil Wars ended, and the Pre-eminence was in Suspence during 14 Years,

A. M. —— 3960 ⎰
B. C. 44

till first *Brutus* and *Cassius* were lost at *Philippi*, and next *Mark Antony* was defeated at *Actium* by OCTAVIANUS, who then conquer'd *Egypt*, and finish'd the Civil Wars: and so the *Grecian* Monarchy being fully ended, the ROMAN Empire began In the Year of *Rome* 719 —— *A. M.* 3974 ⎰ Before the Christian Era —— 30 ⎱

CHAP.

CHAP. VI.

From AUGUSTUS *till the* Havock *of the* 𝔊oth𝔰.

ROME, now the Miſtreſs of the known World, became the Center of Learning a of Imperial Power, and arrived at her *Zenith* under

OCTAVIANUS, now called *Sebaſtos,* or AUGUSTUS CÆSAR, who patroniz'd the Fraternity as their Illuſtrious *Grand Maſter,* (ſo call'd always by the *old* MASONS) with his Deputy AGRIPPA, who adorned the *Campus Martius,* and built the Grand *Portico* of the ROUTNDA *Pantheon,* with many more charming Piles mention'd in Hiſtory.

VITRUVIUS the Learned, the principal *Warden,* by his Writings has Juſtly acquir'd the Character of the Father or Teacher of all accurate Architects, and clever Connoiſſeurs to this Day.

AUGUSTUS firſt employ'd his *Fellow Crafts* in repairing all the publick Edifices (a moſt needful Work after the Wars) and in rebuilding ſome of 'em. But alſo he built the Bridge of *Ariminum;* and at *Rome* the *Temple* of MARS the *Avenger,* the *Temple* of Apollo, the *Rotunda* call'd *Galucio,* the great and ſumptuous *Forum,* the principal and magnificent *Palace* of AUGUSTUS, with ſome leſſer Palaces, the fine *Mauſoleum,* the accurate *Statue* in the *Capitol,* the curious *Library,* the *Portico,* and the *Park* for People to walk in, *&c.* Nay, He fill'd the *Temples* of *Rome* with the moſt coſtly *Statues,* and wittily ſet up *That* of CLEOPATRA (of maſſy Gold brought from *Egypt*) in the *Temple* of VENUS.

In thoſe Golden Days of AUGUSTUS, the Eminent following his Example, built above 100 *Marble Palaces* at *Rome,* fit for the greateſt

greateſt Kings ; and every ſubſtantial Citizen rebuilt their Houſes too in *Marble*, all joining in the ſame Diſpoſition of adorning *Rome :* whereby many *Lodges* appear'd, in City and Suburbs, of the *Free* and *Accepted Maſons :* ſo that AUGUSTUS, when a dying, juſtly ſaid, *I found* Rome *built of* Brick, *but I leave it built of* Marble !

Therefore the preſent Remains of *antient Rome* in his Time, and of ſome following Emperors, are ſo accurate, that They are the beſt Patterns of *true Maſonry* extant, the Epitome of all the old *Grecian Architecture*, commonly expreſſed by the AUGUSTAN STILE : and we now wiſh to arrive at its glorious Perfection in *Wiſdom*, *Strength* and *Beauty*.

But before the Death of AUGUSTUS, we muſt travel into *Judæa*. The *High Prieſts* of *Jeruſalem* had been *Provincial Grand Maſters* there, under the Kings of *Egypt* then Sovereigns of the *Jews*, till SELEUCUS *Philopater* King of   *A. M.* 3824 } *Syria* ſeiz'd *Judæa*, or *Paleſtin*. His Son *viz.*   *B. C.* 180 }

ANTIOCHUS *Epiphanes* cruelly perſecuted the *Jews* till reſcued by the valiant *Aſmonæan* Prieſt *Judas Maccabæus :* for long after *Zerubbabel* and *Jeſhua* the High Prieſt, an ordinary Prieſt, call'd *Aſmonæus*, appear'd, not of the Houſe of *Jeſhua*, but only of the Courſe of *Joarib*, the Great Grand Father of *Mattathias*, the brave Prieſt of *Modin* and Father of MACCABÆUS.

For the lineal Succeſſor of *Jeſhua* was ONIAS IV. (Son of *Onias* III. the laſt good *High Prieſt*) who being depriv'd of his Right by the *Syrian* Kings, went to *Egypt*, where He got leave to build a **Temple** at *Heliopolis*, like That of *Jeruſalem*, for the *Jews* in *Egypt* and *Cyrene*, then more numerous and opu lent than thoſe in *Judæa*. This *Temple* was founded *A. M.* 3855 }
But the *Aſmonæans* or *Maccabees* fought their   *B. C.* 149 }

Way to Pre-eminence, } It ſtood ſplendid till   *A. D.* ___ 73 }
againſt the *Syrian* Kings, }   during Years 222
and alſo obtain'd it as } Till deſtroy'd by *Veſpaſion* the Emperor.
High Prieſts and Princes of the *Jews*, during about 130 Years, till *Mark Antony* and *Octavicnus* got the *Senate* of *Rome* to create

HEROD

HEROD the *Edomite*, or *Idumean Jew*, King of *Judæa* in the *Capitol A. M.* 3964, and by the Help of the *Romans*, HEROD conquer'd ANTIGONUS, and mounted the Throne at *Jerusalem*

See the ⎫	A. M. ———	3367 ⎫
Margin ⎬	Before the Christian Era	37 ⎬
Below. ⎭	Before the Birth of Christ	33 ⎭

---

* MATTATHIAS the *Asmonæan* Priest died *A. M.* 3837. *B. C.* 167. And three of his Sons ruled the *Jews*, viz.

| 1 JUDAS MACCABÆUS died 3843 acted as High Priest and Ruler | 2 JONATHAN owned a Free Prince and High Priest. Murder'd 3860 | 3 SIMON the King and High Priest, erected over *Jonathan*'s Grave a lofty Monument of *white Marble* |

ruled independent of the *Gentiles*, till murder'd *A. M.* 3868

4 JOHN HYRCANUS succeeded Father *Simon*, till he died 3897

| 5 ARISTOBULUS I. reign'd one year, viz. *A. M.* 3898 | 6 ALEXANDER JANNÆUS reign'd 27 years, and died *A. M.* 3925. leaving the Crown to |

7 ALEXANDRA his Widow, and *Hyrcanus* wore the Mitre, till she died *A. M.* 3934

| 8 HYRCANUS, after his Mother died, was *King* and *High-Priest* 3 Months, till deprived by his Brother. He was restored by POMPEY only to the *Mitre*, till captivated by the *Parthians*, who set up ANTIGONUS 3964. *Hyrcanus* was beheaded by *Herod, A. M.* 3974 | 9 ARISTOBOLUS II. usurped 6 Years till deposed by POMPEY 3940 and poisoned ——— 3955 |

| ALEXANDRA Wife of her first Cousin, viz. | ALEXANDER beheaded 3995 | 10 ANTIGONUS set up by the *Parthians* 3964. reign'd 3 Years, till conquer'd by *Herod* and crucify'd by the *Romans* ——— 3967 |

| * * HEROD I. an *Idumæan Jew*, created at *Rome* K. of *Judæa* 3964 conquer'd *Antigonus* and began to reign 3967 ⎫ and in the last Year ⎬ of his Reign —— 33 ⎭ | MARIAMNE *Herod*'s Queen, was by him beheaded 3975. and by his Order her two Sons were strangled, but they left a Royal Race | ARISTOBULUS III. made *High Priest* by *Herod*, till drown'd in a Bath without Issue 3969 |

Christ *A. M.* —— 4000 was born but the *first* Year of our *A. D.* or *Christian Era*, is *A. M.* 4004. See Page 2.

He got rid of all the *Afmonæans*, made the *Sanhedrim* ufe-
lefs, and fet up *High Priefts* at his Pleafure. But for all his
great Faults,

HEROD became the greateſt Builder of his Day, the Patron or
Grand Maſter of many *Lodges*, and fent for the moſt expert *Fellow
Crafts* of *Greece* to affiſt his own *Jews*: For after the Battle of
Actium B. C. 30. Before *Chriſt*'s Birth 26.

HEROD, being reconciled to *Auguſtus*, began to fhew his mighty
Skill in *Maſonry*, by erecting a fplendid *Grecian* THEATRE at
Jeruſalem, and next built the ſtately City *Sebaſte*, (fo called from
Sebaſtos or *Auguſtus*) formerly *Samaria*, with a curious little *Temple*
in It like That of *Jeruſalem*. He made the City *Cæfarea* the beſt
Harbour in *Paleſtine*, and built a *Temple* of white Marble at
Paneas ——the Cities *Antipatris*, *Phaſaelis* and *Cypron*, and the
Tower of *Phaſael* at *Jeruſalem*, not Inferior to the *Pharo* of *Alex-
andria*, &c.

But his moſt amazing Work was his Rebuilding of the **Temple**
of ZERUBBABEL ; for having prepared Materials (which with
thoſe of the old Temple were enough) and proper Inſtruments,
HEROD employ'd 10000 *Maſons* (befides Labourers) and marſhall'd
'em in *Lodges* under 1000 Prieſts and Levites that were ſkilful
Architects, as *Maſters* and *Wardens* of the *Lodges*, and acted as
GRAND MASTER himſelf with his Wardens HILLEL and
SHAMMAI, two learned *Rabbins* of great Reputation.

He began to pull down the *Temple* of *Zerubbabel*, not all at
once, but Piece by Piece, and levelled the Foot-ſtone of this
Temple of *Jeruſalem*, viz.

After the founding of the *ſecond Temple*
518 Years

In the 21ſt Year of *Herod* and 13 Year | *A. M.* ——— 3987 ⎫
of *Auguſtus* and 29th *Julian* Year. ⎬ Before the *Chr. Æra* 17 ⎬
In the 4th Year of *Olympiad* CXC. and | ⎭
of *Rome* 732. | Before *Chriſt*'s Birth 14

Juſt 46 Years before the ſecond Paſſover of *Chriſt*'s Miniſtry
ſor the *Jews* faid 46 *Years was this Temple in Building*, John xi. 20.

The

The *Holy Place*, and the *Holy of Holiest* in the West, and the great *Portico* in the East, were finish'd at a wondrous Cost, and in the short Space of 1 Year and 6 Months } 9 Y. and 6 M. and the Rest design'd by *Herod* in 8 Years more.

When the *Fraternity* celebrated the *Cape Stone* with great Joy and in due Form, and the King solemniz'd Its *Dedication* by Prayer and Sacrifice, on his Coronation Day, of the 31st Year of his Reign, } * *A. M.* ———— 3997 } and 23d of *Augustus* *. Before the Christian Era 7 } Before *Christ's Birth*

Josephus describes It †, as he † *Antiq.* lib. xv. cap xi. view'd It, with the Additions built after *Herod* died, a number of the most curious and magnificent Marble Edifices that had been rais'd since the Days of SOLOMON ; yet more after the *Grecian Stile*, and much Inferior to *Solomon's* TEMPLE in Extent and Decoration, tho' larger than That of *Zerubbabel*, and was by the *Romans* esteemed the same : for *Tacitus* calls It the same that *Pompey* walk'd thro'.

But It was not fully finish'd, in all Its Appartments, till about 6 Years before It was destroy'd, *viz.* A. D. 64.

At length

AUGUSTUS having shut up the *Temple* of *JANUS* ; for that all the World was at Peace, In the 26th Year of his Empire, after the Conquest of *Egypt*,

The WORD was made *FLESH*, or the LORD JESUS CHRIST IMMANUEL was born, the Great Architect or *Grand Master* of the *Christian* Church.

After *Solomon's* Death	971 }	In the Year of the *Julian Period* 4710
In the Year of *Rome*	745 }	In the Year of *Masonry* or *A.M.* 4000
In the Year of *Herod*	34 }	B. C. or Before the *Christ. Æra* 4

King HEROD died a few Months after the *Birth* of CHRIST, and, notwithstanding his vast Expence in *Masonry*, He died rich.

After the Birth of *Christ* 4 Years, or when CHRIST was going in his 4th Year, The CHRISTIAN Era begins *A. M.* 4004.

Commonly call'd ANNO DOMINI, ——— 1.

See the Margin of Page 2.

G

And when *Chrift* was aged near 18 Years, the *Great* Augustus died at *Nola* in *Campania*, Aug. 19. —— A. D. 14
In the Year of *Rome* 761 ⎰ In the *Vulgar* Year of *Mafonry* 4014
After he had reign'd 44 ⎱ tho' the accurate Year is 4018
Years : when TIBERIUS I. his Collegue began to reign alone, who alfo encouraged the *Craft.*

In his 20th Year after *Auguftus,* or the *Vulgar A. D.* 34.
The LORD JESUS CHRIST, aged 36 Years, and about 6 Months, was Crucified, without the Walls of *Jerufalem,* by *Pontius Pilat* the *Roman* Governor of *Judæa,* and rofe again from the Dead on the 3d Day, for the Juftification of all that believe in him.

Tiberius banifh'd *Pontius Pilat* for his Injuftice to Christ ; and next Year That Emperor died *A. D.* 35

The Augustan Stile was well cultivated, and the clever *Craftsmen* were much encouraged by fome following Emperors. Thus even

NERO, for all his grofs Faults, rais'd his brazen *Statue* in *Via Sacra* 110 Foot high ; and built his guilded Palace, a Nonfuch.

VESPASIAN, who commenced *A. D.* 68. fent his brave Son Titus to fubdue the *Jews.* Titus took in *Jerufalem,* when a Soldier, without Orders, fet fire to the Temple⎱ A. D. —— 70
Vespasian fhut the *Temple* of Janus, and built ⎰ after Chrift's⎱
the *Temple* of Peace. He rais'd his famous ⎰ Crucifixion ⎱ 36
Amphi-Theatre, when the rich Composite⎰
Order was firft ufed. He order'd the *Jewifh Temple* in *Egypt* to be demolifh'd, *A. D.* 73. and died *A. D.* 77.

TITUS reign'd but 2 Years.	DOMITIAN fucceeded Brother
He had built his *Triumphal* Arch	*Titus,* and rebuilt the *Temple* of
with fine Ingravings ; and a	Jupiter *Capitolinus,* moft magni-
ftately Palace with the famous	ficent, overlaid It with Plates of
Statue of *Laocoon* of one Stone,	Gold, and had all the *Columns*
and died *A. D.* 79.	cut at *Athenes.*

Domitian built alfo the *Temple* of MINERVA, and That of the *Flavians* ; and rais'd a *Palace* more Grand and Rich than
That

That of *Augustus*, with stately Galleries in the Portico, besides Halls, Baths and beautiful Apartments for his Women. He died *A. D.* 93. succeeded by NERVA, who died — 95. after he had adopted

TRAJAN, whose Warden was *Apollodorus*, the Architect, He laid his wonderful Bridge over the *Danube*, built his noble *Circus* and *Palace*, his two *Triumphal* Arches, the one at *Ancona* still standing, and the other at *Rome*, afterwards pull'd to Pieces to adorn the *Arch* of CONSTANTIN: besides *Trajan* erected his famous COLUMN, a Pattern of the Kind, well known to all Connoisseurs. He died *A. D.* 114.

ADRIAN succeeded, a learned Designer, and even a dexterous Operator, repair'd the publick Edifices, like a Wise *Grand Master*, built *Adrian*'s Wall in *Britain*, his commodious Bridge at *Rome*, and his famous *Mausoleum* or MOLES ADRIANI, with accurate *Collonading*, and died *A. D.* 135.

ANTONINUS PIUS rais'd his curious Column, and died *A. D.* 159.

MARCUS AURELIUS countenanced the Artists till he died *A. D.* 178.

———————⌒———————

COMMODUS, tho' educated a *Designer*, turn'd vicious; and, in his Time, *Painting* and *Sculpture* began to decline at *Rome*, tho' not yet *Architecture*. He died *A. D.* 191.

SEVERUS built his *Corinthian Epizone* at *Rome*, and *Murfever* in *Britain*. He died at *York A. D.* 209.

———————⌒———————

CORACALLA erected his splendid *Circus*, and died *A. D.* 215. Nor find we much more till

CONSTANTIN the *Great*, who commenced in *Britain* Emperor of *Rome*, A. D. 306. He repair'd and beautify'd *Jerusalem*, *Drepanum*, *Troy*, *Chalcedon*, *Thessalonica*, &c. and rear'd at *Rome* the last *Triumphal* Arch in the *Augustan Stile*.

For He removed his Throne from *Rome* to *Bizantium*, which he call'd now *Constantinople*, and also carried off all the portable Monuments of Art from *Italy*, and the best Artists to embellish his

new

new Metropolis, where He built at a vaſt Rate, many artful Piles, *Forums, Hippodroms, Temples* or *Churches, Porticos, Fountains,* a *ſtately Imperial Palace and Senate Houſe,* a *Pillar* of *Porphyre* of 8 Stones, about 87 Foot high above the Pedeſtal, and the amazing *Serpentin Pillar* with his own *Equeſtrian Statue,* &c. He died *A. D.* 336.

See *Petrus Gyllius* his Antiquities of *Conſtantinople,* tranſlated into *Engliſh* by Mr *Ball, A.* D 1729.

CONSTANS brought with him to *Rome* the famous Architect HORMISDAS the King of *Perſia's* Son, who was juſtly aſtoniſh'd at the antient Structures and Statues, and declared them inimitable : for now all the *Arts of Deſigning* dwindled at *Rome,* as They flouriſh'd at *Conſtantinople.* Nay the *Chriſtians,* in Zeal againſt Heathen Idolatry, demoliſh'd many curious Things ; till

The *Roman Empire* was partition'd between two Brothers, *viz.*

VALENTINIAN 1. Emperor of the *Weſt* at *Rome.* Now the *Chriſtians* at *Rome* adorn'd their old Church of St. *Peter's* with the Columns of *Adrian's Mole,* but could not follow the Juſt Proportions of the Antients. He died *A. D.* 374. and this Empire was ſoon ingroſſed by the *Eaſtern* ;

and VALENS Emperor of the *Eaſt* at *Conſtantinople,* who was diſtreſs'd by the *Goths,* and died without Iſſue, *A. D.* —— 378 THEODOSIUS *the Great* ſucceeded, who built a fine *Column* like That of *Trajan,* with his brazen *Statue* on the Top of It, and a great *Circus.*

THEODOSIUS gloried in being the *Potron* of all the *Deſigners* and *Operators* (the ſame as *Grand Maſter*) and loved them ſo well, that by a Law, he exempted *all the Craft* from Taxation.

The Northern Nations of *Europe,* the *Goths, Vandals, Huns. Allemans, Herules, Sweves, Dacians, Alans, Franks, Gepidans, Saxons, Angles, Longobards,* and many more, had gradually grown powerful as the *Roman Empire* decay'd, and invaded *Greece, Aſia, Gaul, Spain* and *Africa,* nay *Italy* Itſelf, over-running the polite World like a Deluge, with warlike Rage and groſs Ignorance, the Enemies of *Arts* and *Sciences.*

But THEODOSIUS ſtopt their Carrier, became ſole Emperor of the *Eaſt* and *Weſt,* and died A. D 395.

TH o

THEODOSIUS divided the Empire between his two Sons, *viz.*

HONORIUS, Emperor of the *West* at *Rome*, in whose Reign *Alaricus* the warlike *Visogoth* took in *Rome* A.D. 409.

HONORIUS died A.D. 423.

VALENTINIAN III. succeeded, in whose Reign ATTILA the *Hun* laid *Italy* waste, and would have destroy'd *Rome* but for the Prudence of the Bishop. When he died *A.D.* ——— 455

Ten *nominal* Emperors succeeded. Mean while *GENSERICUS* the *Vandal* came from *Carthage*, and plunder'd *Rome* 456
At last

AUGUSTULUS, the Tenth of those *Nominal* Emperors, fairly abdicated for fear of *Odoacer* King of the *Herules* 475
So ended the *Western* Empire,
when

The GOTHIC Kings of *Italy* succeeded, *viz.* ODOACER King of *Italy* reign'd 17 Years, till slain by

THEODORIC the *Goth.* A. D. 492 He and his Race reign'd Kings of *Italy* during 48 Years, till *A. D.* 540. when

TOTILA was elected King of *Italy*. But maliciously designing to extinguish the Name and Memorial of old *Rome*, *TOTILA* set it on fire during 13 Days, and had demolish'd about two Thirds of that lofty Metropolis of the World, before he was beat off by *Bellisarius*, A.D. 547
O *Gothic* Ignorance!

And here we may date the *Total Departure* of the AUGUSTAN STILE in *Italy* and the *West*.

See Its *Revival* in the next Chapter.

ARCADIUS Emperor of the *East* at *Constantinople*, who inriched that City with many fine Structures, and his lofty *Pillar*, with a Stair in the Heart of It, 147 Foot high. He died *A. D.* 408.

THEODOSIUS, *Jun.* erected there *Statues, Columns* and *Obelisks*, the Spoils of *Greece, Egypt* and *Asia*; repair'd the great Church of St. *Sophia*, and died 449

The following Emperors of the *East* supported the *Lodges* or Academies of the Artists or *Craftsmen*, down to

JUSTINIAN I. who began A. D. ——— 526. He restor'd the whole *Roman* Empire almost to its Pristin Glory.

Nay, in laudable Zeal for the AUGUSTAN STILE, He sent his General, the brave BELLISARIUS, with an Army against *TOTILA* the *Goth*, whom he forced to run away; and so *Bellisarius* saved as much of old *Rome* as he could
A.D. 547
JUSTINIAN

JUSTINIAN I. by his General *Narſes*, deſtroy'd TOTILA 551
He collected the *Roman* Laws in his *Codex Juſtinianus*; and expended 34 Millions of Gold in rebuilding the Church of St. *Sophia*, which he intended to be equal, in Decoration, to SOLOMON's Temple, tho' in vain.

When this learned *Grand Maſter* died A. D. 565
JUSTIN II. ſucceeded, who upon the Death of *Teyas* the laſt *Gothic* King of *Italy* A. D. 568. appointed the EXARCHS of *Ravenna* to ſucceed the *Roman Couſuls*, to rule *Italy* by the *Roman* Laws, and to ſtop the Incurſions of the *LONGOBARDS* ; which They did, till the laſt *Exarch* was expell'd by *Luitprandus* King of *Lombardy*, A. D. 741.

The *LONGOBARDS* began to reign in the North of *Italy* (from them called *Lombardy*) the ſame time with the *Exarchs* of *Ravenna*, till conquer'd by CHARLE MAIN, who captivated *Deſiderius* the laſt King of *Lombardy*, A. D. 771. But to return,

JUSTIN II. died *A. D.* 582. ſucceeded by TIBERIUS II. and he by MAURICUS murder'd PHOCAS, and he was murder'd by

HERACLIUS, who commenced *A. D.* 610. Father of CONSTANTIN III. Father of CONSTANS II. Father of CONSTANTIN IV. Father of JUSTINIAN II. murder'd *A. D.* 710. When the *Eaſtern* Emperors called the *Iconoclaſtes*, or Deſtroyers of Images, began. So that here we may date the Departure of the AUGUSTAN STILE from the *Eaſt* ; after the *Havock* of TOTILA 163 Years.

Thus the AUGUSTAN STILE was quite loſt, and the Loſs was publick.

Now the 12th Year of HERACLIUS *A. D.* 622. is the firſt Year of the *Mahometan* HEGIRA. And ſo if from this *A. D.* 1737
We ſubſtract Years 621
——
The preſent *Anno Hegiræ* is 1116
But the *Grand Deſign* of the MAHOMETANS was not to cultivate *Arts* and *Sciences*, but to convert the World by *Fire* and *Sword* : So that Architecture in *Aſia* and *Africa* ſuffer'd by them as in *Europe* by the *GOTHS*.

For

For when the *Gothic Nations*, and thofe conquer'd by them, began to affect ftately Structures, They wanted both Heads and Hands to imitate the Antients, nor could They do it for many Ages (as in the next Chapter) yet not wanting Wealth and Ambition, They did their beft: and fo the more Ingenious gradually coalefced in Societies or *Lodges*, in Imitation of the Antients, according to the remaining Traditions that were not quite obliterated, and hammer'd out a *New Stile* of their own, call'd the GOTHIC.

But tho' This is more expenfive than the *old Stile*, and difcovers now to us the Ignorance of the *Architect*, and the Improprieties of the *Edifice* ; yet the Inventions of the *Artifts* to fupply the Want of good old Skill, and their coftly Decorations, have manifefted their great Efteem of the *Royal Art*, and have render'd their *Gothic* Structures *Venerable* and *Magnificent* ; tho' not Imitable by Thofe that have the true *High Tafte* of the *Grecian* or AUGUSTAN STILE.

CHAP. VII.

The REVIVAL *of* Old Architecture, *or the* AUGUSTAN *Stile.*

THE *Royal Art* lies dead and buried ftill in the *Eaft*, by the wilful Ignorance of the *Mahometan* Nations. But firft in *Italy* It began to peep from under Its Rubbifh in *Tufcany* : for the *Pifans* brought from *Greece* a few Marble *Columns* and other Fragments of *old Mafonry* for their new Cathedral carried on by BUSCHETTO the *Greek*, who firft began to imitate the Antients.

After TOTILA'S *Havock*,	A. D. 547
Years ——	466
	A. D. 1013

He join'd with Others to form a *New Lodge*, for that laudable Imitation, built St. *John's* at *Pifa*, and educated many Artifts that long'd for the *Revival*, till IL BUONO flourifh'd at *Ravenna*, and built at *Venice* the Steeple of St. *Mark*. A. D. 1152.

OLTRO·

Oltromontano and Bonnano built the Steeple of *Pisa* .174
Marchione of *Arezzo* rais'd the Marble Chappel of
Presepio at St. *Mary Majore* ———————— 1216
James the *German* built the firſt fine Edifices of *Florence*,
whoſe Son Jacopo Arnolpho Lapo, with the Painter
Cimaboius, deſign'd the Cathedral of St. *Mary Delfiore* 1298

CHARLES of *Anjou*, King of *Naples*, was the *firſt Prince*
that publickly encouraged the *Revival* of the *Arts* of *Deſigning*,
by employing the ſaid *Cimaboius* and *Nicholas Piſan* to build an
Abby in the Plain of *Taglia Cotzo*, where CHARLES had defeated
the Pretender *Conradin*. JOHN PISAN, ſon of *Nicholas*, built for
the King his new Caſtle of *Naples*. This Royal Patron, (the ſame
as *Grand Maſter*) of the *Revivers*, died *A. D.* 1285. And his
Succeſſors inriched the Kingdom of *Naples* with learned Architects,
and ſplendid Edifices.

Cimaboius and the *Piſans*, educated many fine *Maſters*
and *Fellow Crafts*; particularly,

Giotto the Architect; till the ⎰ After Totila's *Havoke* 547 ⎱
Florentines arrived at a pretty good ⎱ Years ———— 753 ⎰
Imitation of the Antients, which ⎰
was diſcover'd in all the Parts of ⎱ ————
the Church in St. *Miniate*. A. D. 1300

Giotto and his Pupils formed an Academy of *Deſigners*, or a
learned *Lodge* at *Florence*, who, like thoſe of old at *Athenes* and
Sicyon, inlightened *all Italy*, by ſending forth excellent Connoiſſeurs
and dexterous Operators in all the Arts of *Deſigning*.

Andrew Pisan, one of them, was made a Magiſtrate of
Florence; and many of 'em afterwards flouriſh'd Wealthy at *Piſa*,
Ravenna, *Venice*, *Urbino*, *Rome*, and *Naples*.

Laurentio Ghiberto, educated there, conducted for ſome
Time the Raiſing of the ſaid St. *Mary Delfiore*, and framed the
Two Brazen Gates of St. *John*'s, of which, long afterwards, *Michael
Angelo* ſaid in Rapture, that they were worthy of being the *Gates*
of *Paradiſe*.

Do-

DONATELLO next appear'd with *Andrea Verrochio*, the Mafter of *Piedro Perrugino* and *Leonardo da Vinci*, prodigious Men! Alſo *Dominigo Ghirlandaio* the Mafter of *Michael Angelo* and *Maiano*, and other ſublime and profound Architects.

Yet the *Gothic* Stile was not quite left off at *Florence*; till

BRUNELESCHI, having ſtudied at *Rome* the Beauty and Accuracy of the old *Roman* Buildings there ſtanding or proftrate, return'd full fraught to *Florence*, where He eſtablifh'd the ample and com- pleat Uſe of the *Doric*, *Ionic*, *Corinthian* and *Compofite* ORDERS ; and ſo the GOTHIC STILE was wholly laid aſide there, and the AUGUSTAN STILE was entirely Reviv'd.

}
After TOTILAH's *Havock* 547 }
Years juſt ——— 853 }
A. D. 1400

This *happy* REVIVAL was alſo much owing to the Coun- tenance and Encouragement given to the Learned, by the *Princes* of the Houſe of MEDICIS.   Thus

1. JOHN *de Medicis* Duke of *Florence*, became the learned *Patron* of the *Revivers*, or their *Grand Mafter*, and carefully ſupported the ſaid *Lodge*, or Academy of Maſters and Connoiſſeurs, at *Florence*, till he died A. D. 1428.

---

2. COSMO I. *de Medicis*, educated in that ſame Academy, ſucceeded his Father as Duke of *Flo- rence*, and *Grand Mafter* of the *Revivers*.   He erected a fine *Library* of the beſt Manuſcripts brought from *Greece* and *Afia*, and a curious *Cabinet* of the rareſt and moſt valuable Things that could be gather'd.   He eſtablifh'd very great Commerce by Sea and Land, and juſtly acquir'd the Title of *Pater Patriæ*, the Father of his Country, and died A. D. 1464.

LAURENTIO *de Medicis*, a Lord in *Florence*, ſlain 1474.

JOHN JULIAN *de Medicis*, the moſt beautiful Youth and the moſt excellent Connoiſſeur in true old Archi- tecture in all *Florence*.

3 PETER I. *de Medicis* upheld the Lodge, and died Duke of *Florence* A. D. 1472.
But he was not ſo Eminent as either his Father or his Son.   3. *Peter* I.

This

H

3. *Peter* I.

4 LAURENTIO I. *de Medicis* Duke of *Florence*, stiled the *Magnificent*, was both *Horace* and *Mecenas*, and *Grand Master* of the *Revivers*. He inrich'd his Grandfather's *Library* and *Cabinet* at a vast Expence; and erected a *great Gallery* in his Garden, for educating the more promising Youth; among whom young *Michael Angelo*, as a Favourite, was admitted to the Duke's Table.

This kind Grand Master died 9 *April* 1492.

JULIAN *de Medicis* slain 1478 whose natural Son

JULIUS *de Medicis* was elected POPE *Clement* 7. 1523. He was besieged by *Ch.* v. and forced the *Florentines* to submit to his Kinsman Duke *Alexander* 1531. He was a most Ingenious Architect and carried on St. *Peter's* at *Rome*, till he died, 1534.

This Jo. JULIAN was also a dexterous operator, to the great Honour of the *Fellow Crafts*. He died 1498.

LEWIS, call'd JOHN *de Medicis*, was educated at *Florence* in Mathematical Learning: but his Genius was for War, and so affected the *military Architecture* He died 1526.

5 PETER II. *de Medicis* succeeded Duke of *Florence*, upheld his Father's curious Works, and countenanced the Academies and *Lodges*, till He died 1504.

JOHN *de Medicis* was elected POPE LEO X. 1513. a zealous Patron of the *Revivers* at *Rome*, especially in Carrying on the *gorgeous Cathedral* of St. PETERS, till He died *A. D.* 1521.

By his Wife Duke *Peter* had

By his Mistress Duke *Peter* had

6 LAURENTIO II. *de Medicis* succeeded his Father 1504, Duke of *Florence*, and *Patron* of the *Revivers*, till he died without Issue. 1519

7 ALEXANDER *de Medicis*, who succeeded *Laurentio* as Duke of *Florence* 1519, and by the Emperor *Charles* V. was made the first absolute Duke *A.D.* 1531. He patroniz'd the *Designers* and *Operators*, till He died without Issue, *A. D.* 1537.

LEWIS

Lewis, or John *de Medicis*.

8 Cosmo II. *de Medicis*, succeeded Duke *Alexander* 1537. as absolute Duke of *Florence*. He Instituted the *Knights* of the Order of St. *Stephen* 1561. Pope Pius V. and the Emperor *Ferdinand* I. gave him the Title of Great Duke of *Tuscany* A. D. 1569.

He was the chief Patron, or *Grand Master*, of all the *Italian* Designers and Craftsmen in *Architecture, Painting, Sculpture, Statuary, Carving* and *Plastering*. He Instituted the famous Academy or *Lodge* at *Pisa* for the Improvement of Disciples and *Enter'd Prentices*. He made such beautiful Alterations in the Buildings of *Florence*, that, like *Augustus*, when a dying, He said, *I found the City built of Brick and course Stone, but I leave It built of Polish'd Marble*. He died aged only 55 Years, A. D. 1574. So much for the *Revivers* of the *Art*, in the House of *Medicis*. But to return.

After the *Revival* of the Augustan Stile in *Italy*, A. D. 1400.

Leon Baptista Alberti was the first Modern that wrote of *Architecture*, and many excellent *Masons* flourish'd in this 15th Century ; but more were born and educated, that prov'd the Wonders of the World in the next Century, and will be ever mention'd in the *Lodges* with the greatest Honour, for Improving the *Revival*, as if the *Augustan Age* It self had revived, under the generous Encouragement of the *Popes*, the *Princes* and *States* of *Italy*, the Patrons of the many Lodges then constituted. Thus

BRAMANTE, the learned Monk of *Urbino*, studied *Masonry* at *Milan* under Cæsariano ; and after having narrowly examin'd all the Remains of the Antients throughout *Italy*, He was employ'd by 3 successive *Popes* to build at *Rome* the *Cloister* of the Church of *Peace*, the Palace of the *Chancery*, and St. *Laurence* in *Damaso*. He adorn'd many old Churches with *Frontispieces* of his own Designing, built the pretty little St. *Peters* in *Mont Orio*, rais'd some Buildings in the *Vatican* and in the Palace of *Belvidere*.

Pope Julius II. the learned Patron or *Grand Master* of *Rome*, retain'd *BRAMANTE* as his Architect and Grand *Warden*, 1503 and order'd him as Master of Work, to draw the Grand Design

of

of St. PETERS new CATHEDRAL in *Rome*, the largeſt and moſt accurate *Temple* now in all the Earth: and the ſaid POPE with BRAMANTE led a ſolemn Aſſembly of *Cardinals*, *Clergymen* and *Craftsmen*, to level the *Foot-Stone* of Great St. PETER's in due Form, A. D. 1507.

BRAMANTE conducted that Work 7 Years, till he died, and was buried in It by POPE LEO X. duly attended by his *Craftsmen*, A. D. 1514.

RAPHAEL of *Urbino*, the *Prince* of *Painters*, had learn'd *Maſonry* of his unkle *Bramante*, and ſucceeded him in ſurveying St. *Peter's*, till he died, aged only 37 Years, on his own Birth-Day, 6 *April* 1520. when he was to be made a *Cardinal* by POPE LEO X. and with a univerſal Mourning was buried in the *Rotunda Pantheon*.

JOCUNDE of *Verona*, and ANTONY SAN GALLO ſucceeded *Raphael* at St. *Peter's*, till They died A. D. 1535. when POPE PAUL III. preferr'd to that Office

MICHAEL ANGELO, the greateſt *Deſigner* of his Time, and in his laſt Years the greateſt *Architect*, who finding fault with *San Gallo*'s Draughts, made a new Model of St. *Peter's*, according to which that *lofty Temple* was finiſh'd.

This *Grand Maſter* leaving his Warden PIRRO LIGORIO at St. *Peter's*, erected the new *Capitolium*, the Palace of *Farneſe*, and other accurate Structures. He had before built the *Mauſoleum* in St. *Peter's ad Vincula*, with the curious Statue of *Moſes*, the fine Front of St. *Laurence* at *Florence*, by order of *Pope* LEO X, the *Sepulchre* of the *Houſe* of *Medicis* by order of Duke *Alexander*, and the *Apoſtolical* Chamber at *Rome*.

MICHAEL ANGELO certainly carried on *Maſonry* to Its higheſt Perfection, till he died at *Rome* aged 90 Years, on 17 *Feb.* 1564. highly eſteem'd by all the Princes of *Europe*; and COSMO, the Great Duke of *Tuſcany*, ſtole his Corps from *Rome*, reſolving that ſince he could not have ANGELO alive, He would have him dead, and ſolemnly buried him in St. *Croſs* at *Florence*, attended by the *Fraternity*, and order'd *Vaſario* to deſign his Tomb inrich'd with the three great Marble Statues of *Architecture*, *Painting* and *Sculpture*.

James

James Barotzi da VIGNOLA fucceeded *Michael Angelo* at St. *Peters*, by order of *Pope* PAUL V. but *Ligorio* the Grand *Warden*, for altering *Angelo*'s Defign, was turn'd out by *Pope* GREGORY XIII. VIGNOLA, befides his accurate Edifices at *Rome* and elfewhere, defign'd for *Philip* II. King of *Spain*, the famous ESCURIAL, and St. *Laurence*, Mafterpieces of Art. He publifh'd a Book of the *Orders*, and the Beauty of his *Profiles* is much admired. He defign'd the Church of *Jefus* at *Rome*, the Caftle of *Caprarola* and the fide of the Palace of *Farnefe* that is next the *Tiber*, and died at *Rome*, aged 66. *A. D.* 1573.

MADERNI fucceeded *Vignola* at St. *Peters*, and built the ftately *Frontifpiece* of that vaft *Temple*, about the Time that *Pope* GREGORY XIII. made a *New Calendar*, or began the NEW STILE call'd, from him, the *Gregorian*, the firft Year of which is *A. D.* 1582. *Gregory* dying 1585. was fucceeded by *Pope* SEXTUS QUINTUS, who employ'd

DOMINICO FONTANA in many curious Buildings, and to move the *Egyptian Obelisks* into publick Places erect. After which *Fontana* was chief Ingeneer of *Naples*, and built the magnificent Palace of the *Vice Roy*.

Tis endlefs to mention the ingenious Contemporaries of thofe *great Mafters*, the other accurate *Revivers* and Improvers of the Royal *Art*, fuch as

BALDASSARE PERUZZI, who defign'd and made the Model of the Palace of *Chighi*, and his Difciple *Sebaftian Serglio.* ——*Julio Romano*, the chief Difciple of *Raphael*, built for the Duke of *Mantua* his Palace of △ *Delta*, ——*Lombard* of *Milan*— *James Sanfovino*, recommended by Pope *Leo* X. to the *Venetians* ———— *Jerom Genga* built for Duke *Guido Baldo* his Palaces at *Urbino* and *Pefaro.* —*Pellegrino Tibaldi* built the great Church of *Milan*, and its Dome was made by *John James de la Porta*—Sir *Baccio Bandinelli*, who was knighted by Pope *Clement* VII. for being a moft excellent *Sculptor.* ——*Benvenuto Cellini* —— *Daniel da Volterra* built pretty St. *Helens* in the great Church of *Trinity dell Monte at* Rome.—— *Perrin del Vaga* built at *Genua* the Grand Palace of Prince *Doria*, and was an inimitable *Plafterer*, a fine Art then much in Requeft.

At

At *Venice* also the *Revival* was carried on ; for *Jocunde* of *Verona*, above-mention'd, built the *Stone Bridge*, and erected the stately *Gates* of *Verona*.

When *CHARLES* V. besieged *Rome* 1525, MICHAEL ANGELO retir'd to *Venice*, when the *Doge* got him to design the famous *Bridge* of *Realto*.

JAMES SANSOVINO constituted a *Lodge* of *Architects* (or *Masters*) at *Venice*, artfully supported the *Dome* of St. *Mark* then in Danger *, embellish'd the *Palace* and *Treasury*, and forti- * 1527 fy'd the whole Republick as 𝕲𝖗𝖆𝖓𝖉 𝕸𝖆𝖘𝖙𝖊𝖗 of *Masons*.

But at *Venice* the *Augustan Stile* was also well improv'd by the learned VINCENT SCAMOTZI, DANIEL BARBARO, and the great
ANDREA PALLADIO.

PALLADIO's excellent Genius was highly discover'd by the sacred Edifices, the Palaces and Seats of Pleasure, and the other charming Buildings of his, throughout the State of *Venice.* He wrote also with great Judgment of the ORDERS of *Old Architecture*, and of the *Temples* of the *Antients* ; which is a noble Monument of his Merit, useful to all Ages. He died renowned A. D. 1580.

Thus *Italy* was again the *Mistress* of the *World*, not for Imperial Power, but for the *Arts* of *Designing* revived from *Gothic Rubbish.*

But from the *first Revival*, the *Masons* began to form *New Lodges* (called by the Painters *Academies* or *Schools*, as all *true Lodges* ought to be) far more elegant than the former *Gothic Lodges* ; for instructing Disciples or *Enter'd Prentices*, for preserving the *Secrets* of the *Fraternity* from Strangers and *Cowans*, and for Improving the *Royal Art*, under the Patronage of the *Popes* and the *Italian* Princes and *States*, as could be more amply prov'd.

After shewing in *Part* II. how the *Romans* brought the *Augustan Stile* into *Britain*, and carried it off with 'em ; and how the *Gothic Stile* prevailed there, till the *Union* of the *Crowns.* I shall shew how the *Augustan Stile* was revived in this Island by INIGO JONES, in *Part* III.

PART

PART II.

The History of MASONRY *in* BRITAIN, *from* JULIUS CÆSAR, *till the* Union *of the* Crowns, 1603.

CHAP. I.

From JULIUS CÆSAR *to the First Arrival of the* SAXONS *in* Britain.

HISTORY fails to tell, how long the *Europeans* in the *North* and *West* had lost their original Skill brought from *Shinar* before the *Roman* Conquest: but leaving our Brother *Masons* of other Nations to deduce their History of the *Royal* Art in their own Manner, we shall carry on our Deduction in the *Britannic* Isles.

CÆSAR in his Commentaries gives us the first certain Account of *Britain.* He landed at *Dover* on the 20*th* of August, and next Year He reached *London* ; but pursued not his Conquests, because of his Design to

$$\left.\begin{array}{l} \text{A. M.} \quad — \quad 3949 \\ \textit{B.C. or Christ. Era} \quad 55 \\ \textit{Before Christ's Birth} \quad 51 \end{array}\right\}$$

be the GRAND MASTER of the *Roman* Republick. Yet the *Romans* did not follow his Tract during about 97 Years, even till

AULUS PLAUTIUS came from the Emperor *Claudius,* A. D. 42 NextYear CLAUDIUS came himself, and afterwards he sentOSTORIUS SCAPULA, who was succeded by several *Roman* Lieutenants, that soon formed *Lodges* for building Castles and other Forts to secure
their

their Conquefts: till the Emperor VESPASIAN fent his brave Lieutenant, about A. D. 77. *viz.*

JULIUS AGRICOLA, who conquer'd as far as the *Iftmus*, between the Firths of *Clyde* and *Forth*, which he fortifi'd by a Wall of Earth againft the *Northerns*. But after he was recall'd, the *Northerns* got over the *Wall*, and made bold Incurfions into the *South*, till

ADRIAN the Emperor came himfelf, [A. D. 120] and finding the War tedious and hazardous, rather chofe to fence the *Roman* Provnice by a Rampart from *Tine Mouth* to *Solway Firth*. Bu afterwards *Antoninus Pius* fent

LOLLIUS URBICUS, who fubdued the *Brigantes*, and repuls'd the *Northerns*, even beyond *Agricola*'s Wall, which he fortify'd with Caftles ——— A. D. 131.

After this we read of *Lud*, or LUCIUS, a *Britifh* King under the *Romans*, who became Chriftian, and built Churches: while the War was carried on in the *North* with various Succefs, till the *Northerns* forced VIRIUS LUPUS to purchafe Peace with a great Sum of Money. This inraged the Emperor, *viz.*

SEPTIMIUS SEVERUS, who came with a great Army [A. D. 207] vowing to extirpate them, but could not, even tho' he penetrated to the *Northern Sea*; and having loft 50000 Men in the Expedition, he was forced to imitate ADRIAN, and rais'd his old Rampart into a *Stone Wall*, call'd of old MUR SEVER, or Wall of *Severus*, alfo *Greme's Dyke*, or *Piɛt's Wall*.

When NONNIUS PHILIPPUS [A. D. 238] came from the Emperor *Gordian*, EMILIUS CRISPINUS, his Mafter of Horfe, a fine Architeɛt, built a pretty *Temple* at *Caerlifle*, the *Altar* Stone of which was lately found there, near old *Mur Sever*.

The *South Brittons* had been long foftned in their Manners by the *Romans*, and affeɛted their Politenefs, wearing the *Roman* Drefs, and fpeaking *Latin*; and abounding alfo in *Commerce*, they improv'd in Arts and Sciences, and found the *Roman* Conqueft was a great Blefling to the Conquer'd, beholding with Pleafure their Country, formerly all grotefque and wild, now adorn'd with venerable *Temples*, folemn *Courts* of Juftice, ftately *Palaces* and

Manfions,

Manfions, large and beautiful *Cities*, regular *Forts* and *Caftles*, convenient *Bridges*, &c.

The joint Emperors *Dioclefian* and *Maximian* employ'd CARAUSIUS as their Admiral againft the *Saxon* Pirates, who being at Peace with the *Picts*, and gaining the Army, put on the *Purple* and was own'd by the other Two. A. D. 287.

CARAUSIUS encouraged the *Craft*, particularly at *Verulam*, (now St. *Albans, Hertfordfhire*) by the worthy Knight, ALBANUS, who afterwards turn'd Chriftian, and was call'd St. *Alban*,(the Proto Martyr in *Britain* under the *Dioclefian* Perfecution) whom CARAUSIUS employ'd (as the old Confti-

> This is afferted by all the old Copies of the *Confti-tutions*, and the old *Englifh Mafons* firmly believ'd it.

" tutions affirm) to inviron that City with a StoneWall, and to build
" him a fine *Palace* ; for which that *Britifh* King made St. ALBAN
" the Steward of his Houfhold and chief Ruler of the Realm.

" St. ALBAN loved *Mafons* well, and cherifhed them much,
" and he made their Pay right good, *viz. Two Shillings per Week*,
" *and Three Pence to their Cheer* ; whereas before that Time,
" through all the Land, *a Mafon had but a Penny a Day, and his*
" *Meat*, until St. *Alban* amended it. He alfo obtained of the
" King a Charter for the *Free Mafons*, for to hold a general
" Council, and gave it the Name of *Affembly*, and was thereat
" himfelf as *Grand Mafter*, and helped to make *Mafons*, and
" gave them good Charges, *&c.*

When *Dioclefian* and *Maximian* abdicated, A. D. 303.

CONSTANTIUS CHLORUS fucceeded Emperor of the *Weft*, a Lover of Arts and Sciences, and much encouraged the *Craft*, till he died at *York*, A. D. 306. the fame Year that his *Britifh* Emprefs HELENA girt *London* with a Stone Wall.

CONSTANTIN the *Great*,their Son,born in *Britain*, fucceeded,who partition d *South Britain* into four Provinces. During his Reign the *Chriftian* Religion flourifh'd, the *Britons* enjoy'd Peace and Plenty, and old *Roman Mafonry* appear'd in many ftately and curious Piles, till he died, A. D. 336.

I

After

After which, the *Northerns* joining the *Saxon* Pirates, invaded the *South*, till A. D. 367. when

THEODOSIUS (Father of the Emperor *Theodosius the Great*) came from the Emperor *Valentinian* I. and bravely beat them back, even over *Agricola*'s Wall, which he fortified with new *Castles* and *Forts*; and recovering the Land of the *old Meats* between the two Walls, he made it a fifth Province, calling it *Valentia*. He also beautified *London*, repair'd all the Cities and Forts, and left *Britain*, A. D. 374.

MAXIMUS (call'd the Tyrant) came next from the Emperor *Gratian*, who put on the *Purple*, sail'd into *Gaul* but was defeated in *Italy* by *Theodosius Magnus*, and beheaded A. D. 388.

CONSTANTIN, a common Soldier, for the Sake of his fortunate Name, was chosen by the *Southerns* to be their Leader, who also put on the *Purple*, sail'd into *Gaul*, and was there defeated and beheaded by the Emperor *Honorius*. And now

HONORIUS, not being able to protect the *Southerns* against the *Northerns*, fairly renounced his Sovereignty over *Britain*, the next Year after ALARIC had took in *Rome*, viz. A. D. 410. Yet

ÆTIUS, the General of *Valentinian* III, being victorious in *Gaul*, from Pity sent the *Britons* one Legion under GALLIO, who repell'd the *Northerns* beyond *Mur Sever*, which he rebuilt of Stone Work 8 Foot broad, and 12 Foot high : and being recall'd, he left the *South Britons* to defend themselves against the *Northerns*, and carried off his *Legion*, A. D. 426.

tho' the *Roman* Soldiers did not at All depart till   A. D. 430.

In the Vulgar Year of *Masonry*, 4430.

After *Cæsar*'s Invasion,   486 Years.

After *Aulus Plautius* came, 389

During which Time, the *Romans* had propagated *Masonry* in every Garrison, and had built fine Places past Number, even to the *North Border*, or the Wall of AGRICOLA, near which, at the *Forth*, they rais'd the little *Temple* of their *God* TERMINUS, that stands to this Day, now call'd by the Vulgar, *Arthur's Oven*, a curious *Rotunda* in Shape of the *Pantheon* at *Rome*, 20 Foot high

high, and near 20 Foot in Diameter. Nay, in Times of Peace the *Northerns* might learn of the *Romans* to extend the *Art* to the fartheft *North* and *Weſt*, or the ULTIMA THULE.

But true *old Maſonry* departed alſo from *Britain*, with the *Roman Legions* : for tho' many *Roman* Families had ſettled in the *South*, and were blended with the *Britons*, who had been well educated in the *Science* and the *Art*, yet the ſubſequent Wars, Confuſions and Revolutions in this Iſland, rnin'd ancient Learning, till all the fine Artiſts were dead without Succeſſion.

For the *Northerns* hearing that the *Roman Legions* were never to return, broke through *Mur Sever*, ſeiz'd all the Land *North* of the *Humber*, and ravaged the *South* the more eaſily, that the *Southerns* were divided by petty Kings, till they choſe a *General Monarch*, *viz.* A. D. 445

VORTIGERN, who being unable to retrieve Affairs, got the Conſent of his Nobles to invite the SAXONS in Lower *Germany* to come over and help him : and ſo *Prince* HENGIST, with 2000 *Saxons* landed in *Thanet* upon *Kent*, A. D. 449.

CHAP. II.

From the Firſt Arrival of the SAXONS, To WILLIAM the Conqueror.

THE SAXONS having aſſiſted *Vortigern* to repulſe the *Scots* and *Piƈts* beyond the *Humber*, built THONG CASTLE in *Lincolnſhire* ; and being daily recruited from lower *Germany*, and the River *Elb*, they reſolved to ſettle here ; and after much Bloodſhed in many Battles between the *Britons* and *Saxons*, they founded and eſtabliſh'd their HEPTARCHY, or *Seven Kingdoms*, viz.

1. Kingdom of KENT, founded by HENGIST, A. D. 455.
2. Kingdom of SUSSEX, by ELLA, —— 491.
3. Kingdom of WESSEX, by CHERDICK, — 519.
4. Kingdom of ESSEX, by ERCHENWYNE, — 527.
5. Kingdom of NORTHUMBRIA, by IDA the *Angle* 547.
6. Kingdom of EAST ANGLES, by UFFA, —— 571.
7. Kingdom of MIDLE ANGLES or MERCIA, by CRIDA. 584.

I 2

And

And as the *Anglo Saxons* encreas'd, the *Britons* loft Ground; till after the Death of AMBROSIUS *Aurelius*, and his brave Son King ARTHUR, the *Britons* had no *Grand Monarch*, but only a few petty Kings: but after CRIDA landed, many of them fubmitted to him (as to other *Saxon* Kings) many fled to *Cornwal*, and by Sea to *Armorica*, (call'd ftill *Bretagne* in *France*) and many went to *North Britain* among the *Scoto Walenfes*; tho' the greater Part fled beyond the *Severn*, where they were coop'd in between the Mountains and the *Irifh* Sea, A. D. 589.

The *Anglo Saxons*, who had always call'd the *Britons* GUALISH or *Walifhmen*, now call'd their Settlement beyond the *Severn* WALISHLAND or WALES, call'd ftill by the *French* GALLES from the GAULS their Progenitors. And here they elected the noble CADWAN their King, the Progenitor of the *Chriftian* Kings and *Princes* of WALES.

During the horrid Wars, fince the Departure of the *Roman Legions*, about 160 Years, Mafonry was extinguifh'd: nor have we any Veftige of it, unlefs we reckon that of STONE HENG, and allow, with fome, that AMBROSIUS, King of the *Britons*, rais'd that famous Monument on *Salisbury Plain*, by the Art of *Marvellous* MERLIN (whom the Populace counted a *Conjurer* and *Prophet*) in Remembrance of the *bloody Congrefs*, when HENGIST murder'd 300 *Britifh* Nobles. Others think it an old *Celtic Temple* built by the *Britons* long before the *Romans* came here: and fome have counted it only a *Danifh* Monument. But the great INIGO JONES, and his Kinfman Mr. JOHN WEB, have learnedly prov'd it to be a *Roman Temple*, the largeft Piece of Antiquity in the Ifland.

See STONE HENG reftored.

The ANGLO SAXONS came over all rough, ignorant Heathens, defpifing every Thing but War; nay, in Hatred to the *Britons* and *Romans*, they demolifh'd all acurate Structures, and all the glorious Remains of antient Learning, affecting only their own barbarous Manner of Life, till they became *Chriftians*; as appears from *Bede*, the *Saxon* Annals, and other good Vouchers: therefore we have no Account of *Mafonry* in their firft Settlements.

But

But where the WELCH dwelt, we find the earlieft Accounts, at leaft, of *Sacred* Architecture ; as at GLASTONBURY in *Devonfhire* ; *Padftow* in *Cornwal* ; *Caerleon* or *Chefter*, afterwards tranflated to St. *Afaph's* in *Flintfhire* ; *Llan Twit*, or Church of *Iltutus* ; *Llan Badarn Vawr*, or Church of *Great St. Patern* ; the Monaftry of *Llan Carvan* ; *Bangor* in *Caernarvonfhire* ; *Holyhead* in *Anglefey* ; *Llandaff* in *Glamorganfhire* ; *Menevia*, or St. *David's* in *Pembrokefhire* ; and many more Churches, Monaftries, and Schools of Learning.

Some pous *Teachers* came from *Wales* and *Scotland*, and converted many of the *Anglo Saxons* to Chriftianity ; but none of their Kings till A. D. 597. when AUSTIN, and forty more *Monks*, came from *Pope* GREGORY 1. and baptized ETHELBERT King of *Kent* ; and in about 60 Years, *all* the *Kings* of the HEPTARCHY were baptized.

Then affecting to build Churches and Monaftries, Palaces and fine Manfions, they too late lamented the ignorant and deftructive Conduct of their Fathers, but knew not how to repair the publick Lofs of *old Architecture* : yet being zealous, they follow'd the *Gothic Stile*, then only ufed, and rear'd foon

They alfo built many *Palaces* and *Caftles*, and fortified their *Cities*, efpecially on the Borders of each Kingdom. This requir'd many *Mafons*, who foon form'd themfelves into Societies, or *Lodges*, by Direction of Forreigners that came over to help them.

The Cathedral of *Canterbury*, A. D. 600
That of *Rochefter*, 602
St. *Paul's London*, 604
St. *Peter's Weftminfter*, 605
And a great many more defcrib'd in the *Monafticon Anglicanum*.

Thefe many *Saxon Lodges* gradually improved, till

ETHELBERT King of *Mercia* and *general* Monarch fent to CHARLES MARTEL, the Right Worfhipful *Grand Mafter* of *France* (Father of *King Pippin*) who had been educated by Brother *Mimus Græcus* : He fent over from *France* [about A.D. 710] fome expert *Mafons* to teach the SAXONS thofe *Laws* and *Ufages* of the antient Fraternity that had been happily preferv'd from the *Havock* of the *Goths* ; tho' not the *Auguftan Stile* that had been long loft in

the

the *West*, and now alfo in the *Eaſt*. This is ſtrongly aſſerted in all the *old Conſtitutions*, and was firmly believ'd by the old *Engliſh* Maſons.

The CLERGY now found it convenient to ſtudy *Geometry*, and *Architecture*, ſuch as it was ; becauſe the noble and wealthy, nay *Kings* and *Queens*, thought it meritorious·to build *Churches*, and other *pious* Houſes, where ſome of them ended their Days in ſweet Retirement : for thoſe *holy Houſes* were all under the Direction of the Clergy ; and the *Lodges* were held in Monaſtries before the Inundation of the *Danes*. Yet at firſt they built moſtly of *Timber* only, till

BENNET, the Abbot of *Wirral*, introduced the Uſe of *Brick* and *Stone*, about A. D. 680 : ſo that even the *Gothic Stile* was but in its Infancy during the *Heptarchy*, which laſted from *Hengiſt's*

Arrival. —— A. D. 449 ⎫
At laſt   during Years 381 ⎭

EGBERT, King of *Weſſex*, by Policy and Conqueſt, ⎫ *A.D.* 830.
became Sovereign of the other ſix Kingdoms,   ⎭

and the *Angles* being moſt numerous, he call'd his united Kingdom ENGLAND, and all the People ENGLISHMEN : tho' the *Welch*, the *Iriſh*, and *Scots* Highlanders, call them ſtill SAXONS, after thoſe that firſt came with *Hengiſt*. Thus

1. EGBERT, the *firſt* King of *All England*, A. D. 830. fortified his Sea Ports, and died A. D. 836.

2. ETHELWOLPH employ'd St. *Swithin* to repair the pious Houſes, and died, A. D. 857.

3. ETHELBALD.	4. ETHELBERT.	5. ETHELRED I.	6. ALFRED the *Great*, the *4th*
died 860.	died 866.	died 872.	Son, who commenc'd A.D. 872 ſubdu'd the *Danes*, tho' not expell'd them ; he increaſed his *Navy Royal*, fortify'd and rebuilt many Towns, and founded the Univerſity of *Oxford*.
in whoſe Reigns the *Danes* ſettled in *Eaſt Anglia* and *Northumbria*, pillaging and demoliſhing the pious Houſes.			

King

King ALFRED had about him the beſt *Architects*, and employ'd the *Fellow-Crafts* wholly in *Brick* or *Stone*. The *beſt* KING of *England*, and died illuſtrious, A. D. 900.

7. EDWARD *Senior*, left *Maſonry* to the Care, firſt cf *ETHRED*, the Deputy King of *Mercia*, the Husband of *Edward*'s Siſter ELFREDA, the glorious Heroin, who by her Valour expell'd the *Danes* out of *Mercia*, and fortified many Towns and Caſtles to prevent their Incurſions. Next the King put his learned Brother *ETHELWARD* at the Head of the *Fraternity*, and founded the Univerſity of *Cambridge* that had been long a Nurſery of the Learned. The King died 924. leaving 3 Kings and a Queen.

8. ATHELSTAN the eldeſt Son ſucceeded, tho' only the Son of a *Concubine*, and at firſt left the *Craft* to the Care of his Brother *Edwin*, call'd in ſome Copies his *Son :* for in all the *old Conſtitutions* It is written to this Purpoſe, *viz.*

" That tho' the antient Records of the Brotherhood in *England*,
" were moſt of them deſtroy'd or loſt in the Wars with the *Danes*,
" who burnt the *Monaſtries* where the Records were kept ; yet
" King *Athelſtan* (the Grandſon of King *Alfred*) the firſt anointed
" King of *England*, who tranſlated the *Holy Bible* into the SAXON
" Language, when he had brought the Land into Reſt and Peace,
" built many great Works, and encouraged many *Maſons*
" from *France* and elſewhere, whom He appointed Overſeers
" thereof : they brought with them the *Charges* and *Regulations*
" of the foreign *Lodges*, and prevail'd with the King to increaſe
" the Wages.

" That *Prince* EDWIN, the King's Brother, being taught
" *Geometry* and *Maſonry*, for the Love he had to the ſaid Craft,
" and to the honourable Principles whereon it is grounded, pur-
" chaſed a *Free Charter* of King *Athelſtan* his Brother, for the
" *Free Maſons* having among themſelves a CORRECTION,
" or a Power and Freedom to regulate themſelves, to amend
" what

" what might happen amifs, and to hold an yearly *Communication*
" in a General *Affembly*.

 " That accordingly *Prince* Edwin fummon'd all the *Free* and
" *Accepted Mafons* in the Realm, to meet him in a *Congregation*
" at YORK, who came and form'd the *Grand Lodge* under him
" as their *Grand Mafter*, A. D. 926.

 " That they brought with them many old Writings and Re-
" cords of the *Craft*, fome in *Greek*, fome in *Latin*, fome in
" *French*, and other Languages ; and from the Contents thereof,
" they fram'd the CONSTITUTIONS of the *Englifh Lodges*,
" and made a Law for Themfelves, to preferve and obferve the
" fame in all Time coming, *&c. &c. &c.* "

 But good *Prince* Edwin died before the King [A. D. 938]
without Iffue, to the great Grief of the *Fraternity* ; though his
Memory is fragrant in the *Lodges*, and honourably mention'd in
all the *old Conftitutions*.

 Some *Englifh* Hiftorians fay that Edwin being accufed of a
Plot, the King fet him adrift in a Boat without Sail and Oars ;
that Edwin protefting his Innocence, went aboard and jumpt into
the Sea ; and that his Efquire was drove into *Picardy*.

 But the Hiftorian *Malmsbury* disbelieves the whole Story as
grounded only on fome *old Ballad*, and becaufe of *Athelftan*'s
known Kindnefs and Love to all his Brothers and Sifters : and
Huntingdon writes of the Lofs of Edwin by Sea, as a very fad
Accident, and a great Misfortune to *Athelftan*, who was very
fond of him.

 King Athelstan built many Caftles in *Northumbria* to bridle
the *Danes* (whom he had fubdu'd) and the famous *Abby* of St. *John*
at *Beverley* (lately repair'd for Divine Service) and *Melton Abby* in
Dorfetfhire ; He rebuilt the City of *Exeter*, and repair'd the old
Church of the Culdees at *York*. He died without Iffue, 940.

9. Edmund I.

𝕾𝖆𝖝𝖔𝖓 Kings of *England*.

9 EDMUND I. succeeded Brother *Athelstan*, repaired the Cities and Churches, and leaving two Sons, died, *A. D.* 946.

10 EDRED succeeded his Brother *Edmund*, rebuilt *Glastonbury*, and died without Issue 955.

11 EDWI succeeded his Uncle *Edred*, and died without Issue, 959.

12 EDGAR built and rebuilt about 48 pious Houses, by the Direction of St. *Dunstan*, 𝕲𝖗𝖆𝖓𝖉 𝕸𝖆𝖘𝖙𝖊𝖗, and several more expert Masters. He also rigg'd out a good Navy, which prevented the Invasions of the *Danes*, and died 975.

13 EDWARD *Junior*, call'd the *Martyr*, died without Issue 979.

14 ETHELRED II. was always distressed by the *Danes*, and contrived their Massacre, *A. D.* 1002.

ETHELRED, upon the Death of *Swen Otto*, returned, but died inglorious 1016.

By his first Wife he had

16 EDMUND II. *Ironsides* reigned in the *West* till murder'd, *A. D.* 1017. Father of Prince

By his 2d Wife *Ethelred* had

20. EDWARD the

𝕯𝖆𝖓𝖎𝖘𝖍 Kings of *England*.

THYRA. Daughter of *Edward Senior* (according to the *Danish* Historians) was married to GORMO III. King of *Denmark*, and bore to him,

HAROLD VIII. King of *Denmark*.

SWEN OTTO, King of *Denmark*, who finding that *Ethelred* neglected his Fleet, allowed his *Danes* to invade *England* every Year, and they left many 𝕷𝖔𝖗𝖉 𝕯𝖆𝖓𝖊𝖘, to oppress the poor *English*. But hearing of the Massacre, SWEN OTTO sail'd over with great Force, and drove *Ethelred* into *Normandy*. And so, 15 SWEN OTTO was King of *England* — 1013 but died suddenly — 1014

17 CANUTUS or *Knut Magnus*, after the Death of King EDMUND *Ironsides*, was crown'd King of *all England*, *A. D.* 1017.

He built the Abby of St. *Edmund's-Bury*, and died — 1036. Father of 18 HA-

𝕾𝖆𝖝𝖔𝖓 Kings of *England.*　𝕯𝖆𝖓𝖎𝖘𝖍 Kings of *England.*

Prince *Edward* who died at *London* 1057.	the *Confeſſor,* who ſucceeded King *Hardy-Knut* in the Throne of *England,* 1041.	18 HAROLD I. *Harefoot,* King of *England,* died without Iſſue. *A.D.* 1039.
Prince *Edgar Atheling* died without Iſſue.	MARGARET, Wife of MALCOLM *Keanmore,* King of *Scotland.*	He collected the *Saxon* Laws in a Body. In his Reign	19 HARDY-KNUT, King of *England,* the laſt of the *Daniſh* race, died without Iſſue, *A. D.* 1041.

Arts and Sciences flouriſh'd. 𝕷𝖊𝖔𝖋𝖗𝖎𝖈𝖐 the Wealthy Earl of *Coventry,* at the Head of the *Free Maſons,* built the Abby of *Coventry,* and Others built 12 more pious Houſes. The King rebuilt *Weſtminſter-Abby,* tho' not as it now ſtands, and died without Iſſue on 5 *Jan.* 106⅚, when the Nobles and People choſe,

21. HAROLD II. Son of Earl *Goodwin,* who reign'd nine Months, even till WILLIAM the *Baſtard,* the Duke of *Normandy,* ſlew *Harold* bravely fighting in the Battle of *Haſtings* in *Suſſex,* where the *Engliſh* were totally routed by the *Normans,* on the 14th of *October, A. D.* ———————————— 1066.

In the vulgar Year of *Maſonry* 5066.
After *Hengiſt*'s Arrival ——— 617.
After the End of the *Heptarchy,* 236.

As for the 𝕯𝖆𝖓𝖊𝖘, having no Princely Head, They had ſubmitted to the *Saxon* Kings, and daily loſing their Genealogy, They were gradually blended with the *Anglo-Saxons,* having much the ſame Language.

CHAP.

CHAP. III.

MASONRY *in* England *from* WILLIAM *the* Conqueror *to King* HENRY IV.

1. WILLIAM I. the *Conqueror*, having settled *England*, appointed Gundulph Bishop of *Rochester*, Roger de *Montgomery* Earl of *Shrewsbury* and *Arundel*, and other good Architects, to be at the Head of the *Fellow Crafts*, first in civil and military Architecture, building for the King the *Tower* of *London*, and the Castles of *Dover*, *Exeter*, *Winchester*, *Warwick*, *Hereford*, *Stafford*, *York*, *Durham*, and *New-Castle* upon *Tine* ; whereby the proud *Normans* bridled the *English*.

Next in *sacred* Architecture, building *Battle-Abby* near *Hastings*, in memory of his Conquest, St. *Saviour's Southwark*, and 9 more pious Houses ; while Others built 42 such, and 5 Cathedrals. The King brought many expert *Masons* from *France*, and died in *Normandy, A. D.* 1087.

2. WILLIAM II. *Rufus*, succeeded his Father, and employ'd his Architects and Craftsmen in building a new Wall round the *Tower*, and in rebuilding *London-Bridge* ; and by Advice of his *Grand Lodge* of *Masters*, He built the Great Palace of *Westminster*, with large *Westminster-Hall*. 270 Foot long, and 74 Foot broad, the largest one Room upon Earth ; and 4 pious Houses, while Others built 28 such. He died without Issue, *A. D.* 1100.

3. HENRY I. *Beau Clerc*, born at *Selby* in *Yorkshire*, succeeded Brother *William*, tho' the eldest Brother *Robert* Duke of *Normandy*, was alive.

Now the *Norman* Barons, perceiving their great Possessions in *England* depended only on Royal Pleasure ; and finding the Laws of the *Anglo-Saxons* to be better for securing Property than the Laws of *Normandy* ;

Normandy; the 𝕹𝕺𝖗𝖒𝖆𝖓𝖘 began to call themfelves ENGLISHMEN, to affert the *Saxon-Rights*, and prevail'd with this King to grant them the firft 𝔐𝔞𝔤𝔫𝔞 ℭ𝔥𝔞𝔯𝔱𝔞, or larger *Paper* and Deed of *Rights* in this firft Year of his Reign, *A. D.* 1100.

This King built the great Palace of *Woodftock*, and a little one at *Oxford* to converfe with the Learned, and 14 pious Houfes, while Others built about 100 fuch, befides many fine Manfions. He died *A. D.* 1135. fucceeded by his Nephew, *viz.*

King HENRY I. by his Wife MAUD (Daughter of MAL-COLM *Keanmore* King of *Scotland* by his Wife MARGARET the *Saxon* Heirefs of *England*) left only a Daughter *viz.*

MAUD the *Emprefs*, who next married 𝔊𝔢𝔬𝔣𝔣𝔯𝔢𝔶 *Plantagenet* Count of *Anjou*, *A.D.* 1127.

She came over, tho' too late, to affert her Claim (to which her Father had fworn the whole Kingdom, even *Stephen* alfo) and

4. STEPHEN, Count of *Boulloign*, Son of ADELA Daughter of *William* the *Conqueror*, by the Power of the Clergy. During the Civil Wars between him and MAUD the *Emprefs*, the Nobles and Gentry, being courted by both, laid hold of the Occafion to build about 1100 Caftles, that proved afterwards very convenient for them in the *Barons Wars*; fo that the *Mafons* were as much employ'd as the Soldiers, under their 𝔊𝔯𝔞𝔫𝔡 𝔐𝔞𝔰𝔱𝔢𝔯 *Gilbert de Clare* Marquis of *Pembroke*, by whom the King built 4 Abbies and 2 Nunneries, with St. *Stephen*'s Chapel in the Palace of *Weftminfter*: While Others built about 90 pious Houfes. King *Stephen* died without Iffue Male,

the laft of the Royal *Normans.* } *A. D.* ———— 1154. After the *Conqueft* 88 Years.

fought like a brave Heroine; but refufing to confirm *Magna Charta*, fhe was deferted: And her beft Friends dying, fhe was forced to re-turn to *Anjou*, A. D. 1147. But her Son HENRY came over and afferted his Claim, till King *Stephen* agreed that *Henry* fhould fuc-ceed him,

Accordingly, when *Stephen* died,

The

The *PLANTAGENETS* of *Anjou* commenced, *viz.*

1. HENRY II. *Plantagenet*, Count of *Anjou* became King of *England*, *A. D.* 1154, who fortify'd fome Caftles againft the *Welch* and *Scots*, built fome little Palaces, and 10 pious Houfes, while Others built about 100 fuch. The *Grand Mafter* of the *Knights Templars* erected their Society and built their 𝕮𝖊𝖒𝖕𝖑𝖊 in *Fleetftreet*, *London*. The King died *A. D.* 1189.

2. RICHARD I. much abroad, died without Iffue 1199; yet in this Reign about 20 pious Houfes were built.	3. King JOHN fucceeded Brother *Richard*, and firft made his Chaplain

𝕻𝖊𝖙𝖊𝖗 *de Cole-Church* 𝕲𝖗𝖆𝖓𝖉 𝕸𝖆𝖘𝖙𝖊𝖗 of the *Mafons* in rebuilding *London-Bridge* of Stone, which was finifh'd by the next Mafter *William Almain*, *A. D.* 1209. Next 𝕻𝖊𝖙𝖊𝖗 de *Rupibus* Bifhop of *Winchefter* was 𝕲𝖗𝖆𝖓𝖉 𝕸𝖆𝖘𝖙𝖊𝖗, and under him *Geoffrey Fitz Peter* was chief Surveyor or *Deputy* Grand Mafter, who built much for the King ; while Others built about 40 pious Houfes. The King died *A. D.* 1216, fucceeded by his Son,

4. HENRY III. a Minor of nine Years. When 𝕻𝖊𝖙𝖊𝖗 de *Rupibus*, the old *Grand Mafter*, came to be the King's Guardian, he levell'd the *Footftone* of *Weftminfter* Abby, in that Part call'd *Solomon*'s Porch, *A. D.* 1220.

PETER Count of *Savoy* (Brother of the Queen's Mother) built the Palace of *Savoy* in the *Strand London :* And *John Balliol*, Lord of *Bernard* Caftle in *Durham*, (Father of JOHN King of *Scotland*) founded *Balliol College* in *Oxford*. The *Templars* built their *Domus Dei* at *Dover*, and Others built 32 pious Houfes. The King died *A. D.* 1272.

5. EDWARD I. being deeply engaged in Wars, left the *Craft* to the Care of feveral fucceffive *Grand Mafters*, as 𝖂𝖆𝖑𝖙𝖊𝖗 𝕲𝖎𝖋𝖋𝖆𝖎𝖉 Archbifhop of *York*, 𝕲𝖎𝖑𝖇𝖊𝖗𝖙 de *Clare* Earl of *Glocefter*, and 𝕽𝖆𝖑𝖕𝖍 Lord of *Mount Hermer*, the Progenitor of the *Montagues* ; and by thefe the King fortify'd many Caftles, efpecially againft the

the *Welch*, till they fubmitted to him, *A. D.* 1284, when *Edward* the King's Son and Heir was born at *Caermarthen*, the firft *Englifh* Prince of *Wales*.

The King celebrated the *Cape-ftone* of *Weftminfter* Abby, *A. D.* 1285, juft 65 Years after it was founded. But that *Abby* and the *Palace* being burnt down, 1299, the King order'd the Palace to be repair'd, but was diverted from repairing the *Abby* by his Wars in *Scotland.* In this Reign *Merton* College *Oxford*, the Cathedral of *Norwich*, and about 20 more pious Houfes were founded. The King died in his Camp on *Solway Sands*, 7th of *July*, 1307.

6. EDWARD II. made **Walter Stapleton** Bifhop of *Exeter* *Grand Mafter*, who built *Exeter* and *Oriel* Colleges in *Oxford*; while Others built *Clare-Hall Cambridge*, and 8 pious Houfes. The King died *A. D.* 1327.

7. EDWARD III. became the Patron of Arts and Sciences. He fet up a Table at *Windfor*, 600 Feet round, for feafting the gallant *Knights* of all Nations, and rebuilt the Caftle and Palace of *Windfor*, as a *Royal* **Grand Mafter**, by his feveral Deputies or Mafters of Work, *viz.*

1. **John** de *Spoulee*, call'd *Mafter* of the *Ghiblim*, who rebuilt St. *George*'s Chapel; where the King conftituted the *Order* of the *Garter*, *A. D.* 1350.

2. **William a Wickham**, at the Head of 400 *Free Mafons*, rebuilt the Caftle ftrong and ftately, *A. D.* 1357, and when he was made Bifhop of *Winchefter*, A. D.——1367. then next

3. **Robert** *a Barnham* fucceeded at the Head of 250 *Free Mafons*, and finifh'd St. *George*'s great Hall, with other Works in the Caftle, *A. D.* 1375.

4. **Henry Yevele** (call'd at firft, in the old Records, the King's *Free Mafon*) built for the King the *London Charter-houfe*, *King's-Hall Cambridge*, *Queenborough Caftle*, and rebuilt St. *Stephen*'s Chapel, now the Houfe of Commons in Parliament.

5. **Simon Langham**, Abbot of *Weftminfter*, who repair'd the Body of that Cathedral as it now ftands.

The

The King also founded the Abby of *Eaftminfter* near the *Tower*; and his laudable Example was well follow'd; for the Queen endow'd *Queen's College Oxford*, while Others built many ftately Manfions, and about 30 pious Houfes, for all the expenfive Wars of this Reign.

The CONSTITUTIONS were now meliorated; for an old Record imports, " *that in the glorious Reign of* King EDWARD III. *when Lodges were many and frequent, the* Grand Mafter *with his* Wardens, *at the Head of the* Grand Lodge, *with Confent of the* Lords *of the Realm, then generally* Free Mafons, *ordain'd,*

That for the future, at the Making or Admiffion of a Brother, the Conftitutions *fhall be read, and the* Charges *hereunto annexed.*

That Mafter Mafons, *or* Mafters of Work, *fhall be examined whether they be* able of Cunning *to ferve their refpective* Lords, *as well the Higheft as the Loweft, to the Honour and Worfhip of the forefaid Art, and to the Profit of their Lords; for they be their* Lords *that employ and pay them for their Travel.*

That when the Mafter *and* Wardens *prefide in a Lodge, the* Sheriff, *if need be, or the* Mayor, *or the* Alderman *(if a Brother) where the Chapter is held, fhall be* fociate *to the* Mafter, *in help of him againft Rebels, and for upholding the Rights of the Realm.*

That Enter'd Prentices *at their Making fhall be charged not to be* Thieves, *nor* Thieves Maintainers. *That the* Fellow Crafts *fhall travel honeftly for their Pay, and love their Fellows as themfelves; and, That all fhall be true to the* King, *to the* Realm, *and to the* Lodge.

That if any of the Fraternity fhould be fractious, mutinous, or difobedient to the Grand Mafter's *Orders, and after proper Admonitions, fhould perfift in his Rebellion, He fhall forfeit all his Claim to the* Rights, Benefits, *and* Privileges *of a true and faithful Brother, &c.* Concluding with, AMEN, So mote it be.

ED-

King EDWARD III. died 21 *June* 1377.

EDWARD the 𝕭𝖑𝖆𝖈𝖐 Prince of *Wales* died before his Father, *A. D.* 1376. | See the other Sons, with re-spect to the *Succeſſion*, in the *Margin* below. *

8. RICHARD II. ſucceeded his Grandfather, *A. D.* 1377. He employ'd 𝔚𝔦𝔩𝔩𝔦𝔞𝔪 *a Wickham*, Biſhop of *Wincheſter*, *Grand Maſter*, to rebuild *Weſtminſter-Hall* as it now ſtands ; and 𝔚𝔦𝔩𝔩𝔦𝔞𝔪, at his own Coſt, built *New College Oxford*, and founded *Wincheſter College*, while Others built about 15 pious Houſes.

At laſt, while King *Richard* was in *Ireland*, his Couſin *Henry* Duke of *Lancaſter* landed in *Yorkſhire*, rais'd a great Army ſeiz'd King *Richard* upon his Return, got the Parliament to depoſe him, and ſucceeded in the Throne, *A. D.* 1399 ; and next Year *Richard* was murder'd without Iſſue.

---

* The other Sons of King EDWARD III. with reſpect to the Succeſſion.

LIONLEL Duke of *Clarence*, the ſecond Son, left only

PHILIPPA of *Clarence*, Wife of *Edmund Mortimer*, Earl of *March*, Mother of

Roger Mortimer, Earl of *March*, left only

Ann Mortimer, the Heireſs of *Clarence* and *March*.

EDMUND Duke of *York*, the fourth Son, *Patriarch of the* 𝔚𝔥𝔦𝔱𝔢 𝔅𝔬𝔰𝔢, by his Wife *Iſabella*, ſecond Daughter of *Piedro Crudelis*, King of *Caſtile*.

Richard Earl of *Cambridge*, behead-ed 1415.

Richard Duke of *York*, ſlain, 1460.

King EDWARD IV. | King RICHARD III.

JOHN *a Gaunt* Duke of *Lancaſter*, the third Son, Patriarch of the 𝔅𝔢𝔡 𝔅𝔬𝔰𝔢. Wives.
1. *Blanche* of *Lancaſter*, Mother of King *Henry* IV.
2. *Conſtantia*, eldeſt Daughter of *Piedro Crudelis* King of *Caſtile*, Mother of *Katharine* married to *Henry* III. King of *Caſtile*.
3. *Katharine Roet*, his Concubine, whom at laſt he married, and her Children were legitimated by Act of Parliament, but not to inherit the Crown. Mother of

John Beaufort, (not *Plantagenet*) Earl of *Somerſet*.

John Beaufort Duke of *Somerſet*.

Margaret Beaufort, Mother of King HENRY VII.

CHAP.

C H A P. IV.

MASONRY in *England* from HENRY IV.
to the *Royal* TEWDORS.

KING EDWARD III.

JOHN *a Gaunt*, Duke of *Lancaster*, Patriarch of the 𝕽𝖊𝖉 𝕽𝖔𝖋𝖊, or the Royal *Lancastrians*, by his first Wife, *Blanche* of *Lancaster*, had

9. HENRY IV. Duke of *Lancaster*, who supplanted and succeeded King *Richard* II. *A. D.* 1399. He appointed 𝕿𝖍𝖔𝖒𝖆𝖘 *Fitz-Allen* Earl of *Surrey*, to be *Grand Master*; and after his famous Victory of *Shrewsbury*, the King founded *Battle-Abbey* there, and afterwards that of *Fotheringay*. Others built 6 pious Houses, and the *Londoners* founded their present *Guild-Hall*, a large and magnificent Fabrick. The King died 1413.

10. HENRY V. while triumphing in *France*, order'd the Palace and Abbey of *Sheen* (now call'd *Richmond* upon *Thames*) to be rebuilt by the Direction of the *Grand Master* 𝕳𝖊𝖓𝖗𝖞 𝕮𝖍𝖎𝖈𝖍𝖊𝖑𝖊𝖞 Archbishop of *Canterbury*; while Others built 8 pious Houses. The King died *A. D.* 1422.

By his Queen, *Katherine* of *France* (afterwards the Wife of 𝕺𝖜𝖊𝖓 𝕿𝖊𝖜𝖉𝖔𝖗 below.) He had

11. HENRY VI. a Minor of nine Months, in whose third Year an ignorant Parliament endeavour'd to disturb the *Lodges*, tho' in vain, by the following Act, *viz.*

3 *Hen.* VI. Cap. I. *A. D.* 1425.

Title. MASONS *shall not confederate in Chapters and Congregations.*

L   WHEREAS

WHEREAS *by yearly Congregations and Confederacies made by the* Masons *in their General Assemblies, the good Course and Effect of the Statutes of Labourers be openly violated and broken, in Subversion of the Law, and to the great Damage of all the Commons ;* Our Sovereign Lord the King *willing in this Case to provide a Remedy, by the Advice and Consent aforesaid, and at the special Request of the* Commons, Hath Ordain'd and Establish'd,

That such Chapters *and* Congregations *shall not be hereafter holden: And if any such be made, They that cause such* Chapters *and* Congregations *to be assembled and holden, if they thereof be convict, shall be judged for* Felons: *And that other* Masons *who come to such* Chapters *and* Congregations *be punished by Prisonment of their Bodies, and make Fine and Ransom at the King's Will.*

But this Act is explain'd in Judge COKE's Institutes, Part III. fol. 19. where we find that the Cause why this Offence was made *Felony*, is for that the good Course and Effect of the Statutes of Labourers was thereby violated and broken. Now says my Lord *Coke*,

All the Statutes concerning Labourers before this Act, and whereunto this Act doth refer, are repealed by the 5 ELIZ. Cap. 4. about A. D. 1562. whereby the Cause and End of making this Act is taken away, and consequently the Act is become of no Force ; for ceſſante ratione legis ceſſat ipſa lex! *and the Inditement of* Felony *upon this Statute must contain, That those* Chapters *and* Congregations *are to the violating and breaking of the good Course and Effect of the Statutes of Labourers ! which now cannot be so alledged, because those Statutes be repeal'd. Therefore this would be put out of the Charge of Justices of the Peace.*

But this Act was never executed, nor ever frightned the *Free Masons* from holding their *Chapters* and *Congregations*, leſſer or larger ; nor did ever the *Working Masons* desire their Noble and Eminent Brothers to get it repeal'd, but always laugh'd at it: For they ever had, and ever will have their own Wages, while they coalesce in due Form, and carefully preserve the Cement under their own 𝕲𝖗𝖆𝖓𝖉 𝕸𝖆𝖘𝖙𝖊𝖗 ; let *Cowans* do as they please.

Nay even during this King's **Minority**, there was a good *Lodge*
under

under *Grand Master* 𝕮𝖍𝖎𝖈𝖍𝖊𝖑𝖊𝖕 held at *Canterbury*, as appears from the Latin Register of *William Molart* * Prior of *Canterbury* in Manuscript, pap. 88. in which are named *Thomas Stapylton* the Master, and *John Morris* Custos de la Lodge Lathomorum or *Warden* of the Lodge of Masons, with fifteen *Fellow-Crafts*, and three *Enter'd Prentices* all named there. And a Record in the Reign of EDW. IV. says, *the Company of* Masons, *being otherwise termed* Free Masons, *of auntient Staunding and good Reckoning, by Means of affable and kind Meetings dyverse Tymes, and as a loving Brotherhood use to do, did frequent this mutual Assembly in the Tyme of* Henry VI. *in the Twelfth Year of his Most Gracious Reign* viz. *A. D.* 1434. when HENRY was aged thirteen Years.

* Intitled *Liveratio generalis Domini Gulielmi Prioris Ecclesiæ Christi Cantuariensis erga Festum Natalis Domini* 1429.

Grand Master CHICHELEY held also a *Lodge* at *Oxford*, where he built *All-Soul's-College*, and *Bernard*, now St. *John*'s College, &c. till he died 1445. when the King appointed,

𝖂𝖎𝖑𝖑𝖎𝖆𝖒 𝖂𝖆𝖎𝖓𝖋𝖑𝖊𝖊𝖙, Bishop of *Winchester*, to be *Grand Master* in building *Eaton* College near *Windsor*, and *King*'s College *Cambridge*, tho' before the Civil Wars in this Reign, the *Chapel* of it was only finish'd, a Master-Piece of the richest *Gothic* that can hardly be matched. The King also founded *Christ*'s College *Cambridge* (afterwards finish'd by *Margaret Beaufort* Countess of *Richmond*) and his Queen MARGARET of *Anjou* founded *Queen*'s College *Cambridge*. While Ingenious 𝖂𝖆𝖎𝖓𝖋𝖑𝖊𝖊𝖙 at his own Cost built *Magdalene* College *Oxford*; and Others about 12 pious Houses.

So that before the King's Troubles, the *Masons* were much employ'd, and in great Esteem; for the foresaid Record says farther, *That the* Charges *and* Laws *of the* Free Masons *have been seen and perused by our late Soveraign King* Henry VI. *and by the Lords of his most honourable Council, who have allow'd them, and declared, that They be right good and reasonable to be holden, as They have been drawn out and collected from the Records of auntient Tymes,* &c. &c.

At last *Masonry* was neglected during the seventeen Years of the bloody Civil Wars between the two *Royal* Houses of *Lancaster* and *York*, or the 𝕽𝖊𝖉 and 𝖂𝖍𝖎𝖙𝖊 *Roses*: For

L 2

𝕽𝖎𝖈𝖍𝖆𝖗𝖉

Richard Plantagenet, Duke of *York*, Son of *Richard* Earl of *Cambridge*, and *Anne Mortimer* the Heiress of *Clarence* (as in the *Margin* Page 72.) claim'd the Crown in Right of his Mother, *A. D.* 1455. and after twelve sore Battles the **Red** *Rose* lost the Crown, poor King *Henry* VI. was murder'd, and *all* the *Males* of every Branch of *Lancaster* were cut off; after *John a Gaunt's* Offspring had reigned 72 Years, *A. D.* 1471.

White Rose, see Page 72.

Thus *Richard* Duke of *York* slain in the Battle of *Wakefield*, 1460.

---

12 EDWARD IV. crown'd 1561. sometimes a King, and sometimes not a King, till *A. D.* 1471. when EDWARD reigned without a Rival, and employ'd the *Grand Master* **Richard Beauchamp**, Bishop of *Sarum*, to repair the Royal Castles and Palaces after the Wars, and to make the Castle and Chapel of *Windsor* more magnificent; for which the Bishop was made *Chancellor* of the *Garter*.

Great Men also repair'd and built apace; and now the *Londoners* rebuilt their Walls and Gates; while Others rais'd 7 pious Houses. The King died 9 *April* 1483.

---

13 EDWARD V. a Minor, proclaim'd, but not crown'd.

These two Sons were said to be murder'd in the *Tower* by Order of their Uncle and Guardian *Richard* III. on 23 *May*, 1483.

Richard, Duke of *York*.

Elizabeth Plantagenet, Wife of King *Henry* VII. below.

And also the 14 *Kings* call'd *Plantagenets*, of the House of *Anjou*, who had reign'd from King *Stephen's* Death, *A. D.* ——1154
during Years —— 331
till *A. Dom.* —— 1485

14 RICHARD III. kill'd and took Possession, and was crown'd on 6 *July*, 1483. and reign'd a wise and valiant Prince, till he was slain, bravely contending for the Crown with his Rival HENRY *Tewdor* Earl of *Richmond*, in the Battle of *Bosworth Leicestershire*, on the 22 *Aug.* 1485. without legal Issue.

So ended the **White Rose**, or House of *York*:

For

For connecting the Hiſtory.
The GENEALOGY of the Royal TEWDORS
They are clearly deſcended (tho' not in Male Iſſue) from
CADWAN the Firſt, King of *Wales*, (Page 60.) down to
RODERIC *Mawr*, who partition'd his Kingdom into 3 Principa-
lities among his 3 Sons, and died *A·.D.* 876.

1. AMARAWDD, Prince of *North Wales*, whoſe *Male* Iſſue fail'd in LLEWELIN ap *Daffyd*, the laſt Soveraign Prince of *all Wales*, ſlain in Battle, A. D. 1283. when the *Welch* began to ſubmit to the Crown of *England*.	2 CADELH, Prince of *South Wales*, whoſe lineal *Male* Iſſue ended in GRUFFYD ap *Rhyſe*, the laſt Prince of *South Wales*, who died, *A. D.* 1202. But his Siſter, *viz.*	3. MERBYN, Prince of *Powis Land*, ſoon fail'd.

GWENLIAN, was the Wife of Ednyſed Fychan, Lord of *Brynfeingle*.

Gronw *ap Ednyſed*

Theodore, or *Tewdor ap Gronw*.

Gronw ap *Tewdor*.

Tewdor *ap Gronw*, married MARGARET, Grand Daughter of LEWELIN ap *Daffyd*, the laſt Soveraign Prince of *Wales*.

Meredith ap *Tewdor*.

OWEN TEWDOR, ſlain in the Battle of *Mortimer's* Croſs, 1461.

EDWARD III. King of *England*.

JOHN a *Gaunt*, by his third Wife, *Katharine Roet*, Page 72.

JOHN BEAUFORT, Earl of *Somerſet*.

JOHN BEAUFORT, Duke of *Somerſet*, After all the *Males* of *John a Gaunt* were extinct, left his only Child. *viz.*

CHARLES VI. King of *France*.

Queen KATHARINE, Widow of King *Henry* V.

Margaret Beaufort.	Edmund Tewdor, Earl of Richmond.	*Jaſper Tewdor*, Duke of *Bedford*, without legal Iſſue.	*Owen Tewdor*, a Monk.

HENRY VII. *Tewdor*, King of *England*.

CHAP. V.

MASONRY in *England* from King HENRY VII. till the 𝔘𝔫𝔦𝔬𝔫 of the *Crowns*, A. D. 1603.

WHEN King *Richard* III. was flain at *Bofworth*, his Crown was forthwith put upon the Head of the Conqueror, HENRY TEWDOR Earl of *Richmond*, in the Field of Battle, and the Army proclaim'd him.

1. HENRY VII. King of *England*, on 22 *Aug.* 1485. nor did he ever affect another Title and Claim.

But his Wife ELIZABETH PLANTAGENET, Daughter of King *Edward* IV. was truly the Heirefs of all the *Royal* 𝔓𝔩𝔞𝔫𝔱𝔞𝔤𝔢𝔫𝔢𝔱𝔰, and conveyed hereditary Right to her Offspring.

New Worlds are now difcovered,

The *Cape of Good Hope*, A. D. 1487.
and *America*, —————— 1493.

In this Reign the 𝔊𝔬𝔱𝔥𝔦𝔠 *Stile* was brought to it's higheft Perfection in *England*, while it had been wholly laid afide in *Italy* by the Revivers of the old *Auguftan Stile*; as in Part I. Chap. VII.

𝔍𝔬𝔥𝔫 𝔍𝔰𝔩𝔦𝔭, Abbot of *Weftminfter*, finifhed the Repairs of that Abby, *A. D.* 1493. fo as it ftood till the late Reparations in our Time.

The Grand Mafter and Fellows of the Order of St. JOHN at *Rhodes* (now at *Malta*) affembled at their *Grand Lodge*, chofe King HENRY their Protector, *A. D.* 1500.

This *Royal* GRAND MASTER chofe for his Wardens of *England*, the forefaid 𝔍𝔬𝔥𝔫 𝔍𝔰𝔩𝔦𝔭, Abbot of *Weftminfter*, and

Sir 𝔕𝔢𝔤𝔦𝔫𝔞𝔩𝔡 𝔅𝔯𝔞𝔶, Knight of the *Garter*.

or *Deputies*, by whom the King fummon'd a *Lodge* of *Mafters* in the Palace, with whom he walked in ample Form to the *Eaft* End of *Weftminfter* Abby, and

and levell'd the *Footſtone* of his famous Chapel on 24 *June,* 1502. tho' it well deſerves to ſtand clean alone, being juſtly call'd by our Antiquary *Leland* the eighth *Wonder of Art,* the fineſt Piece of *Gothic* upon Earth, and the Glory of this Reign. It's *Capeſtone* was celebrated *A. D.* 1507.

The King employ'd *Grand Warden* 𝕭𝖗𝖆𝖞 to raiſe the middle Chapel of *Windſor,* and to rebuild the Palace of *Sheen* upon *Thames,* which the King call'd 𝕽𝖎𝖈𝖍𝖒𝖔𝖓𝖉; and to enlarge the old Palace of *Greenwich,* calling it 𝕻𝖑𝖆𝖈𝖊𝖓𝖙𝖎𝖆, where he built the pretty Box call'd the *Queen's-Houſe.*

He rebuilt *Baynard* Caſtle, *London,* founded ſix Monaſteries, and turn'd the old Palace of *Savoy* into an *Hoſpital:* while Others built *Braſen-Noſe* College *Oxford,* *Jeſus*'s and St. *John*'s Colleges *Cambridge,* and about 6 pious Houſes; till the King, aged only 54 Years, died at *New Richmond,* on 22 *April,* 1509. leaving three Children, *viz.*

2. Henry VIII. *Tewdor,* Prince of *Wales,* aged 18 Years, ſucceeded his Father, *A. D.* 1509.	Margaret *Tewdor,* firſt the Wife of *James* IV. King of *Scotland,* next of *Archibald Dowglaſs,* Earl of *Angus;* next of *Henry Stewart,* Lord *Methuen.*	Mary *Tewdor,* firſt the Wife of *Lewis* XII. King of *France;* and next of *Charles Brandon,* Duke *Suffolk.*

Cardinal 𝖂𝖔𝖔𝖑𝖘𝖊𝖞 was choſen *Grand Maſter,* who built *Hampton-Court;* and next rear'd *White-Hall,* the College of *Chriſt*'s Church *Oxford,* and ſeveral more good Edifices, which upon his Diſgrace were forfeited to the Crown, *A. D.* 1530.

𝕿𝖍𝖔𝖒𝖆𝖘 𝕮𝖗𝖔𝖒𝖜𝖊𝖑𝖑 Earl of *Eſſex* was the next Patron of the *Craft* under the King, for whom he built St. *James*'s Palace, *Chriſt*'s Hoſpital *London* and *Greenwich* Caſtle. Mean while

The King and Parliament threw off the old Yoke of the *Pope*'s Supremacy, and the King was declared the Supreme Head of the Church *A. D.* 1534. and *Wales* was united to *England,* *A. D.* 1536.

The

The *pious Houses*, in number about 926. were fuppref'd, *A.D.* 1539.
Cromwell, Earl of *Effex*, being unjuftly beheaded, *A. D.* 1540.
𝕵𝖔𝖍𝖓 𝕮𝖔𝖚𝖈𝖍𝖊𝖙, Lord *Audley*, became *Grand Mafter*.

But the Suppreffion of the religious Houfes did not hurt *Mafonry* ; nay Architecture of a finer Stile gain'd Ground : for thofe *pious* Houfes and their Lands being fold by the King at eafy Rates to the Nobility and Gentry, they built of thofe Ruins many ftately Manfions : Thus Grand Mafter *Audley* built *Magdalen* College *Cambridge*, and his great Houfe of *Audley End*.

King *Henry* VIII. aged near 56 Years, died on 28 *Jan.* 154⅚. and left three Children.

3. EDWARD VI. *Tewdor*, born by Queen *Jane Seymour*, a Minor of 9 Years, under the Regency of his Mother's Brother, EDWARD Duke of *Somerfet*, who eftablifht the *Proteftant* Religion ; and as 𝕲𝖗𝖆𝖓𝖉 𝕸𝖆𝖋𝖙𝖊𝖗 built his Palace in the *Strand*, call'd ftill *Somerfet-Houfe*, tho' forfeited to the Crown, *A. D.* 1552. and when the *Regent* was beheaded, JOHN POYNET, Bifhop of *Winchefter*, was the Patron of the *Free-Mafons* till the King died without Iffue, *A. D.* 1553.

4. MARY *Tewdor*, Daughter of Queen *Katharine* of *Aragon*, aged 38 Years, fucceeded her Brother *Edward*, as Queen Sovereign.

She reftored the *Romifh* Religion, and perfecuted the *Proteftants* ; married *Philip* II. King of *Spain*, and died without Iffue, 17 *Nov.* 1558.

5. ELIZABETH *Tewdor*, Daugh. of Queen *Anne Bollen*, aged 25 Years, fucceeded Sifter *Mary* as Queen Sovereign. She reftored the *Proteftant* Religion, and was declared Supreme Head of the Church. Now Learning of all Sorts revived, and the good old AUGUSTAN STILE in *England* began to peep from under it's Rubbifh: And it would have foon made great Progrefs, if the Queen had affected Architecture : But hearing the *Mafons* had cer-

tain *Secrets* that could not be reveal'd to her (for that fhe could not be *Grand Mafter*) and being jealous of all fecret Affemblies,

fhe

she sent an armed Force to break up their annual *Grand Lodge* at *York*, on St. *John's* Day, 27 *Dec.* 1561.

But Sir 𝕿𝖍𝖔𝖒𝖆𝖘 𝕾𝖆𝖈𝖐𝖛𝖎𝖑𝖑𝖊, *Grand Master*, took Care to make some of the chief Men sent *Free-Masons*, who then joining in that *Communication*, made a very honourable Report to the Queen ; and she never more attempted to dislodge or disturb them, but esteem'd them as a peculiar sort of Men that cultivated Peace and Friendship, Arts and Sciences, without meddling in the Affairs of Church or State.

This Tradition was firmly believ'd by all the old *English* Masons.

In this Reign some Colleges were built, and many stately Mansions, particularly famous *Burleigh-House* : For Travellers had brought home some good Hints of the happy *Revival* of the AUGUSTAN *Stile* in *Italy*, with some of the fine Drawings and Designs of the best Architects ; whereby the *English* began apace to slight the 𝕲𝖔𝖙𝖍𝖎𝖈 *Stile*, and would have entirely left it off, if the Queen had frankly encouraged the *Craft*.

Here it is proper to signify the Sentiment and Practice of the *Old Masons*, viz. That *Kings* and other *Male* Soveraigns, when made *Masons*, are *Grand Masters by Prerogative* during Life, and appoint a *Deputy*, or approve of his Election, to preside over the Fraternity with the Title and Honours of *Grand Master* ; but if the Soveraign is a *Female*, or not a Brother, or a *Minor* under a *Regent*, not a Brother ; or if the *Male* Soveraign or the *Regent*, tho' a Brother, is negligent of the *Craft*, then the *old* Grand Officers may assemble the *Grand Lodge* in due Form to elect a *Grand Master*, tho' not during Life, only he may be annually rechosen while he and they think fit.

Accordingly, when *Grand Master* SACK-VILLE demitted, *A. D.* 1567. FRANCIS RUSSEL, Earl of *Bedford* was chosen in the *North* ; and in the *South* Sir THOMAS GRESHAM, who built the first *Royal Exchange* at *London*, A. D. 1570. Next

This is the Tradition of the *Old Masons*.

CHARLES HOWARD Lord of *Effingham*, was *Grand Master* in the *South* till 1588. then GEORGE HASTINGS Earl of

M

Huntington,

Huntington, till the Queen died unmarried,
on 24 *March*, 160$\frac{2}{3}$. when

The Crowns of *England* and *Scotland* (tho' not yet the Kingdoms) were united in her Succeſſor, *viz.*

JAMES VI. *Stewart*, King of *Scotland*, Son of MARY *Stewart* Queen Soveraign, Daughter of King JAMES V. Son of King JAMES IV. by his Queen MARGARET TEWDOR eldeſt Daughter of HENRY VII. King of *England*, by his Queen ELIZABETH *Plantagenet* the Heireſs of *England*. And he was proclaim'd at *London*, JAMES I. King of *England*, *France* and *Ireland*, on 25 *March*, 1603. See Part III.

CHAP. VI.

MASONRY *in* Scotland *till the* UNION *of the* Crowns.

THE Hiſtory of the *firſt* Kings of the *Scots* in *Albin*, or the *Weſtern* Parts beyond the *Clyde* and the middle *Grampian* Hills ; and alſo that of the *Piɛts* in *Caledonia* along the *German* Sea Coaſt and towards *England*, not containing much to our Purpoſe, we may begin with the Reſtoration of the Kingdom of *Albin* (according to the *Scottiſh* Chronicle) made by

King FERGUS II. *Mac Erch*, A. D. 403.

And even after that Period, the Hiſtory of both theſe Nations conſiſts moſtly of War ; only we learn that the *Piɛts* were a more mechanical and mercantil People than the *Scots*, had built many Cities, and firſt founded all the old ſtrong Caſtles in their Dominion ; while the *Scots* affeɛted rather to be a Nation of Soldiers, till

KENNETH II. *Mac Alpin*, King of *Scots*, demoliſh'd the Kingdom of the *Piɛts*, and so became the *firſt* King of all *Scotland*, A. D. ———— 842. He repair'd the publick Edifices after the Wars, and died, 858.

* See his Race in the Margin of next Page.

But both the Branches of his *Royal* Race were moſtly engaged in War till King MALCOLM II. *Mac Kenneth*, ſucceeded his Couſin King *Grimus*, A. D. 1008. as on the next Page.

For

For King *Malcolm* II. firft compil'd the Laws in the famous Book of *Scotland* call'd REGIAM MAJESTATEM, partition'd the Land into *Baronies*, founded the Bifhoprick of *Aberdeen* (in Memory of his routing the *Norwegians*) A. D. 1017. cultivated *Arts* and *Sciences*, and fortified his Towns and Caftles till he died, leaving only two Daughters, *viz.*

BEATRIX the Eldeft, Wife of 𝔄𝔩𝔟𝔞𝔫𝔞𝔠𝔥 Thane of the *Ifles*.	DOCHA the Younger, Wife of 𝔅𝔢𝔱𝔥-𝔣𝔦𝔫𝔩𝔢𝔤 Thane of *Angus*.
1. DUNCAN I fucceeded his Grandfather, *A. D.* 1033. murder'd by *Mackbeth*-- 1040. but King DUNCAN I. was the *Patriarch* of the following Kings on the next Page.	2. MACKBETH kill'd and took Poffeffion, 1040. built the Caftle of *Dunfinnan* and *Lumfannan*, &c. and much encouraged the *Craft*, till cut off by *Macduff*, A. D. 1057.

* 1. KENETH II. *Mac Alpin* died 858. Father of — 2. DONALD V. fucceeded his Brother *Kenneth* II.

3. CONSTANTIN II fucceeded *Donald* V.	ETHUS fucceeded *Conftantin* II.	
6. DONALD VI. fucceeded *Gregory*.	CONSTANTIN III. fucceeded *Donald* VI.	
8. MALCOLM I. fucceeded *Conftantin* III He received *Cumberland* and *Weftmoreland* from EDMUND I. King of *England*, Father of	9 INDULPHUS fucceeded *Makolm* I 11. CULENUS fucceeded *Duffus*. 13. CONSTANTIN IV. fucceeded *Kenneth* III.	5. GREGORY, Son of King *Congallus*, (who had reign'd before *Kenneth* II.) fucceeded ETHUS. He built *Aberdeen*.

10 DUFFUS, who fucceeded *Indulphus*.	12. KENNETH III. fucceeded *Culenus*, A. D. 976. the Year after *Edgar* King of *England* died. KENNETH enacted the Crown *hereditary* in his Family, and died, *A. D.* 994.	𝔐𝔬𝔤𝔞𝔩𝔩𝔲𝔰 the Prince. 14. GRIMUS fucceeded *Conftantin* IV. and died 1008. 𝔉𝔞𝔫𝔠𝔥𝔬 murder'd by *Mackbeth*. Below
	15. MALCOLM II. fucceeded *Grimus*, A. Dom. 1008.	King

King *Duncan* I.

3. MALCOLM III. *Keanmore,* or *Head Great,* was reſtor'd when *Macbeth* was ſlain, 1057. He built the old Church of *Dunfermling,* a Royal Sepulchre, and levell'd the *Footſtone* of the old Cathedral of *Durham,* which he richly endow'd. He fortified his

4. DONALD *Bane,* or *White* DONALD, *Malcolm's* younger Brother mounted the Throne, *A D.* 1093. and after the Uſurper *Duncan* was ſlain 1095. *Donald* reign'd ti'l hii Nephew King *Edgar* impriſon'd him for Life. *A. D.* 1098.

5. DUNCAN II. a Baſtard of King *Malcolm,* uſurped, *A D.* 1094.

Borders, Caſtles and Seaports, as the Royal 𝕲𝖗𝖆𝖓𝖉 𝕸𝖆𝖘𝖙𝖊𝖗 and Patron of *Arts* and *Sciences,* till he died, *A. D.* 1093.

By his Queen MARGARET, Siſter of Prince *Edgar Atheling,* and Grand-Daughter of King EDMUND *Ironſides,* the *Saxon* Heireſs of *England* (by the *Scots* call'd St. *Margaret.*) He had

6. EDGAR ſucceeded *Donald,* and died without Iſſue, 1107.

────────

Colms's Inch, St. *Michael's* at *Scone,* &c. and patroniz'd the *Craft* till he died, *A. D.* 1124. without Iſſue.

7. ALEXANDER I. ſucceeded Brother *Edgar,* built the Abbies of *Dunfermlin,* and St.

8. DAVID I. ſucceeded Brother *Alexander,* built the Abby of *Holy-Rood* Houſe, and the Cathedrals of four Biſhopricks that he eſtabliſh'd. The Clergy call'd him St. *David* for his great Endowments

MAUD, Wife of *Henry* I. King of *England.*

〜〜〜

MAUD, the Empreſs.

MARY, Wife of *Euſtace,* Count of *Boulogne.*

〜〜〜

MAUD, Wife of King *Stephen.*

to the Church; and the *Maſons* worſhipped him as their beneficent 𝕲𝖗𝖆𝖓𝖉 MASTER, till he died, *A. D.* 1153.

By his Q. MAUD, the Heireſs of *Huntington,* King DAVID I. had

𝕳𝖊𝖓𝖗𝖞, Prince of *Scotland,* died before his Father, 1152. leaving three Sons, *viz.*

9. MALCOLM IV. call'd the *Maiden,* ſucceeded Grand-father *David,* and died without Iſſue, *A. D.* 1165.

10. WILLIAM the *Lion.*   See next Page.

DAVID, Earl of *Huntington.*   See next Page.

10. WILLIAM

10. WILLIAM the *Lion* succeeded Brother *Malcolm*, built a Palace at *Aberdeen*, rebuilt the whole Town of *Perth* after a Fire, and was an excellent **Grand Master**, by the Affistance of the Nobility and Clergy, till he died A. D. 1214. See the next *Page*.

David Earl of *Huntington* died in *England*, A. D. 1219. But all King WILLIAM's Race failing in the *Maiden of Norway*, as on the next Page, the Right of *Succeffion* was in the Heirs of this **David**; and they made the *Competition* for the Crown, as in the Margin below. 10. WIL-

---

Competition of BRUCE and BALLIOL

Prince DAVID Earl of *Huntingdon* had 3 Daughters, *viz.*

1. MARGARET, Wife of Alan Lord of *Galloway*.

DORNAGILLA, Wife of **John Balliol** Lord of *Bernard* Caftle in *Durham*.

1. JOHN BALLIOL, the *Competitor*, as defcended from *David*'s Eldeft Daughter, was declar'd King of *Scotland*, by the Umpire of the *Competition* King EDW. I. of *England*, A. D. 1292. for *John*'s owning him his Superior.

But JOHN revolting, *Edward* depos'd him, 1296. banifh'd him into *Normandy*, and garrifon'd *Scotland* for himfelf. But the *Englifh* were expell'd firft by Sir **William Wallace**, and next by King ROBERT BRUCE. See the next *Margin*.

2. ISABELLE, Wife of ROBERT BRUCE, an *Englifh* Lord, made Lord of *Anandale* in *Scotland*.

ROBERT BRUCE, the *Competitor*, as the *firft Male* from Prince *David*: But his Claim was over-ruled by the Umpire; and *Robert* foon died.

Robert Bruce, Lord of *Anandale*, and by Marriage, Earl of *Carrick*, was by King EDWARD I. made Earl of *Huntington* to make him eafy: And after *John Balliol* was banifh'd, King EDWARD promis'd to make BRUCE King of *Scotland*, in order to engage him againft **Wallace** But next Day after the Battle of *Falkirk*, A. D. 1298. at a Conference or Interveiw.

Wallace.
See the next Margin.

3. ADA, Wife of Lord *Haftings*.

Defcent of the ROYAL STEWARTS from GRIMUS King of *Scotland* who died 1008.

Bancho, Thane of *Loch-Abyr*, murder'd by *Macbeth*, 1040. Page 83.

Fleance fled to *Wales*, and married *Nerfta*, Daughter of GRUFFYD ap *Llewelin*, Prince of *Wales*, and died there.

Walter I. the young *Welchman* came to *Scotland* upon the Reftoration of King *Malcolm Keanmore*, who made him *heritable Lord* **High Stewart.**

WALTER I

10. WILLIAM the *Lion*.

————————————————⌃————————————————

11. ALEXANDER II. rebuilt *Coldingham*, and died, *A. D.* 1249

————————————————⌃————————————————

12. ALEXANDER III. the laſt *Male* from *Duncan* I. died *A.D.* 1285.

⌃

MARGARET, Queen of *Ericus* King of *Norway*.

MARGARET, *the Maiden* of *Norway*, died coming over 1290.
But from the Diſſolution of the *Pictiſh* Kingdom, *A. D.* 842.⎫
the 𝕲𝖔𝖙𝖍𝖎𝖈 𝕾𝖙𝖎𝖑𝖊 was well improv'd in *Scotland* during Years 448.⎬
till the *Maiden* of *Norway* died, and the *Competition* began.⎭

This

King JOHN *Balliol*.	Houſe of BRUCE.	Houſe of STEWART.
	𝖂𝖆𝖑𝖑𝖆𝖈𝖊 convinced	WALTER I. the *Stewart*.
————⌃————	𝕭𝖗𝖚𝖈𝖊 of his Error,	
3. EDWARD *Balliol*,	who never fought more	ALAN the *Stewart*.
wasby King EDW. III	againſt the *Scots*, and	
of *England*, ſent to *Scotl*	died 1303.	ALEXANDER I. the *Stewart*.
and, join'd his Party,		
expell'd young King	————⌃————	WALTER II. the *Stewart*.
David Bruce, and wa	2. ROBERT I. 𝕭𝖗𝖚𝖈𝖊	————⌃————
crown'd *A. D.* 1332	fled to *Scotland*, and	ALEX- | Sir 𝕽obert *Stewart*,
but expell'd———— 1341	was crown'd 1306 And	ANDER | Lord *Darnley*, Pa-
Some ſay his Race	after many ſore Con-	II. the | triarch of the STEW-
are ſtill in *France*.	flicts, he totally routed	*Stewart*. | ARTS of 𝕷ennor,
	King EDWARD II. of	———⌃——— | from whom deſcend-
England at *Bannockburn*, A. D. 1314. obtain'd	JOHN | ed HENRY Lord
an honourable Peace, and died illuſtrious,	the *Stew-* | *Darnley*, Father of
A. D. 1329.	art. | K. *James* VI. below.
4. DAVID II. *Bruce* ſuc-	MARJORY BRUCE	WALTER III. the *Stewart*,
ceeded, a Minor of 8. Years	born of King *Robert's*	the lineal *Male* of the *Old*
born of King *Robert's* ſecond	*firſt* Wife, *Iſabella*,	*Royal Race*, and Patriarch of
Wife, was ſent to *France* till	Daughter of *Donald*,	the *Royal Stewarts*, by his
Edward Balliol was expell'd,	Earl of *Mar*, a no-	Wife *Marjory Bruce*.
He was afterwards captivated	ble *Pict*.	
in *England* till ranſom'd, and		
died without Iſſue, 1370.		
	King ROBERT II. *Stewart*. See the next Margin.	

This had been more amply and accurately difcover'd, if the *Learn'd* of *Scotland* had publifh'd a *Monafticon Scoticanum*, with an Account of the old Palaces and Caftles (as fine as any in *Europe*) before the *Competition* of BRUCE and BALLIOL, in a Chronological Deduction : *A Work long and much defiderated!*

During the *Competition*, MASONRY was neglected ; but after the Wars, King ROBERT I. *Bruce*, having fettled his Kingdom, forthwith employ'd the *Craft* in repairing the Caftles, Palaces and pious Houfes ; and the *Nobility* and *Clergy* follow'd his Example till he died, *A. D.* 1329.

King DAVID II. *Bruce*, after his Reftoration, much affected *Mafonry*, and built *David's Tower* in *Edinborough* Caftle, till he died without Iffue, *A. D.* 1370. leaving the Crown to his Sifter's Son, *viz.*

Royal Stewards. See the laft Margin.

1. ROBERT II. *Stewart*, who left the Care of *Mafonry* to the Eminent Clergy, then very active in raifing fine religious Houfes, till he died *A. D.* 1390.

2. ROBERT III. *Stewart*, being fickly, left the Government to the Care of his Brother Robert Duke of *Albany*, a great Patron of the *Craft*, till the King died *A. D.* 1406.

2. ROBERT

ROYAL STEWARDS. See the laft *Margin*.

1. ROBERT II. *Stewart*, fo call'd from his hereditary Office that now reverted to the *Crown :* and hence the King's Eldeft Son is ftiled the *Prince* and STEWART of *Scotland.* This King was firft the *Earl of Strathern*, till his Uncle King *David* died, *A. D.* 1370. and King *Robert* II. died 1390.

His firft Wife ELIZABETH MUIR, was only *Countefs* of *Strathern*, for fhe died before he was King : Yet her Son, *viz.*

His 2d Wife EUPHEMIA ROSS, was Queen of *Scotland*.

2. ROBERT III. *Stewart* (call'd JOHN *formerly*) fucceeded his Father, *A D* 1390. Upon hearing that his only Son JAMES, in his Voyage to *France*, was captivated by King *Henry* IV. of *England*, tho' in Time of Peace, King *Robert* broke his Heart, 1406.

Walter *Stewart*, Earl of *Athol* who murder'd King *James* I. at *Perth.*

3. JAMES I. *Stewart*, after 18 Years was ranfom'd and crown'd, 1424.

2. *Robert* III.

3. JAMES I. *Stewart*, tho' unjuftly captivated, ruled by his *Regent* the faid *Robert* Duke of *Albany*.

𝔥𝔢𝔫𝔯𝔶 𝔚𝔞𝔯𝔡𝔩𝔞𝔴, Bifhop of St. *Andrews*, was now *Grand Mafter*, and founded the *Univerfity* there, *A. D.* 1411. tho' it was long before a Place of Education.

Robert Duke of *Albany* died *A. D.* 1420. and his Son *Duke* 𝔐𝔲𝔯𝔡𝔬𝔠𝔥 was *Regent* till the King was ranfom'd, reftor'd and crown'd, *A. D.* 1424.

King JAMES I. prov'd the *beft* King of *Scotland*, the Patron of the Learned, and countenanced the *Lodges* with his Prefence as the 𝕽𝔬𝔶𝔞𝔩 *Grand* 𝔐𝔞𝔰𝔱𝔢𝔯 ; till he fettled an Yearly Revenue of 4 Pounds *Scots* (an *Englifh Noble*) to be paid by every *Mafter Mafon* in *Scotland*, to a 𝔊𝔯𝔞𝔫𝔡 𝔐𝔞𝔰𝔱𝔢𝔯 This is the *Tradition* of the chofen by the *Grand Lodge*, and approv'd *Old Scottifh Mafons*, and found by the Crown, one *nobly* born, or an in their Records. eminent *Clergyman*, who had his Deputies in Cities and Counties: and every *new* Brother at Entrance paid him alfo a Fee. His Office impower'd him to regulate in the *Fraternity* what fhould not come under the Cognizance of Law-Courts : to him appeal'd both *Mafon* and *Lord*, or the Builder and Founder, when at Variance; in order to prevent *Law-Pleas*; and in his Abfence, they appeal'd to his *Deputy* or *Grand Warden* that refided next to the Premiffes.

This Office remain'd till the *Civil Wars*, A. D. 1640. but is now obfolete ; nor can it be reviv'd but by a ROAYL *Grand* MASTER. And now the *Mafons* joyfully toafted
TO THE KING AND THE CRAFT.

This excellent King repair'd *Falkland* and his other Palaces, fortified all his Caftles and Sea-Ports, and influenc'd the *Nobility* to follow his Example in much employing the *Craft*, till he was bafely murder'd in the *Dominicans* Abby at *Perth*, by his Uncle *Walter Stewart* Earl of *Atholl*, A. D. 1437. and being juftly lamented by All, his Murderers were feverely punifh'd.

By

By his Wife JOAN BEAUFORT, eldeſt Daughter of *John Beaufort* Earl of *Somerſet*, eldeſt Son of *John a Gaunt*, by his 3d Wife *Katharine Roet*, he had

4. JAMES II. *Stewart*, a Minor of 7 Years, under the Regency of Lord *Calendar*.

In this Reign 𝔚𝔦𝔩𝔩𝔦𝔞𝔪 𝔖𝔦𝔫𝔠𝔩𝔞𝔦𝔯 the great *Earl* of *Orkney* and *Caitneſs* was *Grand Maſter*, and built *Roſlin Chapel* near *Edinborough*, a Maſter Piece of the beſt *Gothic*, A. D. 1441. next Biſhop 𝔗𝔲𝔯𝔫𝔟𝔲𝔩𝔩 of *Glaſgow*, who founded the Univerſity there, A. D. 1454

And the King, when of Age, encouraged the *Craft* till he died, ——————————————————————— } 1460

By his Wife MARY, Daughter of *Arnold* Duke of *Guelders*,

5. JAMES III. *Stewart*, a Minor of 7 Years ſucceeded, and when of Age, he employ'd the *Craft* in more curious Architecture than any King before him, particularly at *Sterling*, where he erected a ſpacious *Hall*, and a ſplendid *Chapel Royal* in the Caſtle, by the Direction firſt of Sir 𝔕𝔬𝔟𝔢𝔯𝔱 𝔠𝔬𝔠𝔨𝔢𝔯𝔞𝔫 *Grand Maſter*, and next of 𝔄𝔩𝔢𝔯𝔞𝔫𝔡𝔢𝔯 Lord *Forbes*, who continued in Office till the King died, *A. D.* 1488.

By his Wife MARGARET Daughter of *Chriſtiern* I. K. of *Denmark*.

6. JAMES IV. *Stewart* aged 16 Years ſucceeded, and by the *Grand Maſter* 𝔚𝔦𝔩𝔩𝔦𝔞𝔪 𝔈𝔩𝔭𝔥𝔦𝔫ſ𝔱𝔬𝔫 Biſhop of *Aberdeen*, the King founded the *Univerſity* there *A. D.* 1494. *Elphinſton* at his own Coſt founded the curious *Bridge of Dee* near *Aberdeen*, finiſh'd by his Succeſſor Biſhop 𝔊𝔞𝔟𝔦𝔫 𝔇𝔲𝔫𝔟𝔞𝔯 an excellent *Grand Maſter*, who built many other fine Structures.

The King delighted moſt in *Ship Building*, and encreas'd his *Navy* Royal, a very Warlike Prince : till aſſiſting the *French* in a Diverſion of War, he was loſt in *Flowden-Field*, A. D. 1513.

By his Wife MARGARET TEWDOR, eldeſt Daughter of *Henry* VII. King of *England*, He had

N   7. JAMES

7. JAMES V. *Stewart*, a Minor of 17 Months; and when of Age he became the ingenious Patron of the Learned, especially of the *Muses*.

In this Reign the noble 𝕲𝖆𝖛𝖎𝖓 𝕯𝖔𝖜𝖌𝖑𝖆𝖘, Bishop of *Dunkeld*, was *Grand Master* till he died, *A. D.* 1522. Next

𝕲𝖊𝖔𝖗𝖌𝖊 𝕮𝖗𝖊𝖎𝖌𝖍𝖙𝖔𝖓 *Abbot* of *Holyrood-House*, till *A. D.* 1527. and then

PATRICK, Earl of *Lindsay* (the Progenitor of our late *Grand Master* CRAWFURD) who was succeeded in that Office by Sir 𝕯𝖆𝖛𝖎𝖉 𝕷𝖎𝖓𝖉𝖘𝖆𝖞, *Lion* King at *Arms*, still mention'd among *Scottish Masons* by the Name of DAVY LINDSAY the *learned Grand Master*; till the King died, 13 *Dec.* 1542.

By his Wife MARY, Daughter of *Claud* of *Lorrain* Duke of *Guise*, He left only

8. MARY *Stewart*, Queen *Soveraign* of *Scotland*, a Minor of 7 Days, who became Queen *Consort* of *France*; and after the Death of her first Husband King *Francis* II. without Issue, she return'd to *Scotland A. D.* 1561. and brought with her some fine Connoisseurs in the AUGUSTAN Stile.

She next married, *A. D.* 1565. HENRY STEWART, Lord *Darnley*, eldest Son of 𝕸𝖆𝖙𝖙𝖍𝖊𝖜 Earl of *Lennox*, the lineal *Male* descended from Sir *Robert Stewart* Lord *Darnley* of the *Old Royal Race*, as in the Margin of Page 86.

She fell out with her Nobles, who dethroned her; and being defeated in Battle, she fled for Shelter into *England* 1568. where Queen ELIZABETH detain'd her a Prisoner, and at last, for Reasons of State, beheaded her on 8 *Feb.* 158$\frac{6}{7}$.

9. JAMES VI. *Stewart*, born 19 *June*, 1566. Upon his Mother's Abdication he was crown'd King of *Scotland*, aged 13 Months, under 4 successive *Regents*; and when aged near 12 Years he assum'd the Government *A. D.* 1578.

He founded the *University* of *Edinburg A. D.* 1580. He sail'd to *Denmark*, and married ANN Princess *Royal*, *A. D.* 1589. when he visited the noble 𝕿𝖞𝖈𝖍𝖔 𝕭𝖗𝖆𝖍𝖊, the Prince of *Astronomers*, in his *Scarlet Island*.

The

The Nobility and Gentry having divided the Spoil of the Church's Revenues, built many ſtately Manſions of the Ruins of the pious Houſes, as was done in *England*; and the *Maſons* began to imitate the *Auguſtan Stile*, under the Direction of ſeveral ſucceſſive *Grand Maſters*.

For after the Death of *Davy Lindſay*, 𝕬𝖓𝖉𝖗𝖊𝖜 𝕾𝖙𝖊𝖜𝖆𝖗𝖙 Lord *Ochiltree* was *Grand Maſter*; next Sir 𝕵𝖆𝖒𝖊𝖘 𝕾𝖆𝖓𝖉𝖎𝖑𝖆𝖓𝖉𝖘 Knight of *Malta*: Then 𝕮𝖑𝖆𝖚𝖉 𝕳𝖆𝖒𝖎𝖑𝖙𝖔𝖓 Lord *Paiſley* (Progenitor of our late *Grand Maſter* ABERCORN) who made King JAMES a *Brother Maſon* and continued in Office till the *Union* of the *Crowns*, A. D. 1603.

Before this Period, not only the Crown was poſſeſs'd of many fine Palaces and ſtrong Caſtles, but alſo the Nobles and Chiefs of Clans had fortify'd themſelves; becauſe of their frequent Feuds or Civil Wars; and the *Clergy* had built many Abbies, Churches, Monaſtries and other pious Houſes, of as fine *Gothic* as any in *Europe*, moſt venerable, ſumptuous, and magnificent.

The *Fraternity* of old met in *Monaſteries* in foul Weather; but in fair Weather they met early in the Morning on the Tops of Hills, eſpecially on St. JOHN *Evangeliſt's Day*, and from thence walk'd in due Form to the Place of Dinner, according to the Tradition of the old *Scots Maſons*, particularly of thoſe in the antient Lodges of *Killwinning*, *Sterling*, *Aberdeen*, &c.

CHAP. VII.

MASONRY in *Ireland* till *Grand Maſter* KINGSTON, A. D. 1730.

THE antient *Romans* having never invaded *Ireland*, we have no good Vouchers of what happened there before St. Patrick in the Days of King LEOGHAIR, about *A. D.* 430. He founded St. *Patricks* at | See Sir *James Ware's* Antiq. Hibern.

Ardmagh,

Ardmagh, and the Priory of St. *Avog* at *Loch-Derg*, near the Cave call'd St. *Patrick*'s *Purgatory:* But afterwards many pious Houses appear'd throughout *Ireland.*

Nor did the *Anglo-Saxons* invade *Ireland:* But 𝔅𝔢𝔡𝔢 and Others, in the 8th Century affirm, that then many *Britons, Saxons* and *Franks* reforted to the Schools of *Ireland* for Education.

But the *Norwegians* and *Danes* conquer'd the moſt Part of the Iſland ; and tho' at firſt they deſtroy'd the pious Houſes, they built many Caſtles and Forts with lofty Beacons, to alarm the whole Country in an Hour ; till they were converted to Chriſtianity by the *Iriſh*, when the *Danes* built many religious Houſes ; as at *Dublin* St. 𝔐𝔞𝔯𝔶's Abbey and *Chriſt Church*, about *A. D.* 984.

At length, BRIEN BOROM, the Grand Monarch of *all Ireland* of *Heber*'s Race, after defeating the *Danes* in many Battels, totally routed 'em, *A. D.* 1039.

> From whom our late *Grand Maſter* INCHIQUIN is deſcended in a lineal Male Race.

So the far greater Part of the *Danes* were forced to fail home, and carried with 'em (as the *Iriſh* affirm) the beſt old *Records* of *Ireland*, an irreparable Damage! But the Learned of Other Nations long to fee the remaining Manuſcripts of *Ireland* publiſh'd with good Tranſlations, and alſo a better *Monaſticon Hibernicum* ; that among other Antiquities, the Veſtiges of their old *Celtic* Architecture might be trac'd, if poſſible ; for the *Auguſtan Stile* had never been there, and the *Gothic* was only introduc'd by St. *Patrick.*

After the Expulſion of the *Danes*, the *Mileſian* Kings of *Ireland* order'd the Palaces, Caſtles and pious Houſes to be repair'd, and much employ'd the *Craft* down to RODERIC O CONNOR, the laſt Monarch of *all Ireland*, who built the wonderful Caſtle of *Tuam* (now demoliſh'd) *A. D.* 1168.

But the *Royal* Branches having made themſelves *Petty Soveraigns*, were imbroil'd in frequent Civil Wars : One of them, *viz.*

DERMOT King of *Leinſter*, being defeated by the Others, came to HENRY II. King of *England*, and got Leave to con-
tract

tract with Adventurers, *viz.* **Richard Strongbow** Earl of *Pembroke,* **Robert** *Fitz-Stephen* of *Cardigan,* and **Maurice** *Fitz-Gerald;* who brought over an Army of *Welch* and *English* to DERMOT's Affiftance, took in *Dublin, Waterford* and many other Places, which they fortify'd and furrender'd into the Hands of their King HENRY II. as foon as he had follow'd 'em into *Ireland,* A. D. 1172.

Kings of ENGLAND now *Lords* of IRELAND.

The *Irish,* not without Reafon, fay, that King HENRY II. did not conquer *Ireland;* only fome of their *Petty* Kings and Princes, rather than be farther imbroil'd in *Civil* Wars, chofe to come under his Protection, and of their own Accord receiv'd the *Laws* of *England,* with the *Freedom* of a Parliament at *Dublin.* But where the *English* prevail'd, *Mafonry* and other Arts were moft encouraged.

Thus the faid STRONGBOW Lord *Warden* of *Ireland* Built the Priory of *Kill Mainham;* while St. *Bar* founded the [*A. D.* 1174] Aboy of *Finbar.*

John De Coucy, Earl of *Kingfail,* rebuilt the Abby [*A. D.* 1183] of St. *Patrick* in *Down,* the Priories of *Nedrum* and St. *John's,* with St. *Mary's* Abby of *Innys,* &c.

In the Reign of RICHARD I. **Alured,** a noble *Dane,* built St. *John's* in *Dublin;* and Archbifhop *Comin* rebuilt [*A. D.* 1190] St. *Patrick's* there, all of Stone, which before was only of Timber and *Watles.*

King JOHN was King of *Ireland* (as the *Irish* affirm) till his Brother *Richard* died, 1199. and afterwards went into *Ireland,* and employ'd **Henry Launders** Archbifhop of *Dublin* and Lord *Juftice,* as *Grand Mafter,* in building the Caftle [*A. D.* 1210] of *Dublin;* while **William** Earl of *Pembroke* built the Priory of *Killkenny.*

King HENRY III. granted *Ireland* a **Magna** [*A. D.* 1216] **Charta** the fame with that of *England.* **Felix O Quadam,** Archbifhop of *Tuam,* rebuilt St. *Mary's Dublin,* and cover'd it with Lead; while **Hugh De Lacy,** Earl of *Ulfter,* [about *A. D.* 1210] founded

founded *Carrick-Fergus*, a Friary in *Down*, the Priory of *Ards*, and famous *Trim Castle*, &c. as 𝕲𝖗𝖆𝖓𝖉 𝕸𝖆𝖘𝖙𝖊𝖗, or Patron of the *Craft*.

The *Native* Princes liv'd pretty well with the *English*, till the Reign of King EDWARD II. when Prince EDWARD BRUCE (Brother of *Robert Bruce* King of *Scotland*) headed the confederated *Irish*, conquer'd the Island, was crown'd *King* of *all Ireland*, and reign'd three Years, till Sir *Roger Mortimer* Earl of *March* landed with a strong *English* Army and slew King *Edward Bruce* in Battle. | A. D. 1315 |

After this, *Masonry* in the *English* Settlements revived; and in the *North* of *Ireland* too, where the *Scots* had gradually settled, and brought with them good *Gothic Masonry*. At last,

The *Natives* regarded the *Kings* of *England* as the lawful *Soveraign* Lords of *Ireland* down to King HENRY VIII. who in Defiance of the *Pope*, proclaim'd himself King of *Ireland*, which was confirm'd in the Parliament at *Dublin*, A. D. 1542.

Kings of ENGLAND now *Kings* of IRELAND.

HENRY King of *Ireland* was succeeded by his Son King EDWARD, and he by his Sister Queen MARY *Tewdor*, who got *Pope* PAUL IV. to make her Queen of *Ireland*; succeeded by her Sister Queen ELIZABETH *Tewdor*, who founded the famous *University* of *Dublin*, A. D. 1591.

Masonry made some Progress in *Ireland* in the Reigns of JAMES I. and CHARLES I. till the *Civil* Wars, when all the Fabrick was out of Joint till the *Restoration* A. D. 1660. After which it was revived by some of the Disciples of *Inigo Jones* in the Reign of CHARLES II. and till the Wars of King JAMES II. But after King WILLIAM had settled the Country, Arts and Sciences were again well cultivated in the Reigns of Queen ANNE and King GEORGE I.

Many are the beautiful Remains of the best *Gothic* Architecture in this fine Island, of which the Learned of *Ireland* can best give a Chronological Deduction. But since the *Revolution* the AUGUSTAN STILE has been much encouraged there, both by the Government and the Nobility and Gentry: So that the Metropolis *Dublin* is now adorned with a stately *Tollsell* or *Town-house*,

an

an excellent *Custom-house*, a curious *Armory* in the Castle, a fine *Library* in the *University*, neat and convenient *Barracks* for the Garrison, a Royal *Hospital* for old Soldiers, *Stephen*'s *Green-Square*, the largest in *Europe*, being an *English* Mile round, or 1760 Yards, *Stephens*'s Hospital, besides Churches and other Edifices rais'd by good Architects, particularly by 𝕿𝖍𝖔𝖒𝖆𝖘 𝕭𝖚𝖗𝖌𝖍 Esq; late *Surveyor* General of *Ireland*, and his Successor Sir 𝕰𝖉𝖜𝖆𝖗𝖉 𝕷𝖔𝖛𝖊𝖙 𝕻𝖊𝖆𝖗𝖈𝖊, the Architect of the new magnificent *Parliament-House* (far beyond *that* of *England*) founded on the 3d *Feb.* 172⅞, when Lord *Carteret*, then Lord *Lieutenant*, the Lords *Justices*, several *Peers* and Members of *Parliament*, some eminent *Clergy*, with many *Free Masons*, attended by the King's *Yeomen* of Guard, and a Detachment of *Horse* and *Foot*, made a solemn Procession thither; and the Lord *Lieutenant*, having in the King's Name level'd the *Footstone* at the *South-side*, by giving it 3 Knocks with a Mallet, the Trumpets sounded, the solemn Croud made joyful Acclamations, a Purse of Gold was laid on the Stone for the Masons, who drank *to the King and the Craft*, &c. And in the Stone were placed Two *Silver Medals* of King GEORGE II. and Queen CAROLINE, over which a Copper Plate was laid with the following Inscription.

SERENISSIMUS ET POTENTISSIMUS
REX GEORGIUS SECUNDUS
PER EXCELLENT. DOMINUM
JOANNEM DOMINUM ET BARON. DE HAWNES
LOCUM-TENENTEM,
ET PER EXCELLENT. DOMINOS
HUGONEM ARCHIEP: ARMACHAN:
THOMAM WINDHAM CANCELL.
GULIEL: CONOLLY DOM: COM: PROLOCUT.
JUSTICIARIOS GENERALES,
PRIMUM HUJUSCE DOMUS PARLIAMENT: LAPIDEM
POSUIT
TERTIO DIE FEBRUARII MDCCXXVIII.

At

At laſt the antient *Fraternity* of the *Free* and accepted MASONS in *Ireland*, being duly aſſembled in their *Grand Lodge* at *Dublin*, choſe a *Noble* 𝕲𝖗𝖆𝖓𝖉 𝕸𝖆𝖘𝖙𝖊𝖗, in Imitation of their Brethren of *England*, in the 3d Year of his preſent Majeſty King GEORGE II. *A. D.* 1730. even our *noble Brother*

JAMES KING Lord Viſcount *Kingſton*, the very next Year after his Lordſhip, had, with great Reputation, been the 𝕲𝖗𝖆𝖓𝖉 𝕸𝖆𝖘𝖙𝖊𝖗 of *England*; and he has introduced the ſame *Conſtitutions* and antient *Uſages*.

He has been annually ſucceeded by noble Brothers in *Solomon's* Chair, and the *Grand Lodge* of *Ireland* are firmly reſolved to perſevere in propagating the Knowledge of the *Noble Science* of GEOMETRY and the *Royal Art* of MASONRY.

PART

PART III.

The 𝕳𝕚𝕗𝕿𝕠𝕣𝕪 of MASONRY in *Britain,* from the UNION of the *Crowns* to thefe Times.

CHAP. I.

The AUGUSTAN STILE in *Britain,* from the *Union* of the CROWNS 1603. till the RESTORATION 1660.

BEFORE this *Period,* fome Gentlemen of fine Tafte returning from their Travels full of laudable Emulation, refolved, if not to excel the *Italian Revivers,* at leaft to imitate them in old *Roman* and *Grecian* MASONRY. But no Remains being here, no Veftiges of the good old AUGUSTAN Stile, thofe ingenious Travellers brought home fome Pieces of *old Columns,* fome curious Drawings of the *Italian Revivers,* and their Books of *Architecture* ; efpecially

INIGO JONES, born near St. *Paul's London,* A. D. 1572. (Son of Mr. *Ignatius* or *Inigo Jones,* a Citizen of *London)* bred up at *Cambridge,* who naturally took to the *Arts of Defigning,* and was firft known by his Skill in *Landskip-Painting* ; for which he was patroniz'd by the noble and learned WILLIAM HERBERT (afterwards Earl of *Pembroke)* at whofe Expence *Jones* made the Tour of *Italy,* where he was inftructed in the *Royal Art* by fome of the beft Difciples of the famous
ANDREA PALLADIO.

INIGO

INIGO JONES, upon his Return, laid aside his *Pencil*, and took up the *Square*, *Level* and *Plumb*, and became the 𝕭𝖎𝖙𝖗𝖚𝖛𝖎𝖚𝖘 𝕭𝖗𝖎𝖙𝖆𝖓𝖓𝖎𝖈𝖚𝖘, the Rival of *Palladio* and of all the *Italian* Revivers; as it soon appear'd after

The UNION of the CROWNS, A. D. 1603.

When the ROYAL TEWDORS expired, and the ROYAL STEWARTS succeeded.

SCOTTISH Kings of all Britain.

1. JAMES I. *Stewart*, now the *first* King of *all Britain*, a *Royal* Brother *Mason*, and *Royal Grand Master* by Prerogative, wishing for proper Heads and Hands for establishing the *Augustan Stile* here, was glad to find such a Subject as 𝕴𝖓𝖎𝖌𝖔 𝕵𝖔𝖓𝖊𝖘; whom he appointed his General *Surveyor*, and approv'd of his being chosen *Grand Master* of *England*, to preside over the *Lodges*.

The King order'd him to draw the Plan of a *new* Palace at *Whitehall*, and so when the old *Banquetting-House* was pull'd down, the KING with *Grand Master* 𝕵𝖔𝖓𝖊𝖘 and his *Grand Wardens*, (the foresaid WILLIAM HERBERT Earl of *Pembroke*, and *Nicholas Stone* the Sculptor,) attended by many Brothers in due Form, and many eminent Persons, walk'd to *Whitehall* Gate, and levell'd the *Footstone* of the *New Banquetting-House* with 3 great Knocks, loud Huzza's, Sound of Trumpets, and a Purse of broad Pieces of Gold laid upon the Stone for the *Masons* to drink

𝕿𝖔 𝖙𝖍𝖊 𝕶𝖎𝖓𝖌 𝖆𝖓𝖉 𝖙𝖍𝖊 𝕮𝖗𝖆𝖋𝖙!

A. D. 1607.

Tho' for want of a Parliamentary Fund, no more was built but the said glorious BANQUETTING-HOUSE, the finest single Room of that large Extent since the Days of *Augustus*, and the Glory of this Reign. Afterwards the lofty Ceiling was adorned by the fine Pencil of *Peter Paul* RUBENS.

The best *Craftsmen* from all Parts resorted to *Grand Master* JONES, who always allow'd good Wages and seasonable Times for Instruction in the Lodges, which he constituted with excellent By-Laws, and made 'em like the *Schools* or *Academies* of the

Designers

Designers in *Italy*. He also held the Quarterly *Communication* * of the 𝔊𝔯𝔞𝔫𝔡 𝔖𝔱𝔬𝔫𝔢 𝔩𝔬𝔡𝔤𝔢 of *Masters* and *Wardens*, and the Annual General Assembly and *Feast* on St. *John's* Day, when he was annually rechosen, till *A. D.* 1618. when the foresaid

> So said Brother 𝔑𝔦𝔠𝔥𝔬𝔩𝔞𝔰 Stone his Warden, in a Manuscript burnt 1720.

WILLIAM Earl of *Pembroke* was chosen *Grand Master* ; and being approved by the King, he appointed 𝔍𝔫𝔦𝔤𝔬 𝔍𝔬𝔫𝔢𝔰 his *Deputy* Grand Master.

Masonry thus flourishing, many eminent, wealthy and learned Men, at their own Request, were accepted as *Brothers*, to the Honour of the *Craft*, till the King died 27 *March* 1625. leaving two Children, *viz.*

2. CHARLES I. *Stewart*, aged 25 Years succeeded ; also a Royal Brother and *Grand Master* by Prerogative : Being well skill'd in all the Arts

Elizabeth Stewart Queen of *Bohemia*.

Princess *Sophia*, Electress of *Brunswig*.

George I. King of Great *Britain*. Below.

of Designing, he encouraged the best foreign *Painters*, *Sculptors*, *Statuaries*, *Plaisterers*, &c. but wanted no Foreigners for Architecture, because none of 'em equall'd his own *Inigo Jones* and his excellent Disciples. When *Grand Master* PEMBROKE demitted, *A. D.* 1630.

HENRY DANVERS Earl of *Danby* succeeded in *Solomon's Chair* by the King's Approbation ; and at his own Cost erected a small, but most accurate Piece of the old Architecture, by the Design of his *Deputy* 𝔍𝔬𝔫𝔢𝔰, even the famous beautiful *Gate* of the *Physic Garden* at *Oxford*, with this Inscription.

GLORIÆ DEI OPTIMI MAXIMI HONORI CAROLI REGIS,
IN USUM ACADEMIÆ ET REIPUBLICÆ, *A. D.* 1632.
HENRICUS COMES DANBY.

THOMAS HOWARD Earl of *Arundel* (the Progenitor of our late *Grand Master* NORFOLK) then succeeded *Danby* at the Head

of

of the Fraternity, a moſt excellent Connoiſſeur in all the *Arts* of *Deſigning*, and the great Reviver of learned Antiquities, who will be ever famous for his *Marmora Arundeliana!* But *Deputy* 𝔍𝔬𝔫𝔢𝔰 was never out of Office; and join'd *Grand Maſter* ARUNDEL, in perſuading 𝔉𝔯𝔞𝔫𝔠𝔦𝔰 𝔘𝔲𝔰𝔰𝔢𝔩 Earl of *Bedford*, to lay out his Grounds of *Covent-Garden* in an Oblong-Square *Eaſt* and *Weſt*, where he built the regular Temple of St. *Paul* with its admirable *Portico*, made Parochial *A. D.* 1635. when

Grand Maſter BEDFORD ſucceeded, and employ'd his *Deputy* 𝔍𝔬𝔫𝔢𝔰 to build the *North* and *Eaſt* Sides of that Square with large and lofty *Arkades* (commonly call'd *Piazzas*) which, with the ſaid Church on the *Weſt* End, make a moſt beautiful Proſpect after the *Italian* or antient Manner.

INIGO JONES ſucceeded *Bedford* in *Solomon*'s *Chair* again; and before the Wars the King employ'd him to build the ſtately great *Gallery* of *Somerſet-Houſe* fronting the *Thames*: And the King intended to carry on *Whitehall* according to *Jones*'s Plan, but was unhappily prevented by the *Civil* Wars: For the *Parliament*'s Army conquer'd the *King* and *Parliament* too, and murder'd him at his own Gate on 30 *January* 164⅞.

Yet even during the Wars, the *Maſons* met occaſionally at ſeveral Places: Thus 𝔈𝔩𝔦𝔞𝔰 𝔄ſ𝔥𝔪𝔬𝔩𝔢 in his Diary Page 15. ſays, *I was made a Free Maſon at* Warrington, Lancaſhire, *with Colonel* Henry Manwaring, *by Mr.* Richard Penket *the Warden, and the Fellow Crafts* (there mention'd) *on* 16 Oct. 1646.

The *Great* INIGO JONES aged 80 Years died at *London*, and was buried in St. *Bennet*'s Church at *Paul*'s Wharf on 26 *June* 1652. the 𝔊𝔯𝔞𝔫𝔡 𝔐𝔞ſ𝔱𝔢𝔯 of *Architects*, who brought the *Auguſtan* Stile into *England*.

He ſhew'd his great Skill alſo in deſigning the magnificent *Rowe* of great *Queen-ſtreet*, and the *Weſt* Side of *Lincoln's-Inn-Fields*, with beautiful *Lindſey-Houſe*, the *Chirurgeons Hall* and *Theatre*, *Shaftſbury-Houſe* in *Alderſgate-ſtreet*, *Southampton-Houſe Bloomſbury* (now the Duke of *Bedford*'s) *Berkeley-Houſe Piccadilly* (now the Duke of *Devonſhire*'s) lately burnt and rebuilt; accurate *York-Stairs* at the *Thames*, &c.   And in the Country, *Gunnersbury-Houſe*

Gunnersbury-House near *Brentford, Wilton-House Wiltshire, Castle-Abby Northamptonshire, Stoke-Park,* &c.

Some of his *best Disciples* met privately for their mutual Improvement till the *Restoration,* who preserved his clean Drawings and accurate Designs (still preserved by the skilful *Architect,* the noble RICHARD BOYLE the present Earl of *Burlington*) and after the *Restoration* they propagated his *lofty Stile.*

CHAP. II.

From the RESTORATION 1660. till the REVOLUTION 1688.

3. CHARLES II. *Stewart,* succeeded his Father, and was magnificently restor'd, aged 30 Years, on his own Birth-Day, 29 *May* 1660. In his Travels he had been made a *Free Mason,* and having observed the exact Structures of foreign Countries, he resolved to encourage the *Augustan* Stile by reviving the *Lodges,* and approv'd their Choice of

HENRY JERMYN Earl of St. *Albans* as their 𝕲𝖗𝖆𝖓𝖉 𝕸𝖆𝖘𝖙𝖊𝖗, who appointed Sir JOHN DENHAM his *Deputy Grand Master,* Sir 𝕮𝖍𝖗𝖎𝖘𝖙𝖔𝖕𝖍𝖊𝖗 𝕿𝖗𝖊𝖓, ⎫ *Grand* ⎧ According to a Copy of the Mr. 𝕵𝖔𝖍𝖓 𝕿𝖊𝖇, ⎭ *Wardens.* ⎩ old *Constitutions,* this *Grand Master* held a *General* Assembly and *Feast* on St. JOHN's Day 27 *Dec.* 1663. when the following *Regulations* were made.

1. *That no Person of what Degree soever, be made or accepted a* Free Mason *unless in a regular Lodge, whereof one to be a* Master *or a* Warden *in that Limit or Division where such Lodge is kept, and another to be a* Craftsman *in the Trade of* Free Masonry.

2. *That no Person hereafter shall be accepted a* Free Mason, *but such as are of able Body, honest Parentage, good Reputation, and an Observer of the Laws of the Land.*

3. *That no Person hereafter who shall be accepted a* Free Mason, *shall be admitted into any* Lodge *or* Assembly, *until he has brought a Certificate of the Time and Place of his Acceptation from the*

Lodge

Lodge that accepted him unto the Master *of that* Limit *or* Division *where such Lodge is kept : And the said Master shall enrol the same in a Roll of Parchment to be kept for that* Purpose, *and shall give an Account of all such Acceptations at every General Assembly.*

4. *That every Person who is now a* Free Mason, *shall bring to the Master a Note of the Time of his Acceptation, to the End the same may be enroll'd in such Priority of Place as the Brother deserves ; and that the whole* Company *and* Fellows *may the better know each other.*

5. *That for the Future the said Fraternity of* Free Masons *shall be regulated and govern'd by* One Grand Master, *and as many* Wardens *as the said Society shall think fit to appoint at every Annual General* Assembly.

6. *That no Person shall be accepted unless he be* 21 *Years old or more.*

Thomas Savage Earl of *Rivers* succeeded St. *Albans* as Grand Master, 24 *June* 1666. who appointed Sir Christopher Wren {Mr. *John Web*, } Grand his *Deputy* ; {Mr. *Grinlin Gibbons*,} *Wardens.* but the *Deputy* and *Wardens* manag'd all Things.

This Year on 2 *Sept.* the Great Burning of *London* happen'd, and the *Free Masons* became necessary to rebuild it. Accordingly,

The *King* and *Grand Master* order'd the *Deputy* Wren to draw up a fine Plan of the new City, with long, broad and regular Streets ; but tho' private Properties hinder'd it's taking Effect, yet that noble City was soon rebuilt in a far better *Stile* than before.

The *King* levell'd the *Footstone* of the *New Royal-Exchange* in solemn Form, on 23 *Oct.* 1667. and it was open'd, the finest in *Europe*, by the Mayor and Aldermen on 28 *Sept.* 1669. Upon the Insides of the *Square* above the *Arkades*, and between the Windows, are the *Statues* of the Soveraigns of *England.* Afterwards the *Merchant* Adventurers employ'd *Grand Warden* Gibbons, to erect in the Middle of the Square the King's *Statue*

to

to the Life, in *Cæsarian* Habit, of white Marble, with an elegant Inscription, * below.

GILBERT SHELDON Archbishop of *Canterbury*, an excellent Architect, shew'd his great Skill in designing his famous *Theatrum Sheldonianum* at *Oxford*, and at his Cost it was conducted and finish'd by *Deputy* 𝔚𝔯𝔢𝔫 and *Grand Warden* 𝔚𝔢𝔟 ; and the *Craftsmen* having celebrated the *Cape-Stone*, it was open'd with an elegant Oration by Dr. *South*, on 9 *July* 1669. D. G. M. 𝔚𝔯𝔢𝔫 built also that other *Master Piece*, the pretty *Musæum* near the *Theatre*, at the Charge of the *University*. Mean while

LONDON was rebuilding apace ; and the Fire having ruin'd St. *Paul*'s Cathedral, the KING with *Grand Master* RIVERS, his Architects and Craftsmen, Nobility and Gentry, Lord Mayor and Aldermen, Bishops and Clergy, &c. in due Form levell'd the *Footstone* of New St. *Paul*'s, design'd by D. G. *Master* 𝔚𝔯𝔢𝔫 A. D. 1673. and by him conducted as *Master of Work* and Surveyor, with his Wardens Mr. *Edward Strong* Senior and Junior, upon a Parliamentary Fund.

The City rear'd beautiful *Moor-Gate*, and rebuilt *Bedlam. Hospital* in the best *Old Stile*, A. D. 1675. and where the Fire

---

* CAROLO SECUNDO CÆSARI BRITANNICO
PATRIÆ PATRI
REGUM OPTIMO CLEMENTISSIMO AUGUSTISSIMO
GENERIS HUMANI DELICIIS
UTRIUSQUE FORTUNÆ VICTORI
MARIUM DOMINO AC VINDICI
SOCIETAS MERCATORUM ADVENTUR. ANGLIÆ
QUÆ PER CCCC JAM PROPE ANNOS
REGIA MAJESTATE FLORET
FIDEI INTEMERATÆ ET GRATITUDINIS ÆTERNÆ
HOC TESTIMONIUM
VENERABUNDA POSUIT
ANNO SALUTIS HUMANÆ MDCLXXXIV.

began

began, the City rais'd the famous *Monument* of White Stone, a fine fluted *Column* of the *Doric* Order, 202 Foot high from the Ground, and the *Shaft* is 15 Foot in Diameter, with an eaſy *Stair* of black Marble within the Shaft leading up to an *Iron Balcony*, guilded at the Top, the higheſt *Column* upon Earth. It's *Pedeſtal.* is 21 Foot Square and 40 Foot high, with moſt ingenious *Emblems* in Baſſo Relievo, wrought by the foreſaid *Gabriel Cibber*, with *Latin Inſcriptions*. It was finiſh'd *A. D.* 1677.

So where the Fire ſtopt at *Temple-Bar*, the City built a fine *Roman* Gate, with the Statues of Queen ELIZABETH and King JAMES I. on the *Eaſt* Side, and thoſe of King CHARLES I. and CHARLES II. on the *Weſt* Side.

The 𝕻𝖍𝖞𝖘𝖎𝖈𝖎𝖆𝖓𝖘 diſcover'd alſo their fine Taſte by their accurate *College*, a *Maſter-Piece* ; and the 𝕷𝖆𝖜𝖞𝖊𝖗𝖘 by the Front of *Middle Temple-Lane*.

And after the Fire, the *Pariſh* Churches were many of 'em elegantly rebuilt, eſpecially St. *Mary-le-Bow* with it's Steeple of ſeveral Orders, and St. *Mary Wool-Church* with it's admirable *Cupola*, &c.

The KING alſo founded *Chelſea-Hoſpital* for old Soldiers, and a moſt curious New *Palace* at *Greenwich* from a Deſign of *Inigo Jones*, conducted by *Grand Warden* 𝖂𝖊𝖇 as *Maſter* of Work; and another *Palace* at *Wincheſter*, deſign'd by *Grand Maſter* WREN, an excellent Pile of the richeſt *Corinthian* Order, cover'd in before the King's Death, but never finiſh'd, and now in Ruins.

The King order'd Sir WILLIAM BRUCE, *Baronet*, *Grand Maſter* of *Scotland*, to rebuild his Palace of *Holyrood-Houſe* at *Edinburg* in the beſt *Auguſtan* Stile, and the *Scottiſh* Secretary-Office at *Whitehall*. G. *Maſter* BRUCE built alſo his own pretty Seat at *Kinroſs*.

So

So that the *Fellow Crafts* were never more employ'd than in this Reign, nor in a more lofty *Stile*; and many *Lodges* were conſtituted throughout the Iſlands by Leave of the ſeveral noble G. Maſters: For after G. *Maſter Rivers* demitted, *A. D.* 1674.

For beſides many other fine *Structures* in and about *London*, many noble *Manſions* in the Country were built or founded; as—*Wing-Houſe Bedfordſhire*—*Chevening* in *Kent*—*Ambroſebury* in *Wiltſhire*—*Hotham-Houſe* and *Stainborough Yorkſhire*—Palace of *Hamilton* in *Clydeſdale*—*Sterling-Houſe* near the Caſtle—*Drumlanrig* in *Nidſdale*, and many more.

GEORGE VILLARS Duke of *Bucks*, an old *Maſon*, ſucceeded as G. *Maſter* of *England*; but being indolent, he left all Buſineſs to his *Deputy* 𝔚𝔯𝔢𝔫 and his *Wardens*; and when he demitted *A. D.* 1679.

HENRY BENNET Earl of *Arlington* ſucceeded, who was too deeply engag'd in Affairs of *State* to mind the *Lodges*: Yet in his *Maſterſhip* the Fraternity was conſiderable ſtill, and many Gentlemen requeſted to be admitted. Thus the foreſaid Brother *Aſhmole* (in his *Diary* Page 66.) ſays,

On the 10 *March* 1682. *I received a Summons to appear next Day at a Lodge in* Maſons-Hall London, *when we admitted into the Fellowſhip of Free Maſons Sir* William Wilſon, *Capt.* Richard Borthwick, *and four more. I was the ſenior Fellow, it being* 35 *Years ſince I was admitted; and with me were Mr.* Thomas Wiſe (*Maſter of the* London Company *of Maſons*) *and eight more old Free Maſons. We all dined at the* Half-Moon *Tavern in* Cheapſide, *a noble Dinner, prepared at the Charge of the new accepted Maſons.*

But many of the Fraternity's *Records* of this and former Reigns were loſt in the next and at the *Revolution*; and many of 'em were too haſtily burnt in our Time from a Fear of making Diſcoveries: So that we have not ſo ample an Account as could be wiſh'd of the *Grand Lodge*, &c.

King *Charles* II. dying on 6 *February* 168⅘. his Brother ſucceeded, *viz.*

4. JAMES II. *Stewart*, aged 51 Years. A moſt excellent *Statue* of him ſtill ſtands in *Whitehall*. But not being a *Brother Maſon*, the *Art* was much neglected, and People of all ſorts were

P   otherwiſe

otherwife engag'd in this Reign : Only upon the Death of Grand Mafter *Arlington* 1685 the *Lodges* met and elected

Sir CHRISTOPHER WREN 𝖌𝖗𝖆𝖓𝖉 𝖒𝖆𝖘𝖙𝖊𝖗, who appointed
Mr. *Gabriel Cibber,* }*Grand Wardens.*{ and while carrying on
Mr. *Edward Strong,* St. *Paul*'s, he annually met thofe Brethren that could attend him, to keep up good old *Ufages,* till the Revolution, when

𝖂𝖎𝖑𝖑𝖎𝖆𝖒 of *Naffau* Prince of *Orange,* landed on 5 *Nov.* 1688. and King JAMES fail'd to *France* on 23 *Dec.* following, and died there on 6 *Sept.* 1701.

CHAP. III.

From the REVOLUTION to *Grand Mafter* MONTAGU, 1721.

UPON King *James*'s going off, the *Convention* of *States* entail'd the Crown of *England* upon King *James*'s two Daughters and their Iffue, *viz.* MARY Princefs of *Orange,* and ANN Princefs of *Denmark :* And failing them on WILLIAM Prince of *Orange ;* for his Mother *Mary Stewart* was King *James*'s eldeft Sifter : But ORANGE was to reign during Life. Accordingly on 13 *Feb.* 168$\frac{8}{9}$.

5. King WILLIAM III. aged 38 Years, ⎫ were proclaim'd *King* and his Wife ⎪ and *Queen,* Joint *So-*
6. Queen MARY II. *Stewart,* aged 26 ⎬ *veraigns* of *England ;* Years, ⎪ and *Scotland* foon
She died at *Kenfington* without Iffue on ⎭ proclaim'd them.
28 *Dec.* 1694.

Particular *Lodges* were not fo frequent and moftly *occafional* in the *South,* except in or near the Places where great Works were carried on. Thus Sir *Robert Claytor* got an *Occafional* Lodge of his Brother *Mafters* to meet at St. *Thomas*'s *Hofpital Southwark,* A. D. 1693. and to advife the Governours about the beft Defign of rebuilding that Hofpital as it now ftands

most

moft beautiful ; near which a *ftated* Lodge continued long after-wards.

Befides that and the *old* Lodge of St. *Paul's,* there was ano-ther in *Piccadilly* over againft St. *James's* Church, one near *Weft-minfter* Abby, another near *Covent-Garden,* one in *Holborn,* one on *Tower-Hill,* and fome more that affembled ftatedly.

The *King* was privately made a *Free Mafon,* approved of their Choice of G. *Mafter* WREN, and encourag'd him in rearing St. *Paul's Cathedral,* and the great *New* Part of Hampton-Court in the *Auguftan Stile,* by far the fineft *Royal* Houfe in *England,* after an old Defign of *Inigo Jones,* where a bright *Lodge* was held during the Building. The King alfo built his *little* Palace of *Kenfington,* and finifh'd *Chelfea Hofpital* ; but appointed the fine *new* Palace of *Greenwich* (begun by King *Charles* II.) to be an *Hofpital* for old *Seamen,* A. D. 1695. and order'd it to be fi-nifh'd as begun after *Jones's* old *Defign.*

This Year our moft noble Brother CHARLES LENNOS Duke of *Richmond* and *Lennox* (Father of the prefent Duke) *Mafter* of a Lodge at *Chichefter,* coming to the annual Affembly and Feaft at *London,* was chofen *Grand Mafter* and approv'd by the King. Sir Chriftopher Wren was his { *Edward Strong,* fen. } *Grand* D. G. *Mafter,* who acted as be- { *Edward Strong,* jun. } *Wardens.* fore at the Head of the *Craft,* and was again chofen *Grand Mafter,* A. D. 1698.

In this Reign *Naval* Architecture was wonderfully improv'd, and the *King* difcover'd his High Tafte in building his elegant Palace at *Loo* in *Holland,* till he died at *Kenfington* 8 *March* 170$\frac{1}{2}$. when

7. ANN *Stewart,* the other Daughter of King *James* II. aged 38 Years, fucceeded as Queen *Soveraign,* Wife of GEORGE Prince of *Denmark :* He was the Patron of *Aftronomers* and *Navigators,* and died at *Kenfington* 28 *Oct.* 1708.

Queen ANN enlarg'd St. *James's* Palace, and after the famous Battle of *Blenheim,* A. D. 1704. demolifh'd the *old* Royal Caftle of *Woodftock* in *Oxfordfhire,* and built in its ftead the Caftle of *Blenheim* for her General *John Churchill* Duke of *Marleborough.*

The

The Queen, in her 5th Year, united the *two* Kingdoms of *England* and *Scotland* into the *one* Kingdom of *Great-Britain* which commenced on 1 *May* 1707.

After the *Union* of the *Crowns* 104 Years.

The *Queen* and *Parliament* enacted the building of 50 new *Churches* in the Suburbs of *London*; and the Surveyors shew'd their Skill in *Buckingham* House and *Marleborough* House in St. *James*'s Park, *Powis* House in *Ormond street*, the *Opera* House in *Haymarket*, and many more about Town: As in the Country the Duke of *Devonshire*'s fine *Chatsworth* in *Derbyshire*, *Stourton Wiltshire*, the Earl of *Carlisle*'s Castle *Howard* near *York*, *Helmsley* House or *Duncomb-Park*, *Mereworth* House in *Kent*, *Wilbury* House in *Wiltshire*, &c. Nay after the Peace of *Utrecht* many rich old Officers in the Army, returning home good Connoisseurs in Architecture, delighted in raising stately Mansions.

But the *Augustan* Stile was mostly richly display'd at *Oxford* in the *New* Chapel of *Trinity* College by Dr. 𝔅𝔞𝔱𝔥𝔲𝔯𝔰𝔱, in *Peek-Water-Square* of *Christ's-Church* College by Dr. 𝔄𝔩𝔡𝔯𝔦𝔤𝔢, in *Queen's-College* by Dr. 𝔏𝔞𝔫𝔠𝔞𝔰𝔱𝔢𝔯 elegantly rebuilt, in *Allhallow*'s Church, the new *Printing* House, &c.

Yet still in the *South* the Lodges were more and more disused, partly by the Neglect of the *Masters* and *Wardens*, and partly by not having a *Noble Grand Master* at *London*, and the annual Assembly was not duly attended.

G. M. WREN, who had design'd St. *Paul*'s *London*, A.D. 1673. and as *Master* of *Work* had conducted it from the *Footstone*, had the Honour to finish that noble *Cathedral*, the finest and largest *Temple* of the *Augustan* Stile except St. *Peter*'s at *Rome*; and celebrated the *Capestone* when he erected the Cross on the Top of the Cupola, in *July* A. D. 1708.

Some few Years after this Sir *Christopher Wren* neglected the Office of *Grand Master*; yet the *Old Lodge* near St. *Paul*'s and a few more continued their stated Meetings till

Queen *Ann* died at *Kensington* without Issue on 1 *Aug.* 1714. She was the last of the Race of King *Charles* I. upon the Throne of *Britain*; for the Others, being *Romans*, are excluded by the

Act

Act of Parliament for settling the *Crown* upon the *Protestant* Heirs of his Sister ELIZABETH *Stewart* Queen of *Bohemia* above, *viz.* on her Daughter the Princess SOPHIA Electress Dowager of *Brunswig-Luneburg*; and she dying a little before Queen ANN, her Son the *Elector* succeeded on the said 1 *Aug.* 1714.

Saxon *Kings* of *Great-Britain*.

1. King GEORGE I. enter'd *London* most magnificently on 20 *Sept.* 1714. and after the Rebellion was over *A. D.* 1716. the few *Lodges* at *London* finding themselves neglected by Sir *Christopher Wren*, thought fit to cement under a *Grand Master* as the Center of Union and Harmony, *viz.* the *Lodges* that met,

1. At the *Goose* and *Gridiron* Ale-house in St. *Paul's Church-Yard*.
2. At the *Crown* Ale-house in *Parker's-Lane* near *Drury-Lane*.
3. At the *Apple-Tree* Tavern in *Charles-street, Covent-Garden*.
4. At the *Rummer* and *Grapes* Tavern in *Channel-Row, Westminster*.

They and some old Brothers met at the said *Apple-Tree*, and having put into the Chair the *oldest Master* Mason (now the *Master of a Lodge*) they constituted themselves a GRAND LODGE pro Tempore in *Due Form*, and forthwith revived the Quarterly *Communication* of the *Officers* of Lodges (call'd the Grand Lodge) resolv'd to hold the *Annual* ASSEMBLY *and Feast*, and then to chuse a GRAND MASTER from among themselves, till they should have the Honour of a *Noble Brother* at their Head.

Accordingly

On St. *John Baptist's* Day, in the 3d Year of King GEORGE I. *A. D.* 1717. the ASSEMBLY and *Feast* of the *Free and accepted Masons* was held at the foresaid *Goose and Gridiron* Ale-house.

Before Dinner, the *oldest Master* Mason (now the *Master of a Lodge*) in the Chair, proposed a List of proper Candidates; and the Brethren by a Majority of Hands elected

Mr.

Mr. ANTONY SAYER Gentleman, *Grand Master* of *Masons*, who being forthwith in- { Capt. *Joseph Elliot*. } *Grand* vested with the Badges { Mr. *Jacob Lamball*, Carpenter, } *Wardens*. of Office and Power by the said *oldest Master*, and install'd, was duly congratulated by the Assembly who pay'd him the *Homage*.

SAYER *Grand Master* commanded the *Masters* and *Wardens* of Lodges to meet the *Grand* Officers every *Quarter* in *Communication*, * at the Place that he should appoint in his Summons sent by the *Tyler*.

> * *N. B.* It is call'd the *Quarterly Communication*, because it should meet *Quarterly* according to antient Usage. And
>
> When the *Grand Master* is present it is a Lodge in *Ample Form*; otherwise, only in *Due Form*, yet having the same Authority with *Ample Form*.

ASSEMBLY and *Feast* at the said Place 24 *June* 1718.

Brother *Sayer* having gather'd the Votes, after Dinner proclaim'd aloud our Brother

GEORGE PAYNE Esq; *Grand Master* of *Masons* who being duly invested, { Mr. *John Cordwell*, City Carpenter, } *Grand* install'd, congra- { Mr. *Thomas Morrice*, Stone Cutter, } *Wardens*. tulated and homaged, recommended the strict Observance of the Quarterly Communication; and desired any Brethren to bring to the Grand Lodge any old *Writings* and *Records* concerning *Masons* and *Masonry* in order to shew the Usages of antient Times: And this Year several old Copies of the *Gothic Constitutions* were produced and collated.

ASSEMBLY and *Feast* at the said Place, 24 *June* 1719.

Brother *Payne* having gather'd the Votes, after Dinner proclaim'd aloud our Reverend Brother

JOHN THEOPHILUS DESAGULIERS, L.L.D. and F.R.S. *Grand Master* of *Masons*, and be- { Mr. *Antony Sayer* foresaid, } *Grand* ing duly invested, install'd, { Mr. *Tho. Morrice* foresaid, } *Wardens*. congratulated and homaged, forthwith reviv'd the old regular and peculiar Toasts or Healths of the *Free Masons*.

Now several *old* Brothers, that had neglected the *Craft*, visited the *Lodges*; some *Noblemen* were also made Brothers, and more *new* Lodges were constituted.

ASSEMBLY

ASSEMBLY and *Feaſt* at the foreſaid Place 24 *June* 1720.

Brother *Deſaguliers* having gather'd the Votes, after Dinner proclaim'd aloud

GEORGE PAYNE Eſq; again *Grand Maſter* of *Maſons*; who being duly inveſted, ⎰ Mr. *Thomas Hobby*, Stone-Cutter, ⎱ Grand inſtall'd, congratu- ⎱ Mr. *Rich. Ware*, Mathematician, ⎰ *Wardens*. lated and homag'd, began the uſual Demonſtrations of Joy, Love and Harmony.

This Year, at ſome *private* Lodges, ſeveral very valuable *Manuſcripts* (for they had nothing yet in Print) concerning the Fraternity, their Lodges, Regulations, Charges, Secrets, and Uſages (particularly one writ by Mr. *Nicholas Stone* the Warden of *Inigo Jones*) were too haſtily burnt by ſome ſcrupulous Brothers, that thoſe Papers might not fall into ſtrange Hands.

At the *Quarterly* Communication or *Grand Lodge*, in *ample* Form, on St. *John Evangeliſt*'s Day 1720. at the ſaid Place

It was agreed, in order to avoid Diſputes on the *Annual* Feaſt-Day, that the *new Grand Maſter* for the future ſhall be named and propoſed to the *Grand Lodge* ſome time before the Feaſt, by the preſent or *old Grand Maſter*; and if approv'd, that the Brother propoſed, if preſent, ſhall be kindly ſaluted; or even if abſent, his Health ſhall be toaſted as *Grand Maſter Elect*.

Alſo agreed, that for the future the *New Grand Maſter*, as ſoon as he is inſtall'd, ſhall have the ſole Power of appointing both his *Grand Wardens* and a *Deputy* Grand Maſter (now found as neceſſary as formerly) according to antient Cuſtom, when *Noble* Brothers were *Grand* Maſters.

Accordingly,

At the **Grand Lodge** in *ample* Form on *Lady-Day* 1721. at the ſaid Place *Grand Maſter* PAYNE propoſed for his Succeſſor our moſt Noble Brother

JOHN Duke of MONTAGU, *Maſter* of a Lodge; who being preſent, was forthwith ſaluted *Grand Maſter Elect*, and his Health drank in *due* Form; when they all expreſs'd great Joy at the happy Proſpect of being again patronized by *noble Grand Maſters*, as in the proſperous Times of *Free Maſonry*.

PAYNE

PAYNE *Grand Mafter* obferving the *Number* of Lodges to en-creafe, and that the General *Affembly* requir'd more Room, pro-pofed the next *Affembly* and *Feaft* to be held at *Stationers-Hall Ludgate-ftreet*; which was agreed to.

Then the *Grand Wardens* were order'd, as ufual, to prepare the Feaft, and to take fome *Stewards* to their Affiftance, Bro-thers of Ability and Capacity, and to appoint fome Brethren to attend the Tables; for that no Strangers muft be there. But the *Grand* Officers not finding a proper Number of *Stewards*, our Brother Mr. 𝕴𝖔𝖋𝖎𝖆𝖍 𝕲𝖎𝖑𝖑𝖊𝖓𝖊𝖆𝖚, Upholder in the *Burrough Southwark*, generoufly undertook the whole himfelf, attended by fome Waiters, *Thomas Morrice*, *Francis Bailey*, &c.

C H A P. IV.

From *Grand Mafter* the Duke of MONTAGU to *Grand Mafter* RICHMOND.

ASSEMBLY and *Feaft* at *Stationers-Hall*, 24 *June* 1721. In the 7th Year of King GEORGE I.

PAYNE *Grand Mafter* with his *Wardens*, the former *Grand* Officers, and the *Mafters* and *Wardens* of 12 Lodges, met the *Grand Mafter Elect* in a *Grand Lodge* at the *King's-Arms* Tavern St. *Paul's Church-yard*, in the Morning; and having forthwith recognized their Choice of Brother MONTAGU, they made fome new Brothers, particularly the noble PHILIP Lord *Stanhope*, now Earl of *Chefterfield*: And from thence they marched on Foot to the *Hall* in proper Clothing and due Form; where they were joy-fully receiv'd by about 150 *true* and *faithful*, all clothed.

After Grace faid, they fat down in the antient Manner of *Mafons* to a very elegant Feaft, and dined with Joy and Glad-nefs. After Dinner and Grace faid,

Brother

Brother PAYNE the old *Grand Master* made See the Form of it at the *first Procession* round the *Hall*, and when re- Richmond, Page 117. turn'd, he proclaim'd aloud the moſt noble Prince and our Brother.

1. JOHN MONTAGU Duke of **Montagu** GRAND MASTER of *Maſons!* and Brother *Payne* having inveſted his *Grace's* WORSHIP with the Enſigns and Badges of his Office and Authority, inſtall'd him in *Solomon's* Chair and ſat down on his Right Hand ; while the Aſſembly own'd the Duke's Authority with due Homage and joyful Congratulations, upon this Revival of the *Proſperity* of *Maſonry.*

MONTAGU *G. Maſter*, immediately call'd forth (without naming him before) as it were careleſly, **John Beal**, M. D. as his *Deputy Grand Maſter*, whom Brother *Payne* inveſted, and inſtall'd him in *Hiram Abbiff's* Chair on the *Grand Maſter's Left Hand.*

In like Manner his *Worſhip* ⎰ Mr. *Joſiah Villeneau* ⎱ Grand call'd forth and appointed, ⎰ Mr. *Thomas Morrice* ⎱ Wardens. who were inveſted and inſtall'd by the laſt *Grand* Wardens.

Upon which the *Deputy* and *Wardens* were ſaluted and congratulated as uſual.

Then MONTAGU *G. Maſter*, with his *Officers* and the *old Officers*, having made the 2d *Proceſſion* round the *Hall*, Brother **Deſaguliers** made an eloquent Oration about *Maſons* and *Maſonry :* And after Great Harmony, the Effect of brotherly Love, the *Grand Maſter* thank'd Brother *Villeneau* for his Care of the *Feaſt*, and order'd him as *Warden* to cloſe the *Lodge* in good Time.

—The **Grand Lodge** in *ample* Form on 29 *Sept.* 1721. at *King's-Arms* foreſaid, with the former *Grand* Officers and thoſe of 16 *Lodges*.

His Grace's *Worſhip* and the *Lodge* finding Fault with all the Copies of the *old Gothic Conſtitutions*, order'd Brother *James Anderſon*, A. M. to digeſt the ſame in a new and better Method.

—The **Grand Lodge** in *ample* Form on St. JOHN's Day 27 *Dec.* 1721. at the ſaid *King's Arms*, with former *Grand* Officers and thoſe of 20 *Lodges.*

Q   MONTAGU

MONTAGU *Grand Mafter*, at the Defire of the *Lodge*, appointed 14 learned Brothers to examine Brother *Anderfon*'s Manufcript, and to make Report. This *Communication* was made very entertaining by the Lectures of fome *old Mafons*.

—𝔊𝔯𝔞𝔫𝔡 𝔏𝔬𝔡𝔤𝔢 at the *Fountain Strand*, in *ample* Form 25 *March* 1722. with former *Grand* Officers and thofe of 24 *Lodges*.

The faid *Committee* of 14 reported that they had perufed Brother *Anderfon*'s Manufcript, *viz.* the *Hiftory, Charges, Regulations and Mafter's Song*, and after fome Amendments had approv'd of it : Upon which the *Lodge* defir'd the *Grand Mafter* to order it to be printed. Mean while

Ingenious Men of all Faculties and Stations being convinced that the *Cement* of the *Lodge* was Love and Friendfhip, earneftly requefted to be made *Mafons*, affecting this amicable Fraternity more than other Societies then often difturbed by warm Difputes.

Grand Mafter MONTAGU's good Government inclin'd the better Sort to continue him in the Chair another Year ; and therefore they delay'd to prepare the *Feaft*.

But *Philip* Duke of *Wharton* lately made a Brother, tho' not the *Mafter* of a *Lodge*, being ambitious of the Chair, got a Number of Others to meet him at *Stationers-Hall* 24 *June* 1722. and having no *Grand* Officers, they put in the Chair the *oldeft Mafter Mafon* (who was not the *prefent* Mafter of a *Lodge*, alfo irregular) and without the ufual decent Ceremonials, the faid *old Mafon* proclaim'd aloud

Philip Wharton Duke of *Wharton* Grand Mafter of *Mafons*, and
{ Mr. *Jofhua Timfon*, Blackfmith, ⎫ *Grand* ⎫ but his Grace ap-
{ Mr. *William Hawkins*, Mafon, ⎰*Wardens.*⎰ pointed no *Deputy*, nor was the *Lodge* opened and clofed in due Form.

Therefore the *noble* Brothers and all thofe that would not countenance Irregularities, difown'd *Wharton*'s Authority, till worthy Brother MONTAGU heal'd the Breach of Harmony, by fummoning

— The 𝔊𝔯𝔞𝔫𝔡 𝔏𝔬𝔡𝔤𝔢 to meet 17 *January* 172½. at the *King's-Arms* forefaid, where the *Duke of Wharton* promifing to be *True* and *Faithful, Deputy Grand* Mafter *Beal* proclaim'd aloud the moft noble Prince and our Brother.

II. PHILIP

II. Philip Wharton Duke of *Wharton* Grand Master of *Masons*, who appointed Dr. Desaguliers the *Deputy* Grand Master,

⎰ *Joshua Timson*, forefaid, ⎱ Grand ⎰ for *Hawkins* demitted as al-
⎱ *James Anderson*, A. M. ⎰ Wardens. ⎱ ways out of Town.

When former *Grand* Officers, with those of 25 *Lodges* paid their Homage.

G. Warden *Anderson* produced the *new* Book of *Constitutions* now in Print, which was again approv'd, with the Addition of the *antient Manner of Constituting a Lodge.*

Now *Masonry* flourish'd in Harmony, Reputation and Numbers; many Noblemen and Gentlemen of the first Rank desir'd to be admitted into the *Fraternity*, besides other Learned Men, Merchants, Clergymen and Tradesmen, who found a *Lodge* to be a safe and pleasant Relaxation from Intense Study or the Hurry of Business, without Politicks or Party. Therefore the *Grand Master* was obliged to constitute more *new Lodges*, and was very assiduous in *visiting* the Lodges every Week with his *Deputy* and *Wardens*; and his *Worship* was well pleas'd with their kind and respectful Manner of receiving him, as they were with his affable and clever Conversation.

— Grand Lodge in *ample* Form, 25 *April* 1723. at the *White-Lion Cornhill*, with former *Grand* Officers and those of 30 *Lodges* call'd over by G. Warden *Anderson*, for no *Secretary* was yet appointed. When

Wharton *Grand Master* proposed for his Successor the Earl of *Dalkeith* (now *Duke* of *Buckleugh*) *Master* of a *Lodge*, who was unanimously approv'd and duly saluted as *Grand Master Elect.*

The *Tickets* for the next *Feast* were order'd to be Ten Shillings each, impress'd from a curious *Copper Plate*, and seal'd with the G. *Master's Seal* of Office, to be disposed of by the *Grand Wardens* and the *Stewards.*

ASSEMBLY and *Feast* on *Monday* 24 *June* 1723. at *Merchant-Taylors-Hall.*

The *Committee* appointed to keep out *Cowans* came early, and the *Stewards* to receive the *Tickets* and direct the Servants.

Q 2   WHARTON

WHARTON *Grand Master* came attended by some eminent Brothers in their Coaches ; and forthwith walking with his *Deputy* and *Wardens* into the *Lodge-Room*, he sent for the *Masters* and *Wardens* of *Lodges*, who came from the *Hall* and form'd the *Grand Lodge* call'd over by Brother *William Cowper*, Esq; now appointed *Secretary*.

Some observing that Brother *Dalkeith* was now in *Scotland*, proposed to the G. *Master* to name another for Successor ; but **Dalkeith**'s *Wardens* declar'd that his Lordship would soon return. Adjourn'd to Dinner.

About 400 Free Masons, all duly clothed, dined elegantly in due Form.

See its Description at *Richmond*, G. M.| After Dinner, Brother WHARTON made the *first Procession* round the Tables, and when return'd, proclaim'd aloud our noble Brother.

III. FRANCIS SCOT Earl of *Dalkeith* **Grand Master** of *Masons.* He had left with the *Wardens* of his *Lodge* a Power to appoint in his Name

Dr. **Desaguliers** his ⎰ *Francis Sorrell*, Esq; ⎱ *Grand-Deputy Grand Master,* ⎱ *John Senex* Bookseller, ⎰ *Wardens.* who fill'd the Chair ; and having thank'd the *Stewards*, order'd *Grand* Warden *Sorell* to close the Lodge in good Time. *

— **Grand Lodge** at the *Crown* in *Threadneedle-street* 25 *Nov.* 1723. in *ample* Form, with former *Grand* Officers and Those of 30 *Lodges.* They agreed on several Things for the Good of *Masonry*, which, with other Things afterwards determin'd at *Grand* Lodges, are dispers'd in the *New Regulations, Committee of Charity,* &c. below : and special Care was taken to prevent Disturbance and preserve Harmony on *Feast-Days.*

— **Grand Lodge** in *ample* Form at the foresaid *Crown* 19 *Feb.* 172¾. with former G. *Officers* and Those of 26 *Lodges.*

— **Grand Lodge** in *ample* Form at the *Crown* foresaid 28 *April* 1724. with former G. *Officers* and Those of 31 *Lodges.*

---

* Stewards that acted at the Feast on 24 *June* 1723. and were publickly thank'd

Mr. *Henry Prude*,	Capt. *Benjamin Hodges*,
Mr. *Giles Clutterbuck*,	Mr. *Edward Lambert*,
Mr. *John Shepherd*,	Mr. *Charles Kent*.

Dalkeith

Dalkeith G. *Master* proposed for his Successor the Duke of *Richmond* and *Lennox* (now also Duke d'*Aubigny*) Master of a *Lodge*, who was joyfully saluted *Grand Master Elect*.

C H A P. V.

From *Grand Master* RICHMOND to *Grand Master* NORFOLK.

ASSEMBLY and *Feast* at *Merchant-Taylors-Hall* on 24 *June* 1724.

DALKEITH *Grand Master* with his *Deputy* and *Wardens* waited on Brother *Richmond* in the Morning at *Whitehall*, who with many Brothers duly clothed, proceeded in Coaches from the *West* to the *East*, and were handsomely received at the *Hall* by a vast *Assembly*. The *Grand Lodge* met, and having confirm'd their Choice of Brother *Richmond*, adjourn'd to Dinner. After Dinner G. Master DALKEITH made the *first* Procession round the Tables, *viz*.

Brother *Clinch* to clear the Way.

| This, as a Specimen, to avoid Repetitions. |

The *Stewards* 2 and 2 a Breast with *white* Rods.

Secretary **Cowper** with the *Bag*, and on his Left the *Master* of a *Lodge* with *One* Great *Light*.

Two other *Great Lights* born by two *Masters* of *Lodges*.

Former *Grand Wardens* proceeding one by one, according to *Juniority*.

Former *Grand Masters* proceeding, according to *Juniority*.

Sorell and **Sener** the two *Grand Wardens*.

Desaguliers D. G. *Master* alone.

On the *Left* Hand.	On the *Right* Hand.
The *Sword* carried by the *Master* of the *Lodge* to which the *Sword* belong'd.	The Book of *Constitutions* on a Cushion carried by the *Master* of the *Senior Lodge*.
RICHMOND *Grand Master Elect*.	DALKEITH *Grand Master*.

During the *Procession*, 3 Times round the *Tables*, the Brethren stood up and fac'd about with the *regular* Salutations; and when return'd

Brother

Brother *Dalkeith* ftood up, and bowing to the *Affembly*, thank'd 'em for the Honour he had of being their *Grand Mafter*, and then proclaim'd aloud the moft noble Prince and our Brother

IV. CHARLES LENNOS Duke of *Richmond* and *Lennox*

𝕲𝖗𝖆𝖓𝖉 𝕸𝖆𝖘𝖙𝖊𝖗 of *Mafons!*

The *Duke* having bow'd to the *Affembly*, Brother DALKEITH invefted him with the proper *Enfigns* and *Badges* of his Office and Authority, inftall'd him in *Solomon*'s Chair, and wifhing him all Profperity, fat down on his Right Hand. Upon which the Affembly join'd in due Homage, affectionate Congratulations and other Signs of Joy.

RICHMOND *Grand Mafter* ftanding up, call'd forth (as it were by Accident) and appointed

𝕸𝖆𝖗𝖙𝖎𝖓 𝕱𝖔𝖑𝖐𝖊𝖘, Efq; { *George Payne* Efq; formerly G.M. } *Grand* his *D. G. Mafter*, { *Francis Sorell* late G. Warden, } *Wardens.* invefted and inftall'd by the laft Deputy in the Chair of *Hiram Abbif.*

William Cowper Efq; was continued *Secretary* by the G. Mafter's returning him the Books, and all of 'em were formally congratu-lated by the *Affembly.* *

RICHMOND *Grand Mafter* made the 2d *Proceffion* round the Tables like the *Firft*, except that Brother DALKEITH walked firft as the youngeft late *Grand Mafter*, clofe after the former *Grand Wardens*; and RICHMOND walk'd *alone* laft of all, with his *De-puty* immediately before him, and his *two G. Wardens* before the *Deputy*, and before them the *Sword* and *Conftitutions.*

When return'd,

The *G. Mafter* began to toaft the regular *Healths*, and due Refpects to our noble Brothers prefent and abfent, particularly to our laft good *Grand Mafter* DALKEITH.

After which, the ufual Expreffions of Joy, Love and Friendfhip

---

* Stewards that acted at the Feaft on 24 *June* 1723. and were publickly thank'd.

These firft 6 acted at the laft Feaft.	Mr. *Henry Prude.*	Capt. *Samuel Tuffnell.*
	Capt. *Benjamin Hodges.*	Mr. *Giles Taylor*
	Mr. *Giles Clutterbuck.*	Capt. *Nathaniel Smith.*
	Mr. *John Shepherd.*	Mr. *Richard Crofts.*
	Mr. *Edward Lambert.*	Mr. *Peter Paul Kemp.*
	Mr. *Charles Kent.*	Mr. *North Stainer.*

went

went round ; and the *Affembly* was moft agreeably entertain'd with Orations, Mufick and Mafon Songs, till the *G. Mafter* order'd his Warden *Payne* to clofe the *Lodge* in good Time.

Now MASONRY was illuftrious at home and abroad, and *Lodges* multiplied.

— 𝕲𝖗𝖆𝖓𝖉 𝕷𝖔𝖉𝖌𝖊 in *ample* Form at the *Crown* forefaid, 21 *Nov.* 1724. with former *Grand* Officers and Thofe of 40 *Lodges.* When Our noble Brother DALKEITH, in Purfuance | See the Committee of *Regulation* XIII. propofed a *Fund* of Gene- | of *Charity.* ral Charity for poor Brothers, which was agreed to by all.

— 𝕲𝖗𝖆𝖓𝖉 𝕷𝖔𝖉𝖌𝖊 in *ample* Form at the *Bell Weftminfter* 17 *March* 172⅘. with former *G.* Officers and Thofe of 36 *Lodges.*

— 𝕲𝖗𝖆𝖓𝖉 𝕷𝖔𝖉𝖌𝖊 in *due* Form at the *Devil Temple-Bar* 20 *May* 1725, with former *G. Officers* and thofe of 38 *Lodges.* D. *G. Mafter* FOLKES in the Chair prompted a moft agreeable *Communication.*

𝕲𝖗𝖆𝖓𝖉 𝕷𝖔𝖉𝖌𝖊 in *Due* Form at the *Crown* forefaid on 24 *June* 1725. when the *Grand* Officers were continued Six Months longer.

— 𝕲𝖗𝖆𝖓𝖉 𝕷𝖔𝖉𝖌𝖊 in *ample* Form at the *Bell* forefaid 27 *Nov.* 1725. with former *G. Officers* and Thofe of 49 *Lodges.* When RICHMOND *G. Mafter* propofed for his Succeffor the Lord *Paifley* (now Earl of *Abercorn*) *Mafter* of a *Lodge,* who was gladly faluted as *Grand Mafter Elect.* And no *Stewards* being appointed, G. M. RICHMOND defired our Brother *John James Heidegger* to prepare the *Feaft* in the beft Manner.

ASSEMBLY and *Feaft* at *Merchant-Taylor's-Hall* on St. JOHN's Day 27 *Dec.* 1725.

Lord PAISLEY being in the Country, had by Letter made the *Duke* of RICHMOND his *Proxy,* and all Things being regularly tranfacted as above, Brother *Richmond* proclaim'd aloud our noble Brother

V. JAMES HAMILTON Lord *Paifley* 𝕲𝖗𝖆𝖓𝖉 𝕸𝖆𝖘𝖙𝖊𝖗 of *Mafons.* Brother RICHMOND as *Proxy* continued in the Chair, and in *G. Mafter* PAISLEY's Name appointed

Dr. 𝕯𝖊𝖘𝖆𝖌𝖚𝖑𝖎𝖊𝖗𝖘 a- ⎰Colonel *Daniel Houghton;* ⎱ *Grand* gain D. *G. Mafter,* ⎱Sir *Thomas Prendergaft,* Bart.⎰ *Wardens.* The *Secretary* was continued, and in both Proceffions the DUKE walk'd *alone.* Brother

Brother *Heidegger* was thank'd for the elegant and fumptuous Feaft, and the *G. Mafter* order'd his Warden *Houghton* to clofe the *Lodge* in good Time.

—𝕲𝖗𝖆𝖓𝖉 𝕷𝖔𝖉𝖌𝖊 in ample Form at the *Bell* forefaid on *Monday* 28 *Feb.* 172⅚ with former *G. Officers* and Thofe of 36 *Lodges*.

—𝕲𝖗𝖆𝖓𝖉 𝕷𝖔𝖉𝖌𝖊 in *ample* Form at the *Crown* forefaid, on *Monday* 12 *Dec.* 1726. with former *G. Officers* and thofe of 30 *Lodges*.

In this long Interval the D. *G. Mafter* duly vifited the *Lodges* till the *Principal* came to Town, who now propofed for his Succeffor the *Earl* of *Inchiquin* Mafter of a *Lodge* and he was gladly faluted as *Grand Mafter Elect*.

No *Stewards*; but Brother *Edward Lambert* undertook to prepare the *Feaft*.

ASSEMBLY and *Feaft* at *Mercer's-Hall* on *Monday* 27 *Feb.* 172⅝. All Things being regularly tranfacted as above, Brother *Paifley* proclaim'd aloud our noble Brother

VI. WILLIAM O BRIEN Earl of *Inchiquin* 𝕲𝖗𝖆𝖓𝖉 𝕸𝖆𝖋𝖙𝖊𝖗 of *Mafons*, who appointed

𝖂𝖎𝖑𝖑𝖎𝖆𝖒 𝕮𝖔𝖜𝖕𝖊𝖗 Efq; (formerly *Secretary*) his D. *G. Mafter*.
{ *Alexander Choke* Efq; } Grand { Mr. *Edw. Wilfon*, was made
{ *William Burdon* Efq; } Wardens. { *Secretary*, and Brother *Lambert* was thank'd for his Care of the *Feaft*.

—𝕲𝖗𝖆𝖓𝖉 𝕷𝖔𝖉𝖌𝖊 in *ample* Form at the *Crown* forefaid on *Wednefday* 10 *May* 1727. with former *G. Officers* and Thofe of 40 *Lodges*, in great Harmony.

During the *Masterfhip* of INCHIQUIN

King GEORGE I. having reign'd near 13 Years, died at *Ofnabruck* where he was born, in his Way to *Hannover*, where he was buried, aged 67 Years, on 11 *June* 1727. when his Son fucceeded, *viz.*

2. King GEORGE II. aged 44 Years, who with his Queen CAROLINE were Crown'd at *Weftminfter* on 11 *Oct.* 1727.

In the laft Reign fundry of the 50 *new Churches* in the Suburbs of *London* were built in a fine *Stile* upon the Parliamentary Fund, particularly the beautiful St. *Mary le Strand*. But
St.

St. *Martin's in Campis* was at the Charge of the Parishioners re-built strong and regular: And it being a *Royal* Parish *Church*, King GEORGE I. sent his Lord *Almoner* and *Surveyor* General, attended by Brother *Gib*, (the Architect of that grand Pile) with many *Free Masons*, in a solemn Procession from the Palace, to level the *Footstone* of the *South East* Corner, by giving it 3 Great Knocks with a Mallet in the King's Name, and laying upon it a Purse of 100 *Guineas*: when the Trumpets sounded, all join'd in joyful Acclamations, and the *Craftsmen* went to the Tavern to drink

𝕿𝖔 𝖙𝖍𝖊 𝕶𝖎𝖓𝖌 𝖆𝖓𝖉 𝖙𝖍𝖊 𝕮𝖗𝖆𝖋𝖙.

The *Inscription* below was cut in the Stone and Lead put upon it. *

In this Reign also the *Art* was display'd in the *New Buildings* in and about *Hanover-Square*, as in the net Houses of the Dukes of *Bolton*, *Montrose*, and *Roxborough*, of Sir *Robert Sutton* and General *Wade*, of the Earl of *Burlington* in *Picadilly*, of the Duke of *Chandois* at *Canons* near *Edger*, the Court of the *Rolls*, *Wanstead-House* in *Epping-Forest* by the Earl of *Tilney*, *Houghton-Hall* in

---

D. S.
SERENISSIMUS REX GEORGIUS
PER DEPUTATUM SUUM
REVERENDUM ADMODUM IN CHRISTO PATREM
RICHARDUM EPISCOPUM SARISBURIENSEM
SUMMUM SUUM ELEEMOSINARIUM
ADSISTENTE (REGIS JUSSU)
DOMINO THOMA HEWET EQUITE AURATO
ÆDIFICIORUM REGIORUM CURATORI PRINCIPALI
PRIMUM HUJUS ECCLESIÆ LAPIDEM
POSUIT
MARTII 19. ANNO DOMINI 1721.
ANNOQUE REGNI SUI OCTAVO.

R   *Norfolk*

Norfolk by Sir *Robert Walpole* Knight of the Garter, Sir *Gregory Page*'s Houſe on *Blackheath*, and many more either finiſh'd or founded before the King's Death that ſhew a fine Improvement in the *Royal Art.*

In the *Firſt* Year of King George II.

— INCHIQUIN *Grand Maſter* aſſembled the *Grand* Lodge in *Quarterly* Communication, with former *G. Officers* and Thoſe of 40 *Lodges* at the *Devil Temple-Bar* on *Saturday* 24 *June* 1727.

— 𝕲𝖗𝖆𝖓𝖉 𝕷𝖔𝖉𝖌𝖊 in *Due* Form at the *Bell* foreſaid on *Saturday* 28 *Oct.* 1727. with former *G. Officers* and Thoſe of 35 *Lodges.* D. G. *Maſter* COWPER in the Chair.

— 𝕲𝖗𝖆𝖓𝖉 𝕷𝖔𝖉𝖌𝖊 in *Due* Form at the *Devil* foreſaid on *Tueſday* 19 *Dec.* 1727. with former *G. Officers* and thoſe of only 18 *Lodges.* D. G. *Maſter* COWPER in the Chair, eloquently excuſed the *Grand Maſter*'s Abſence in *Ireland*, and his ſudden Calling them together; for that the *Feaſt* drew nigh, and that the *Grand Maſter* had, by Letter, impower'd him to propoſe, for his Succeſſor, the Lord *Colerane* Maſter of a *Lodge*, who was forthwith ſaluted as *Grand Maſter Elect.*

No *Stewards* being appointed, Brother *Lambert* again undertook to prepare the Feaſt.

ASSEMBLY and *Feaſt* at *Mercer's-Hall* on St. JOHN's Day *Wedneſday* 27 *Dec.* 1727. All Things being regularly tranſacted as above, D. *Grand Maſter* COWPER proclaim'd aloud our noble Brother

VII. HENRY HARE Lord *Colerane* 𝕲𝖗𝖆𝖓𝖉 𝕸𝖆𝖘𝖙𝖊𝖗 of *Maſons!* who appointed 𝕬𝖑𝖊𝖝𝖆𝖓𝖉𝖊𝖗 𝕮𝖍𝖔𝖐𝖊 Eſq; *Deputy Grand Maſter,*

{ *Nathaniel Blakerby*, Eſq; } *Grand*
{ Mr. *Joſeph Highmore* Painter, } *Wardens.*

Mr. *William Reid* was made *Secretary*, and Brother *Lambert* was thank'd for his Care.

𝕲𝖗𝖆𝖓𝖉 𝕷𝖔𝖉𝖌𝖊 in *Ample* Form at the *Crown* foreſaid on *Wedneſday* 17 *April* 1728. with former *G. Officers* and Thoſe of 27 *Lodges.*   — 𝕲𝖗𝖆𝖓𝖉

— 𝕲𝖗𝖆𝖓𝖉 𝕷𝖔𝖉𝖌𝖊 in *Ample* Form at the *King's-Arms* foresaid on *Tuesday* 25 *June* 1728. with former G. *Officers* and Those of 28 *Lodges.*

— 𝕲𝖗𝖆𝖓𝖉 𝕷𝖔𝖉𝖌𝖊 in *Due* Form at the *Queen's-Head* in *Great Queen-street* on *Tuesday* 26 *Nov.* 1728. with the Earl of I𝔫-chiquin and other former G. *Officers* and Those of 30 *Lodges.* D. G. *Master* 𝕮𝖍𝖔𝖐𝖊 in the Chair excused the *Grand Master's* Absence, and in his Name proposed for Successor the Lord Viscount *Kingston* Master of a *Lodge*, who was well recommended also by Brother Inchiquin, and was forthwith saluted as *Grand Master Elect.*

Brother *Desaguliers* moved to revive the *Office* of *Stewards* to assist the *Grand Wardens* in preparing the *Feast*, and that their Number be 12, which was readily agreed to. See their Names in the Margin below. *

A S E M B L Y and *Feast* at *Mercer's-Hall* on St. John's Day *Friday* 27 *Dec.* 1728. D. *Grand Master* Choke with his *Wardens*, several *noble* Brothers, former *Grand* Officers, and many Brethren, duly clothed, attended the *Grand Master Elect* in Coaches from his Lordship's House in *Leicester-Square* to the Hall *Eastward*: And all Things being regularly transacted as above, D.G. M. *Choke* proclaim'd aloud our noble Brother

VIII. James King *Lord* Viscount *Kingston* 𝕲𝖗𝖆𝖓𝖉 𝕸𝖆𝖘𝖙𝖊𝖗 of *Masons!* who appointed 𝕹𝖆𝖙𝖍𝖆𝖓𝖎𝖊𝖑 𝕭𝖑𝖆𝖐𝖊𝖗𝖇𝖞 Esq; D. G. *Master*, {Sir *James Thornhill*, } Grand {and the *Secretary* was conti-{Mr *Martin O Connor*,} *Wardens*, {nued.

— 𝕲𝖗𝖆𝖓𝖉 𝕷𝖔𝖉𝖌𝖊 in *Ample* Form at the 3 Tons *Swithin's-Alley* near the *Royal-Exchange* 27 March 1729. with former G. *Officers* and Those of 31 *Lodges.*

---

* 𝕾𝖙𝖊𝖜𝖆𝖗𝖉𝖘 that acted on 27 *Dec.* 1728. and were publickly thank'd.

1. Mr. *John Revis.*	7. Mr. *William Wilson.*
2. Mr. *Edwin Ward.*	8. Mr. *William Tew.*
3. Mr. *Samuel Stead.*	9. Mr. *William Hopkins.*
4. Mr. *Theodore Cheriholm.*	10. Mr. *Thomas Reason.*
5. Mr. *William Benn.*	11. Mr. *Thomas Alford.*
6. Mr. *Gerard Hatley.*	12. Mr. *H. Smart.*

— 𝕲𝖗𝖆𝖓𝖉

— 𝕲𝖗𝖆𝖓𝖉 𝕷𝖔𝖉𝖌𝖊 in *Due* Form at the *King's-Arms* forefaid on *Friday* 11 *July* 1729. with former *G. Officers* and Thofe of 26 *Lodges*. D. G. M. BLAKERBY was in the Chair.

𝕲𝖗𝖆𝖓𝖉 𝕷𝖔𝖉𝖌𝖊 in *Ample* Form at the *Devil* forefaid on *Tuefday* 25 *Nov.* 1729. with former *G. Officers* and Thofe of 27 *Lodges*.

KINGSTON *Grand Mafter* at his own Coft provided a curious *Pedeftal*, and a rich *Cufhion* with golden *Knops* and *Fringes* for the *Top* of the *Pedeftal*; a fine *Velvet Bag* for the *Secretary*, and a Badge of *Two golden Pens a-crofs* on his Breaft: For which very handfome Prefents the *Lodge* return'd hearty Thanks in folemn Manner.

𝕲𝖗𝖆𝖓𝖉 𝕷𝖔𝖉𝖌𝖊 in *Due* Form at the *Devil* forefaid on St. JOHN's Day, *Saturday* 27 *Dec.* 1729. with our noble Brother INCHIQUIN and other former *G. Officers*, and Thofe of 32 *Lodges*: when 𝕭𝖑𝖆𝖐𝖊𝖗𝖇𝖞 D. G. Mafter in the Chair, in the Grand Mafter's Name and by his Letter, propofed for Succeffor the Duke of *Norfolk* Mafter of a *Lodge*, who was joyfully faluted *Grand Mafter Elect*.

C H A P. VI.

From *Grand Mafter* NORFOLK to *Grand Mafter* CRAUFURD.

ASSEMBLY and *Feaft* at *Merchant-Taylor's-Hall* on *Thurfday*, 29 *Jan.* 17$\frac{19}{30}$. in the 3d Year of King GEORGE II.

KINGSTON *Grand Mafter* with his *Deputy* and *Wardens*, attended the *Grand Mafter Elect* in the Morning, at his Grace's Houfe in St. *James's-Square*; where he was met by a vaft Num-|This is a Specimen to ber of Brothers duly clothed, and from thence avoid Repetitions.| they went to the Hall *Eaftward* in the following *Proceffion* of 𝕸𝖆𝖗𝖈𝖍, viz.

Brother

Brother *Johnson* to clear the Way.

* *Six* of the *Stewards* clothed proper with their *Badges* and *White Rods*, Two in each Chariot.

Brothers without Diftinction duly clothed, in Gentlemen's Coaches.

The *noble* and *eminent* Brethren duly clothed, in their own Chariots.

Former *Grand Officers* not noble, clothed proper, in Gentlemens Coaches.

Former *noble Grand Mafters* clothed proper, in their own Chariots.

The *Secretary alone* with his *Badge* and *Bag*, clothed, in a Chariot.

The Two *Grand Wardens* clothed proper with their Badges, in one Chariot.

The D. G. *Mafter alone* clothed proper with his Badge in a Chariot.

KINGSTON 𝔊𝔯𝔞𝔫𝔡 *Mafter* clothed proper with his Badge,

NORFOLK G. M. *Elect* clothed only as a *Mafon*.

> in one Coach.

The Duke of *Norfolk*'s Coach of State empty.

The *Stewards* halted at *Charing-Crofs* till the Meffenger brought Orders to move on flowly, and till the Reft follow'd : And when the *Grand Mafter moved* from the Square, Brother *John Pyne* the Marfhal made hafte to the *Hall* to conduct the

Proceffion of 𝔈𝔫𝔱𝔯𝔶 at the *Hall-Gate*, viz.

The 12 *Stewards* ftanding, 6 on each Side of the Paffage, with their *White Rods*, made a Lane.

Brother *Johnfon* to clear the Way.

Former *Grand Wardens* walk'd one by one according to *Juniority*.

Former *D. Grand Mafters* walk'd one by one according to *Juniority*.

Former *Grand Mafters* by *Juniority*, viz.

---

* 𝔖𝔱𝔢𝔴𝔞𝔯𝔡𝔰 that acted on 29 *January* 17$\frac{29}{30}$.

1. Mr. *John Revis.*
2. Mr. *Samuel Stead.*
3. Mr. *Edwin Ward.*
4. Mr. *William Wilfon*
5. Mr. *William Hopkins*
6. Mr. *Thomas Reafon.*
7. Mr. *Gerard Hatley.*
8. Mr. *William Tew.*
9. Mr. —— *Pread*
10. Mr. ——*Bardo*, Senior.
11. Mr. ——*Bardo*, Junior.
12. Mr. *Charles Hoar*

The *firft Eight* acted at the *laft Feaft*, and they were all publickly thank'd for their Care.

Lord

(126)

Lord COLERANE, *Earl* of INCHIQUIN, *Lord* PAISLEY, *Duke* of RICHMOND, *Earl* of DALKEITH, *Duke* of MONTAGU, Dr. DESAGULIERS, GEORGE PAYNE Efq; and Mr. ANTONY SAYER.

Then the *Stewards* clofed, walking Two and Two.

The *Secretary* alone.

The Two *Grand Wardens* together.

The *D. Grand Mafter* alone.

On the *Left* Hand.	On the *Right Hand.*
The 𝕾𝖜𝖔𝖗𝖉 born by the *Mafter* of the *Lodge* to which it be-long'd.	The *Book* of CONSTITUTIONS on the fine *Cufhion* carried by the *Mafter* of the *Senior Lodge.*
NORFOLK *Grand Mafter Elect.*	KINGSTON *Grand Mafter.*

Marfhal Pyne with his *Truncheon Blew*, tipt with *Gold.*

In this Order they decently walk'd into the *Lodge Room* (while the Others walk'd into the *Hall)* and there the *Mafters* and *Wardens* of Lodges received their G. MASTER with Joy and Reverence in due Form. He fat down in his Chair before the *Pedeftal,* cover'd with the rich *Cufhion,* upon which were laid the *Conftitutions* and the *Sword* ; and the G. M. *Elect* on his Right Hand.

After opening the *Lodge,* the laft Minutes were read by the *Secretary,* and the Election of Brother *Norfolk* was folemnly recogniz'd.

Adjourn'd to Dinner, a *Grand Feaft* indeed !

As at *Richmond*, Page 117.
After Dinner and the *firft* Proceffion round the *Tables,* Brother *Kingfton* proclaim'd aloud the moft noble *Prince*, the *firft Duke, Marquis* and *Earl* of *Great Britain,* and our Brother

IX. THOMAS HOWARD Duke of *Norfolk* 𝕲𝖗𝖆𝖓𝖉 𝕸𝖆𝖘𝖙𝖊𝖗 of *Mafons !* and having invefted him and inftall'd him in *Solomon's* Chair, fat down on his Right Hand. Upon which the *Affembly* join'd in their Homage and Congratulations.

NORFOLK *Grand Mafter* forthwith appointed

𝕹𝖆𝖙𝖍𝖆𝖓𝖎𝖊𝖑 𝕭𝖑𝖆𝖐𝖊𝖗𝖇𝖞 Efq; to continue D. G. M.	⎱	Col. *Geo. Carpenter,* now *Lord Carpenter,*	⎰	
The *Secretary* was continued.	⎰	*Tho. Batfon* Efq; Counfellor at Law,	⎱	*Grand Wardens.* And

And having made the 2d *Proceffion* round the Tables (as at *Richmond*) great Harmony abounded, till the G. Mafter order'd G. Warden *Carpenter* to clofe the Lodge in good Time.

— 𝕲𝖗𝖆𝖓𝖉 𝕷𝖔𝖉𝖌𝖊 in *Ample* Form at the *Devil* forefaid on *Tuefday* 21 *April* 1730. with the noble Brothers *Richmond, Inchiquin, Kingfton, Colerane,* and other former *G. Officers,* with thofe of 31 *Lodges.* Much Time was fpent in receiving and beftowing Charity.

𝕲𝖗𝖆𝖓𝖉 𝕷𝖔𝖉𝖌𝖊 in *Due* Form at the *Devil* forefaid on *Friday* 28 *Aug.* 1730. with former *G. Officers* and Thofe of 34 *Lodges.* D. G. *Mafter* BLAKERBY in the Chair.

— 𝕲𝖗𝖆𝖓𝖉 𝕷𝖔𝖉𝖌𝖊 in *Due* Form at the *King's-Arms* forefaid on *Tuefday* 15 *Dec.* 1730. with our noble Brother *Colerane* and other former *G. Officers* and Thofe of 41 *Lodges.* D. G. *Mafter* BLAKERBY in the Chair, moved to poftpone the *Feaft,* the 𝕲𝖗𝖆𝖓𝖉 *Mafter* being at *Venice,* which was agreed to.

— 𝕲𝖗𝖆𝖓𝖉 𝕷𝖔𝖉𝖌𝖊 in *Due* Form at the *Devil* forefaid 29 *Jan.* 173$\frac{0}{1}$. with former *G. Officers* and Thofe of 31 *Lodges.* D. G. *Mafter* BLAKERBY acquainted the *Lodge,* that tho' our Right Worfhipful G. MASTER was now at *Venice,* he was not unmindful of us, but had fent us 3 kind Prefents, *viz.*

1. TWENTY POUNDS to the Fund of *Mafons Charity,* See the *Conftitution* of it, below.

2. A Large *Folio* Book of the fineft Writing Paper for the Records of the *Grand Lodge,* moft richly bound in *Turkey* and guilded, and on the Frontifpiece in Vellum, the *Arms* of *Norfolk* amply difplay'd with a *Latin* Infcription of his noble *Titles.*

3. The *Old Trufty Sword* of GUSTAVUS ADOLPHUS King of *Sweden,* that was wore next by his Succeffor in War the brave 𝖁𝖊𝖗𝖓𝖆𝖗𝖉 Duke of *Sax-Weimar,* with both their Names on the Blade; which the *Grand Mafter* had order'd Brother *George Moody* (the King's Sword-Cutler) to adorn richly with the *Arms* of *Norfolk* in Silver on the Scabbard; in order to be the *Grand Mafter's* 𝕾𝖜𝖔𝖗𝖉 of *State* for the future.

The *Lodge* exprefs'd their grateful Acceptance in their own agreeable Manner. The Feaft was again poftponed.

𝕲𝖗𝖆𝖓𝖉

— 𝕲𝖗𝖆𝖓𝖉 𝕷𝖔𝖉𝖌𝖊 in *Due* Form at the *Devil* forefaid on *Wedneſday* 17 *March* 173⁰₁. with our Brothers RICHMOND and COLERANE and other former *G. Officers*, Lord LOVELL and the Officers of 29 *Lodges*, when D. G. M. BLAKERBY in the Chair propoſed (in the *Grand Maſter's* Name) for Succeſſor, the *Lord Lovel* Maſter of a *Lodge*, who was ſaluted *Grand Maſter Elect*.

ASSEMBLY and *Feaſt* at *Mercer's-Hall* 27 *March* 1731. The *Proceſſion* of ·*March* was from Lord *Lovell's* Houſe in *Great Ruſſel-ſtreet Bloomſbury Eaſtward* to the *Hall*: But Lord LOVEL being ill of an Ague, return'd home, and left Lord COLERANE his Proxy for the Day. All Things being regularly tranſacted as above,

D. G. Maſter *Blakerby* proclaim'd aloud our noble Brother

X. THOMAS COOK Lord *Lovel* 𝕲𝖗𝖆𝖓𝖉 𝕸𝖆𝖘𝖙𝖊𝖗 of *Maſons:* and Lord *Colerane* being inveſted in his Name, appointed 𝕿𝖍𝖔𝖒𝖆𝖘 𝕭𝖆𝖙𝖘𝖔𝖓 foreſaid ⎰*George Dowglas*, M. D.⎱ *Grand Deputy Grand Maſter,* ⎱*James Chambers*, Eſq; ⎰*Wardens.* The *Secretary* was continued, and Brother *George Moody* was appointed *Sword-Bearer.* * See the *Stewards* in the Margin below.

— 𝕲𝖗𝖆𝖓𝖉 𝕷𝖔𝖉𝖌𝖊 in *Ample* Form at the *Roſe* in *Mary-la-Bonne* on *Friday* 14 *May* 1731. with the noble Brothers NORFOLK, INCHIQUIN, COLERANE, and other former *G. Officers*, and Thoſe of 37 *Lodges.* When LOVEL *Grand Maſter* moved that the *Lodge* ſhould now return Thanks to kind Brother *Norfolk* for his *noble* Preſents to the *Fraternity*; which was forthwith done in ſolemn Form, and receiv'd by the *Duke* with Brotherly Affection.

---

* 𝕾𝖙𝖊𝖜𝖆𝖗𝖉𝖘 that acted on 27 *March* 1731. who were all publickly thank'd.

1. *George Dowglas*, M. D.	7. Mr. *John Haines.*
2. *James Chambers*,	8. Mr. *William Millward.*
3. *Thomas Moor*, Eſqs;	9. Mr. *Roger Lacy*
4. *John Atwood*,	10. Mr. *Charles Trinquand.*
5. *Thomas Durant*,	11. Mr. *John Calcot*,
6. Mr. *George Page*,	12. Mr. *John King.*

His

His *Royal Highneſs* FRANCIS Duke of *Lorrain* (now *Grand Duke* of TUSCANY) at the *Hague* was made an *Enter'd Prentice* and *Fellow Craft*, by Virtue of a *Deputation* for a *Lodge* there, conſiſting of Rev. Dr. {*John Stanhope*, Eſq; } *Grand* DESAGULIERS *Maſter*, {*Jn. Holtzendorf*, Eſq; } *Wardens.* and the other Brethren, *viz.* PHILIP STANHOPE Earl of *Cheſterfield* Lord Ambaſſador,— *Strickland* Eſq; Nephew to the Biſhop of *Namur*, Mr. *Benjamin Hadley* and an *Hollandiſh* Brother.

Our ſaid *Royal* Brother LORRAIN coming to *England* this Year, *Grand Maſter* LOVEL formed an Occaſional Lodge at Sir *Robert Walpole*'s Houſe of *Houghton-Hall* in *Norfolk*, and made Brother LORRAIN and Brother THOMAS PELHAM Duke of *Newcaſtle* 𝕸𝖆𝖘𝖙𝖊𝖗-𝕸𝖆𝖘𝖔𝖓𝖘. And ever ſince, both in the *G. Lodge* and in particular *Lodges*, the Fraternity joyfully remember His ROYAL HIGHNESS in the proper Manner.

— 𝕲𝖗𝖆𝖓𝖉 𝕷𝖔𝖉𝖌𝖊 in *Ample* Form at the *Half-Moon Cheapſide*, on *Thurſday* 24 *June* 1731. with former *G. Officers* and Thoſe of 29 *Lodges*.

— 𝕲𝖗𝖆𝖓𝖉 𝕷𝖔𝖉𝖌𝖊 in *Due* Form at the *Devil* foreſaid, on *Friday* 3 *Dec.* 1731. with Lord *Colerane* and other former *Grand Officers*, Capt. *Ralph Far Winter* the *Provincial* Grand Maſter of *Eaſt-India*, and the Officers of 46 *Lodges*.

— 𝕲𝖗𝖆𝖓𝖉 𝕷𝖔𝖉𝖌𝖊 in *Due* Form at the *Devil* foreſaid on *Thurſday* 2 *March* 173½. with the Duke of *Richmond*, and other former *G. Officers*, Viſcount *Montagu*, and the Officers of 37 Lodges.

D. G. *Maſter* BATSON in the Chair propoſed, in the *Grand Maſter's* Name, for Succeſſor, the *Lord* Viſcount *Montagu* Maſter of a *Lodge*, who was immediately ſaluted as *Grand Maſter Elect*.

— 𝕲𝖗𝖆𝖓𝖉 𝕷𝖔𝖉𝖌𝖊 in *Due* Form at the *Devil* foreſaid, on *Thurſday* 13 *April* 1732. with former *G. Officers* and Thoſe of 27 *Lodges*.

ASSEMBLY and *Feaſt* at *Merchant-Taylor's-Hall* on *Wedneſday* 19 *April* 1732. D. Grand *Maſter* BATSON with his *Wardens* attended the *G. Maſter Elect* at his Houſe in *Bloomſbury-Square*; and with ſome noble Brothers, the Dukes of *Montagu* and *Richmond*, the Lord *Colerane*, the Lord *Carpenter*, the Earl of *Strathmore* and

Lord

Lord *Teynham*, and many Others, all duly clothed in Coaches, made the *Proceſſion* of **March** *Eaſtward* to the *Hall*, where all Things being regularly tranſacted as above, D. G. M. *Batſon* proclaim'd aloud our noble Brother.

XI. ANTONY BROWN *Lord* Viſcount *Montagu* **Grand Maſter** of *Maſons*, who appointed **Thomas Batſon** to continue D. G. *Maſter*.
{ *George Rook*, Eſq; } *Grand* { The *Secretary* and *Sword*-
{ *James Moor-Smythe*, Eſq; } *Wardens*. { *Bearer* were continued.

— **Grand Lodge** in *Due* Form at the *Caſtle* in *Drury-Lane*, on *Thurſday* 8 *June* 1732. with the Earl of *Inchiquin* and other former *G. Officers* and Thoſe of 39 *Lodges*.

— **Grand Lodge** in *Due* Form at the *Devil* foreſaid, on *Tueſday* 21 *Nov.* 1732. with Lord *Colerane*, Lord *Southwell*, and other former *G. Officers* and Thoſe of 49 *Lodges*.

— **Grand Lodge** in *Due* Form at the *Devil* foreſaid, on *Tueſday* 29 *May* 1733. with Lord *Southwell*, former *G. Officers* and Thoſe of 42 *Lodges*.

D. G. M. BATSON in the Chair, propoſed, in the *Grand Maſter's* Name, for Succeſſor, the *Earl of Strathmore* Maſter of a *Lodge*; who being in *Scotland*, our *Noble* Brother THOMAS Lord SOUTHWELL undertook to be *Proxy* at the next Feaſt, and was ſaluted now as STRATHMORE *Grand Maſter Elect*.

ASSEMBLY and *Feaſt* at *Mercer's-Hall*, on *Thurſday* 7 *June* 1733. D. G. M. BATSON with his *G. Wardens* attended Lord *Southwell* at his Houſe in *Groſvenor-ſtreet*, and with ſome *Noble* Brothers, and many Others, all duly clothed in Coaches, made the *Proceſſion* of **March** *Eaſtward* to the *Hall*. And all Things being regularly tranſacted as above, D. G. **M.** *Batſon* proclaim'd aloud our Noble Brother

---

* **Stewards** that acted at the Feaſt 19 *April* 1732. who were all publickly thank'd.

George Rook, *James Moor Smythe*, *John Bridges*, *Wyrriot Ormond*, *Arthur Moor*, *Vizal Taverner*, } Eſq;	Colonel *John Pitt*, *Claud Creſpigny*, *William Blunt*, } Eſq; Mr. *Henry Tatam*, Mr. *Thomas Griffith*, Mr. *Solomon Mendez*.

XII. JAMES

XII. JAMES LYON Earl of *Strathmore* 𝕲𝖗𝖆𝖓𝖉 𝕸𝖆𝖘𝖙𝖊𝖗 of *Masons!* His Proxy Lord SOUTHWELL being duly invested and install'd, appointed

𝕿𝖍𝖔𝖒𝖆𝖘 𝕭𝖆𝖙𝖘𝖔𝖓 to con-⎰*James Smythe*, Esq;⎱ Grand
tinue D. G. *Master!* ⎱*John Ward*, Esq; ⎰*Wardens.*
The *Secretary* and *Sword-bearer* were continued. See the *Stewards* below. *

— 𝕲𝖗𝖆𝖓𝖉 𝕷𝖔𝖉𝖌𝖊 in *Ample* Form at the *Devil* foresaid on *Tuesday* 13 *Dec.* 1733. with Sir *Edward Mansel*, Bart. Pro. G. Master of *South Wales*, former *G. Officers*, the Earl of *Crawfurd* and the Officers of 53 *Lodges*.

STRATHMORE *Grand Master* moved, that Business greatly encreasing, the *Grand Lodge* do refer what they cannot overtake at one Time, to the *Committee of Charity*, who can make Report to the next *Grand Lodge*; which was unanimously agreed to. See the *Committee of Charity* below.

D. G. M. 𝕭𝖆𝖙𝖘𝖔𝖓 recommended the *New* Colony of *Georgia* in *North America* to the Benevolence of the particular *Lodges*. And

Brother *Thomas Edwards* Esq; *Warden* of the Duke of *Richmond's Lodge* at the *Horn Westminster*, acquainted this *Grand Lodge* that our Brother Capt. *Ralph Farwinter*, 𝕻𝖗𝖔𝖛𝖎𝖓𝖈𝖎𝖆𝖑 GRAND MASTER of *East-India*, had sent from his *Lodge* at *Bengal* a Chest of the best *Arrack* for the Use of the *Grand Lodge*, and TEN GUINEAS for the *Masons-Charity*; which the *Lodge* gratefully receiv'd and order'd solemn Thanks to be return'd to the 𝕷𝖔𝖉𝖌𝖊 at *Bengal*.

— 𝕲𝖗𝖆𝖓𝖉 𝕷𝖔𝖉𝖌𝖊 in *Due* Form at the *Devil* foresaid on *Monday* 18 *March* 173¾. with former *G. Officers*, the Earl of *Craufurd*, Sir *George Mackenzy*, Bart. and the Officers of 47 *Lodges*: when D. G. M. BATSON in the Chair proposed, in the *Grand Master's* Name, for Successor, the *Earl of Craufurd*, Master of a *Lodge*, who was gladly saluted as *Grand Master Elect*.

---

* 𝕾𝖙𝖊𝖜𝖆𝖗𝖉𝖘 that acted at the Feast 7 *June* 1733. who were all publickly thank'd.

1. *John Ward*	7. *John Mizaubin*, M. D.	
2. *John Poexfen*,	8. Mr. *John Dwight*.	
3. *Henry Butler Pacy*, Esqs;	9. Mr. *Richard Baugh*. Gent.	
4. *John Read*,	10. Mr. *Thomas Shank*,	
5. *William Bushy*,	11. Mr. *James Cosens*,	
6. *Philip Barnes*,	12. Mr. *Charles Robinson*.	

S 2 CHAP.

CHAP. VII.

From *Grand Mafter* CRAUFURD, To the *prefent* G. MASTER CAERMARTHEN.

ASSEMBLY and *Feaft* at *Mercer's-Hall* on *Saturday* 30 *March* 1734. D. G. M. BATSON with his G. *Wardens* attended the *Grand Mafter Elect* at his Houfe in *Great Marlborough-ftreet,* with Noble Brothers, and many Others, all duly clothed in Coaches, and made the *Proceffion* of MARCH *Eaftward* to the *Hall* with a Band of *Mufick,* viz. *Trumpets, Hautboys, Kettle-Drums* and *French-Horns,* to lead the *Van* and play at the *Gate* till all arrive: and all Things being regularly tranfacted as above,

D. G. M. *Batfon* proclaim'd aloud, the *firft Earl* of *Scotland* and our Noble Brother

XIII. JOHN LINDSAY *Earl* of *Craufurd* 𝕲𝖗𝖆𝖓𝖉 𝕸𝖆𝖘𝖙𝖊𝖗 of *Mafons,* who appointed Sir **Cecil Wray,** Baronet, D. G. *Mafter,* {*John Ward,* Efq; ⎱ Grand {Brother *John Revis* was {Sir *Edward Manfel,* Bart. ⎰ Wardens. ⎰ made *Grand Secretary,* and Brother *Mody* was continued *Sword-bearer.* After the 2d *Proceffion* round the Tables, much Harmony abounded. *

— 𝕲𝖗𝖆𝖓𝖉 𝕷𝖔𝖉𝖌𝖊 in Ample Form at the *Devil* forefaid on *Monday* 24 *Feb.* 173⁴⁄₅. the Dukes of *Richmond* and *Buccleugh,* and other former Grand Officers, the Earl of *Belcarras,* the Vifcount *Weymouth,* and the Officers of 47 Lodges.

---

* 𝖘𝖙𝖊𝖜𝖆𝖗𝖉𝖘 that acted at the Feaft 30 *March* 1734. who were all publickly thank'd.

1. Sir *Edward Manfell* Baronet.	7. *Richard Rawlinfon,* L. L. D. and F. R. S.
2. *Charles Holtzendorf,* ⎫	8. *Fotherby Baker,*
3. *Ifaac Mueve,* ⎪	9. *Samuel Berrington,*
4. *Prefcot Pepper* ⎬ Efqs;	10. *John Pitt,* Gentlemen.
5. *Chriftopher Nevile,* ⎪	11. *William Varelft*
6. *Richard Matthews,* ⎭	12. *Henry Hutchinfon.*

CRAWFURD

CRAUFURD *Grand Master* made a very handsome Speech, excusing his not calling them together sooner, even because of the Elections for Parliament and other publick Business ; and proposed for his Succeffor the *Lord* Viscount *Weymouth* Master of a *Lodge,* who was forthwith saluted as *G. Master Elect.*

Brother *Anderson,* Author of the *Book* of CONSTITUTIONS, representing that a *new Edition* was become neceffary, and that he had prepared Materials for it, the GRAND MASTER and the *Lodge* order'd him to lay the same before the present and former *Grand Officers* ; that they may report their Opinion to the G. Lodge. Also the Book call'd the *Free Mason's Vade Mecum* was condemn'd by the G. Lodge as a pyratical and filly Thing, done without Leave, and the Brethren were warned not to use it, nor encourage it to be sold.

— **Grand Lodge** in *Ample* Form at the *Devil* foresaid on *Monday* 31 *March* 1735. with former *Grand Officers* and Those of 41 *Lodges.*

CRAUFURD *Grand Master,* in a judicious Speech, proposed several Things for the Good of the *Fraternity,* which were approv'd, and the Substance of 'em are in the *New Regulations* and *Committee* of *Charity,* below.

Brother *Anderson* was order'd also to insert in the New Edition of the Constitutions, the PATRONS of *antient* **Masonry** that could be collected from the Beginning of Time, with the *Grand Masters* and *Wardens,* antient and modern, and the Names of the *Stewards* since G. M. *Montagu.* Never more Love and Harmony appear'd.

ASSEMBLY and *Feast* at *Mercer's-Hall* on *Thursday* 17 *April* 1735.

CRAUFURD *Grand Master* with his *Deputy* and *Wardens,* and the noble Brothers the Dukes of *Richmond* and *Atholl,* the Marquis of *Beaumont,* the Earls of *Winchelsea, Weems, Loudoun* and *Balcarras,* the Lord *Cathcart* and Lord *Vere Berty,* with many Other Brothers all duly clothed, attended the *Grand Master Elect,* and from his House in *Grovenor-Square* made the PROCESSION of **March** with the band of *Musick* leading the Van *Eastward* to the *Hall.* And

All

All Things being regularly tranfacted as above, Brother *Crau-furd* proclaim'd aloud our noble Brother *

XIV. THOMAS THYNNE, *Lord* Vifcount *Weymouth* 𝕲𝖗𝖆𝖓𝖉 𝕸𝖆𝖘𝖙𝖊𝖗 of *Mafons*; who appointed 𝕵𝖔𝖍𝖓 𝖂𝖆𝖗𝖉 Efq; *D. G. Mafter.*

{ Sir *Edward Manfel*, Bart.　　　　} Grand { The*Secretary*
{ *Martin Clare*, A. M. and F. R. S. } *Wardens.* { and *Sword-bearer* continued.

— 𝕲𝖗𝖆𝖓𝖉 𝕷𝖔𝖉𝖌𝖊 in *Due* Form at the *Devil* forefaid on *Thurf-day* 24 *June* 1735. with former *G. Officers* and Thofe of 31 *Lodges.*

D. G. *Mafter* WARD in the Chair, in an excellent Speech recommended *Temper* and *Decency.* The Brothers that ferved the Office of *Stewards* ever fince *Grand Mafter* the Duke of MONTAGU, addrefs'd the *Grand Lodge* for certain *Privileges,* which were granted. See the *New Regulation* 23.

— 𝕲𝖗𝖆𝖓𝖉 𝕷𝖔𝖉𝖌𝖊 in *Due* Form at the *Devil* forefaid on *Thurf-day* 11 *Dec.* 1735. with former *G. Officers* and Thofe of 57 *Lodges.* GEORGE PAYNE, Efq; formerly *Grand Mafter.* in the Chair ; *Martin Clare* the G. W. acted as *Dep. Gr. Mafter,* and

{ *James Anderfon*, D. D. { Grand 　 { pro Tempore.
{ *Jacob Lamball*,　　　　 { *Wardens.* {

Brother *Rigby* from *Bengall,* who brought from thence 20 GUINEAS for the *Charity.*

Sir *Robert Lawley* Mafter of the *Stewards Lodge,* with his *Wardens* and 9 more, with their *new Badges,* appear'd full 12 the *firft* Time.

The 𝕷𝖔𝖉𝖌𝖊 order'd a Letter of Thanks to be fent to the *Lodge* at *Bengal* for their very generous and kind Prefents.

---

* 𝕾𝖙𝖊𝖜𝖆𝖗𝖉𝖘 that acted at the *Feaft* on 17 *April* 1735. who were all publickly thanked.

1. Sir *Robert Lawley*, Baronet,
2. *William Græme*, M. D. and F. R. S.
3. *Martin Clare*, A. M. and F. R. S.
4. *John Theobald*, M. D.
5. *Charles Fleetwood*, Efq;
6. *Thomas Beech*, Efq.
7. Captain *Ralph Farwinter*,
8. *Meyer Shamberg*, M. D.
9. *Robert Wright*, Gentleman,
10. *Thomas Slaughter*, Laceman,
11. *James Nafh*, Gentleman,
12. *William Hogarth*, Painter.

𝕲𝖗𝖆𝖓𝖉

— **Grand Lodge** in Due Form at the *Devil* forefaid on *Tuef-day* 6 *April* 1736. with the Duke of *Richmond*, the Earl of *Craufurd* and other former *G. Officers*, the Earl of *Loudoun*, the *Stewards* Lodge and 5 prefent *Stewards*, with the *Officers* of 61 Lodges.

D. G. *Mafter* WARD in the *Chair* propofed fome *Rules of Communication* that were approved and now make the 40th GENERAL REGULATION. Below.

Then he propofed, in the *Grand Mafter*'s Name, for Succeffor, the *Earl* of *Loudoun* Mafter of a *Lodge*, who was forthwith faluted as *Grand Mafter Elect*.

ASSEMBLY and **Feaft** at *Fifhmongers-Hall* on *Thurfday* 15 *April* 1736. D. G. *Mafter* WARD with his *Wardens* and the noble Brothers, the Duke of *Richmond*, the Earls of *Craufurd* and *Albemarle*, Vifcount *Harcourt*, Lord *Erefkine*, Lord *Southwell*, Mr. *Anftis* **Garter** King at *Arms*, Mr. *Brody* **Lion** King at *Arms*, with many other Brothers all duly clothed, attended the *Grand Mafter Elect*; and from his Houfe in *Whitehall* made the *Proceffion* of *March*, with the Band of Mufick, *Eaft-ward* to the *Hall:* Where all Things being regularly tranfacted as above, *

D. G. *Mafter Ward* proclaim'd aloud, our noble Brother

XV. JOHN CAMPBELL Earl of *Loudoun* **Grand Mafter** of *Mafons*, who appointed **John Ward**, Efq; to continue *Deputy* ⎰Sir **Robert Lawley**, Baronet,⎱ *Grand* *Grand Mafter*, ⎱**William Graeme**, M. D. and F. R. S.⎰*Wardens.* and continued the *Secretary* and *Sword-bearer.*

---

* STEWARDS that acted at the *Feaft* on 15 *April* 1736. who were publickly thank'd.

1. *Edward Hody*, M. D. and F. R. S	7. Mr. *Benjamin Gafcoyne*,
2. *James Ruck*, jun. Efq;	8. *James Styles*, Efq;
3. Mr. *Charles Champion*,	9. Mr. *Walter Weldon*,
4. Mr. *John Gocwland*,	10. Mr. *Richard Sawle*,
5. *John Jeffe*, Efq;	11. Mr. *James Pringle*,
6. *Ifaac Shamberg*, jun. M. D.	12. Mr. *Francis Blythe*.

— **Grand**

— 𝕲𝖗𝖆𝖓𝖉 𝕷𝖔𝖉𝖌𝖊 in *Ample* Form at the *Devil* forefaid on *Thurfday* 17 *June* 1736. with the Earl of *Craufurd* and other former *G. Officers*, the *Stewards* Lodge, the *new* Stewards, and the *Officers* of 36 *Lodges.*

G. 𝖂𝖆𝖗𝖉𝖊𝖓 𝕲𝖗𝖆𝖊𝖒𝖊 acted ⎱ Lord 𝕰𝖗𝖊𝖘𝖐𝖎𝖓𝖊, ⎰ *GrandWardens* as D. G. *Mafter* pro tempore. ⎰ Capt.——*Young*, ⎱ pro tempore.

— 𝕲𝖗𝖆𝖓𝖉 𝕷𝖔𝖉𝖌𝖊 in *Due* Form at the *Devil* forefaid on St. JOHN *Evangelift's* Day, *Monday* 27 *Dec.* 1736. with former *G. Officers*, the *Stewards* Lodge, the *prefent* Stewards, and the *Officers* of 52 Lodges.

Sir ROBERT LAWLEY Sen. G. W. was in the Chair as *Grand Mafter* pro tempore.

𝖂𝖎𝖑𝖑𝖎𝖆𝖒 𝕲𝖆𝖊𝖒𝖊 J. G. W. was ⎱ *Martin Clare*, ⎰ G. *Wardens Deputy* G. *Mafter* pro tempore, ⎰ *Jacob Lamball*, ⎱ pro tempore.

The curious *By-Laws* of the *Lodge* at *Exeter* were publickly read and applauded, and a Letter of Thanks was order'd to be fent to them for their handfome Beneficence to the General *Charity.*

— 𝕲𝖗𝖆𝖓𝖉 𝕷𝖔𝖉𝖌𝖊 in *Ample* Form at the *Devil* forefaid on *Thurfday* 13 *April* 1737. with the Earl of *Craufurd* and other former *G. Officers*, the Earls of *Weems, Hume* and *Darnley*, the *Stewards* Lodge, the *prefent* Stewards, and the *Officers* of 75 *Lodges.* After the Affair of *Charity* was over,

LOUDOUN *Grand Mafter* propofed for his Succeffor the Earl of *Darnley* Mafter of a *Lodge*, who was forthwith faluted as *Grand Mafter Elect.*

ASSEMBLY and 𝕱𝖊𝖆𝖘𝖙 at *Fifhmongers-Hall* on *Thurfday* 28 *April* 1737.

LOUDOUN G. *Mafter* with his *Deputy* and *Wardens*, the noble Brothers, the Duke of *Richmond*, the Earls of *Craufurd* and *Weemes*, Lord *Grey* of *Grooby*, the *Stewards* and many other Brothers all duly clothed, attended the *Grand Mafter Elect* at his Houfe in *Pall-Mall*, and made the *Proceffion* of *March Eaftward* to the *Hall* in a very folemn Manner, having 3 Bands of Mufick, Kettle-Drums, Trumpets and *French* Horns,

properly

properly difpofed in the *March* : Where all Things being regularly tranfacted as above, *

The Earl of *Loudoun* proclaim'd aloud our noble Brother

XVI. EDWARD BLYTHE Earl and Vifcount *Darnley*, Lord *Clifton*, 𝕲𝖗𝖆𝖓𝖉 𝕸𝖆𝖘𝖙𝖊𝖗 of *Mafons*, who continued

𝕵𝖔𝖍𝖓 𝖂𝖆𝖗𝖉, Efq; {Sir *Robert Lawley*, Baronet,   } Grand
D. *Grand Mafter*, {*William Græme*, M. D. and F. R. S. } *Wardens.*
and continued the 𝕾𝖊𝖈𝖗𝖊𝖙𝖆𝖗𝖞 and *Sword-bearer*.

— 𝕲𝖗𝖆𝖓𝖉 𝕷𝖔𝖉𝖌𝖊 in *Ample* Form at the *Devil* forefaid on *Wednefday* 29 *June* 1737. with the Earl of *Loudoun* and other former *G. Officers*, the *Stewards Lodge*, the *New* Stewards and the *Officers* of 49 Lodges.

On 5th *Nov.* 1737. an Occafional *Lodge* was held at the *Prince* of *Wales's* Palace of *Kew* near *Richmond, viz.*

The *Rev.* Dr. DESAGULIERS (formerly *Grand Mafter*) 𝕸𝖆𝖘𝖙𝖊𝖗 of this *Lodge*,

Mr. *William Gofton*, Attorney at Law, *Senior* { *Grand* }
Mr. *Erafmus King*, Mathematician,   *Junior* { *Warden.* }

The Right Hon. *Charles Calvert* Earl of *Baltimore*, the Hon. Colonel *James Lumley*, the Hon. Major *Madden*, Mr. de *Noyer*, Mr. *Vraden* ; and when formed and tiled,

His *Royal* Highnefs FRIDERIC *Prince* of WALES was in the ufual Manner introduced, and made an *Enter'd Prentice* and *Fellow Craft.*

Our faid *Royal* Brother FRIDERIC was made a 𝕸𝖆𝖘𝖙𝖊𝖗 𝕸𝖆𝖘𝖔𝖓 by the fame *Lodge*, that affembled there again for that Purpofe. And ever fince, both in the *Grand Lodge* and in particular *Lodges*, the *Fraternity* joyfully remember his ROYAL HIGHNESS and his SON, in the proper Manner.

---

* STEWARDS that acted at the *Feaft* on 28 *April* 1737. who wore publickly thank'd

1. Sir *Bouchier Wray*, Baronet,	7. *Lewis Theobald* M. D.
2. *George Bothomley*, } Efq;	8. Mr. *Thomas Jeffreys*, Merchant,
3. *Charles Murray*, }	9. Mr. *Peter Leigh*,
4. Capt. *John Lloyd*,	10. Mr. *Thomas Boehm*,
5. Capt. *Charles Scot*,	11. Mr. *Benjamin Da Cofta*,
6. Mr. *Pet. Mac-Culloch*, Surgeon.	12. Mr. *Nathaniel Adams*.

T   *George*

— Grand Lodge in *Ample* Form at the *Devil* forefaid on *Wednefday* 25 *January* 173⅞. with the Earl of *Loudoun*, Dr. *Defaguliers*, *George Payne*, *Nathaniel Blakerby*, *Thomas Batfon*, Efq; Dr. *Anderfon*, and other former Grand *Officers*, Lord *George Graham*, the *Stewards* Lodge, the *prefent* Stewards and the *Officers* of 66 Lodges. After the Affair of *Charity* was over,

The Grand Lodge approved of this *New* Book of *Conftitutions*, and order'd the Author Brother *Anderfon* to print the fame, with the Addition of the *New Regulation* IX. See the *Approbation* below.

—Grand Lodge in *Ample* Form at the *Devil* forefaid on *Thurfday* 6 *April* 1738.
DARNLEY G. *Mafter* in the Chair, John Ward, D. G. *Mafter*, *William Graeme*, fen. G. W. ⎱pro tem-⎰ The Earl of *Inchi-*
James Anderfon, Jun. G. W. ⎰ pore. ⎱*quin*, Dr. *Defaguliers*, *George Payne*, late G. *Mafters*, *John Hammerton* Efq; Provincial G. M. of *Carolina*, *Thomas Batfon* late D. G. M. *Nath. Blakerby* Treafurer, the Marquis of *Caernervon*, the *Stewarts* Lodge, the *prefent* Stewards and the *Officers* of 60 Lodges. After the Affair of *Charity* was over,

Nathaniel Blakerby, Efq; the *Treafurer*, having juftly cleared his Accounts, demitted or laid down his *Office*. Upon which the *Grand Mafter* and the *Lodge* appointed the *Secretary* Revis to be *Treafurer*.

DARNLEY G. *Mafter* propofed for his Succeffor the Marquis of *Caernarvon* Mafter of a *Lodge*, who was forthwith faluted as *Grand Mafter Eleɛt*.

ASSEMBLY and Feaft at *Fifhmongers-Hall* on *Thurfday* 27 *April* 1738.

DARNLEY *Grand Mafter* with his *Deputy* and *Wardens*, the noble Brothers *Richmond*, *Inchiquin*, *Loudoun* and *Colerane*, late Gr. *Mafters*, Earl of *Kintore*, Lord *Grey* of *Grooby*, the *Stewards* and a great many other Brothers all duly clothed, attended the *Grand Mafter Eleɛt* at his Houfe in *Grovenor-ftreet*, and made the *Proceffion* of *March*, with the Band of Mufick, *Eaftward* to the *Hall*, where all Things being regularly tranfaɛted as above,

The

The Earl of *Darnley* proclaim'd aloud our noble Brother

XVII. HENRY BRIDGES Marquis of *Caernarvon*, Son and Heir apparent to the Duke of *Chandos*, Knight of the *Bath*, and one of the *Bed-Chamber* to our *Royal* Brother FRIDERIC Prince of *Wales*, 𝕲𝖗𝖆𝖓𝖉 𝕸𝖆𝖘𝖙𝖊𝖗 of *Masons*, who appointed 𝕵𝖔𝖍𝖓 𝖂𝖆𝖗𝖉, Efq; to continue Deputy Grand Mafter, Lord 𝕲𝖊𝖔𝖗𝖌𝖊 𝕲𝖗𝖆𝖍𝖆𝖒, ⎰ *Grand* ⎱ and continued the 𝕾𝖊𝖈𝖗𝖊𝖙𝖆𝖗𝖞 Capt. *Andrew Robinfon*, ⎱ *Wardens.* ⎰ and *Sword-bearer.* *

Brother *Revis* the *Secretary* declin'd the Office of *Treafurer*; becaufe, he faid, that one Perfon fhould not take upon him both *Offices*, for that the One fhould be a *Check* upon the Other.

— 𝕲𝖗𝖆𝖓𝖉 𝕷𝖔𝖉𝖌𝖊 in *Due* Form at the *Devil* forefaid on *Wednefday* 28 *June* 1738.

Lord GEORGE GRAHAM, S. G. W. in the Chair, as *Grand Mafter*, 𝖂𝖎𝖑𝖑𝖎𝖆𝖒 𝕲𝖗𝖆𝖊𝖒𝖊, M. D. as D. G. *Mafter* pro tempore, Capt. *Andrew Robinfon* as fen. ⎰ *Grand* ⎱ with former *Grand* Mr. *Benjamin Gafcoyne* as jun. ⎱ *Warden.* ⎰ Officers, the *Stewards* Lodge, the *prefent* Stewards and the *Officers* of 61 Lodges.

The Minutes of the laft *Quarterly* Communication and of the *Committe* of Charity were read and approved. Moft of the Time was fpent in receiving the *Charity* of the *Lodges*, and in relieving poor Brothers.

Brother *Revis* the *Secretary* having declin'd the Office of *Treafurer*, the *Lodge* defired him to act as fuch, till One to their Mind can be found.

---

* STEWARDS that acted at the *Feaft* on 27 *April* 1738. and were publickly thank'd.

1. Capt. *Andrew Robinfon.*
2. *Robert Foy*, Efq; ⎰
3. *James Colquhon*, ⎱ Efq;
4. *William Chapman*, ⎰
5. Mr. *Mofes Mendez*,
6. Mr. *George Monkman*,
7. *Stephen Beaumont*, M. D.
8. Mr. *Stephen Le Bas*,
9. Mr. *Henry Higden*,
10. Mr. *Chriftopher Taylor*,
11. Mr. *Simon de Charmes.*
12. Mr. *Harry Leigh.*

The old Stewards named their Succeffors for next Annual Feaft, *viz.* Hon. *John Chichefter*, Efq; Capt. *Charles Fitzroy*, *John Giff*, Efq; *Nathaniel Oldham*, Efq; Mr. *Alexander Pollock*, Surgeon, Mr. *Richard Robinfon*, Confectioner, Mr. *Henry Robinfon*, Mr. *Ifaac Barrett*, Mr. *Samuel Lowman*, Mr. *Edward Mafters*, Mr. *Thomas Adamfon*, Mr. *Jofeph Harris.* A Lift

A *List* of the GRAND MASTERS or *Patrons* of the 𝔉𝔯𝔢𝔢 𝔐𝔞𝔰𝔬𝔫𝔰 in *England*, from the Coming in of the *Anglo-Saxons* to thefe Times, who are mention'd in this Book.

— AUSTIN the *Monk*, the firf *Archbifhop* of *Canterbury*, appear'd at the Head of the *Craft* ir founding the *old Cathedral*, unde *Ethelbert* King of *Kent.*   Page 61

—BENNET Abbot of *Wirrall* undei *Kenred* King of *Mercia* (call'd by Miftake in this Book *Ethelbert*) whc wrote to *Charles Martel.*   62

—St. SWITHIN under the *Saxon* King *Ethelwolph.*   *Ibid*

—King ALFRED the Great.   *Ibid.*

—ETHRED the Deputy King of *Mercia*,
—Prince ETHELWARD the Learned, both under King *Edward* Senior.   63

—Prince EDWIN under his Brother King *Athelftan.*   *Ibid.*

—St. DUNSTAN Archbifhop of *Canterbury* under King *Edgar.*   65

—King EDWARD the *Confeffor*, and
—LEOFRICK Earl of *Coventry.*   66

—ROGER de *Montgomery* Earl of *Arundel*, and
—GUNDULPH Bifhop of *Rochefter*, both under King *William* I. the Conqueror, and alfo under King *William* II. *Rufus.*   67

—King HENRY I. *Beauclerk.*   68

—GILBERT DE CLARE Marquis of *Pembroke* under King *Stephen.*   *Ibid.*

—The GRAND MASTERS of the *Knights* 𝔗𝔢𝔪𝔭𝔩𝔞𝔯𝔰 under King *Henry* II.   Page 69

—PETER de *Cole-Church*, and
—WILLIAM ALMAIN, under King *John.*   *Ibid.*

—PETER de *Rupibus*, and
—GEOFFREYFITZPETER, under King *Henry* III.   *Ibid.*

—WALTER GIFFARD Archbifhop of *York*,
—GILBERT de CLARE Earl of *Glocefter*,
—RALPH Lord of *Mount-Hermer*, all under King *Edward* I.   *Ibid.*

—WALTER STAPLETON Bifhop of *Exeter* under K. *Edward* II.   70

—King EDWARD III. and under him.

—JOHN de SPOULEE Mafter of the 𝔊𝔥𝔦𝔟𝔩𝔦𝔪,
—WILLIAM a WICKHAM Bifhop of *Winchefter*,
—ROBERT a BARNHAM,
—HENRY YEUELE the King's *Free-Mafon*,
—SIMON LANGHAM Abbot of *Weftminfter*, alfo under King *Richard* II.   72   *Ibid.*

—THOMAS FITZ-ALLAN Earl of *Surrey* under King *Henry* IV.   73

—HENRY

I. JOHN

THE

THE OLD
CHARGES

OF THE

FREE and Accepted MASONS,

Collected by the *Author* from their old *Records*, at the Command of the *Grand Master* the present Duke of MONTAGU.

Approved by the 𝕲𝖗𝖆𝖓𝖉 𝕷𝖔𝖉𝖌𝖊, and order'd to be printed in the first Edition of the *Book* of *Constitutions* on 25 *March* 1722.

I. CHARGE. *Concerning* GOD *and Religion.*

 MASON is obliged by his Tenure to observe the Moral Law, as a true *Noachida*; and if he rightly understands the *Craft*, he will never be a Stupid Atheist, nor an Irreligious Libertin, nor act against Conscience.

In antient Times the *Christian Masons* were charged to comply with the *Christian* Usages of each Country where they travell'd or work'd : But *Masonry* being found in all Nations, even of divers Religions, they are now only charged to adhere to that Religion in which all Men agree (leaving each Brother to his

own

own particular Opinions) that is, to be Good Men and True, Men of Honour and Honesty, by whatever Names, Religions or Persuasions they may be distinguish'd: For they all agree in the 3 great *Articles* of NOAH, enough to preserve the Cement of the Lodge. Thus *Masonry* is the Center of their Union and the happy Means of conciliating Persons that otherwise must have remain'd at a perpetual Distance.

II. CHARGE. Of the *Civil* 𝕸𝖆𝖌𝖎𝖘𝖙𝖗𝖆𝖙𝖊, *Supreme* and *Subordinate.*

A *Mason* is a peaceable Subject, never to be concern'd in Plots against the State, nor disrespectful to *Inferior* Magistrates. Of old, Kings, Princes and States encourag'd the Fraternity for their *Loyalty*, who ever flourish'd most in Times of Peace. But tho' a *Brother* is not to be countenanced in his *Rebellion* against the State ; yet if convicted of no other Crime, his Relation to the *Lodge* remains indefeasible.

III. CHARGE. Concerning 𝕷𝖔𝖉𝖌𝖊𝖘.

A LODGE is a Place where *Masons* meet to work in : Hence the *Assembly*, or duly organiz'd Body of *Masons*, is call'd a LODGE ; just as the Word *Church* is expressive both of the *Congregation* and of the *Place* of Worship.

Every Brother should belong to some *particular Lodge*, and cannot be absent without incurring Censure, if not necessarily detain'd.

The Men made *Masons* must be *Freeborn* (or no Bondmen) of mature Age and of good Report, hail and sound, not deform'd or dismember'd at the Time of their making. But no *Woman*, no *Eunuch*.

When Men of *Quality*, Eminence, Wealth and Learning apply to be made, they are to be respectfully accepted, after due Examination : For such often prove Good *Lords* (or Founders) of Work, and will not employ *Cowans* when true *Masons* can be had ; they also make the best *Officers* of *Lodges*, and the best
Designers,

Designers, to the Honour and Strength of the *Lodge* : Nay, from among them, the *Fraternity* can have a *Noble* 𝕲𝖗𝖆𝖓𝖉 𝕸𝖆𝖘𝖙𝖊𝖗. But thofe Brethren are equally fubject to the *Charges* and *Regulations*, except in what more immediately concerns Operative *Mafons*.

IV. CHARGE. Of 𝕸𝖆𝖘𝖙𝖊𝖗𝖘, 𝖂𝖆𝖗𝖉𝖊𝖓𝖘, *Fellows* and *Prentices*.

All Preferment among *Mafons* is grounded upon real Worth and perfonal *Merit* only, not upon *Seniority*. No MASTER fhould take a *Prentice* that is not the Son of honeft Parents, a perfect Youth without Maim or Defect in his Body, and capable of learning the *Myfteries* of the *Art* ; that fo the *Lords* (or Founders) may be well ferved, and the *Craft* not defpifed ; and that, when of Age and Expert, he may become an *Enter'd Prentice*, or a *Free-Mafon* of the loweft Degree, and upon his due Improvements a *Fellow-Craft* and a *Mafter-Mafon*, capable to undertake a *Lord*'s Work.

The WARDENS are chofen from among the *Mafter-Mafons*, and no Brother can be a *Mafter* of a *Lodge* till he has acted as *Warden* fomewhere, except in extraordinary Cafes ; or when a *Lodge* is to be form'd where none fuch can be had : For then 3 *Mafter-Mafons*, tho' never *Mafters* or *Wardens* of Lodges before, may be conftituted *Mafter* and *Wardens* of that *New Lodge*.

But no Number without 3 *Mafter-Mafons* can form a *Lodge* ; and none can be the GRAND MASTER or a GRAND WARDEN who has not acted as the *Mafter* of a *particular* Lodge.

V. CHARGE. Of the 𝕸𝖆𝖓𝖆𝖌𝖊𝖒𝖊𝖓𝖙 *of the* Craft *in Working.*

All *Mafons* fhould work hard and honeftly on Working-Days, that they may live reputably on Holy-Days ; and the Working-Hours appointed by Law, or confirm'd by Cuftom, fhall be obferv'd.

A *Mafter-Mafon* only muft be the Surveyor or *Mafter of Work*, who fhall undertake the *Lord*'s Work reafonably, fhall truly

U   difpend

difpend his Goods as if they were his own, and fhall not give more Wages than juft to any *Fellow* or *Prentice.*

The *Wardens* fhall be true both to *Mafter* and *Fellows*, taking Care of all Things, both within and without the *Lodge*, efpecially in the *Mafter's* Abfence; and their Brethren fhall obey them.

The *Mafter* and the *Mafons* fhall faithfully finifh the *Lord's* Work, whether *Tafk* or *Journey*; nor fhall take the Work at *Tafk* which hath been accuftomed to *Journey.*

None fhall fhew Envy at a Brother's Profperity, nor fupplant him or put him out of his Work, if capable to finifh it.

All *Mafons* fhall meekly receive their Wages without Murmuring or Mutiny, and not defert the *Mafter* till the *Lord's* Work is finifh'd: They muft avoid ill Language, calling each Other *Brother* or *Fellow*, with much Courtefy, both within and without the *Lodge.* They fhall inftruct a younger Brother to become bright and expert, that the *Lord's* Materials may not be fpoiled.

But *Free* and Accepted *Mafons* fhall not allow *Cowans* to work with them; nor fhall they be employ'd by *Cowans* without an urgent Neceffity: And even in that Cafe they muft not teach *Cowans*, but muft have a *feparate* Communication.

No *Labourer* fhall be employ'd in the proper Work of *Free-Mafons.*

VI. CHARGE. Concerning *Mafons* 𝕭𝖊𝖍𝖆𝖛𝖎𝖔𝖚𝖗.

1. 𝕭𝖊𝖍𝖆𝖛𝖎𝖔𝖚𝖗 in the *Lodge* before *Clofing.*

You muft not hold private Committees or feparate Converfation without Leave from the *Mafter*; nor talk of any Thing impertinent; nor interrupt the *Mafter* or *Wardens*, or any Brother fpeaking to the *Chair*; nor act ludicroufly while the *Lodge* is engaged in what is ferious and folemn: But you are to pay due Reverence to the *Mafter, Wardens* and *Fellows*, and put them to worfhip.

Every Brother found guilty of a Fault fhall ftand to the *Award* of the *Lodge*, unlefs he appeals to the *Grand Lodge*; or unlefs a

Lord's

Lord's Work is retarded: For then a particular Reference may be made.

No private Piques, no Quarrels about Nations, Families, Religions or Politicks muſt be brought within the Door of the Lodge: For as *Maſons*, we are of the oldeſt *Catholick Religion* above hinted, and of all Nations upon the *Square*, *Level* and *Plumb*; and like our Predeceſſors in all Ages, we are reſolv'd againſt political Diſputes, as contrary to the Peace and Welfare of the *Lodge*.

2. 𝕭𝖊𝖍𝖆𝖛𝖎𝖔𝖚𝖗 *after the* Lodge *is cloſed and the* Brethren *not gone,*

You may enjoy yourſelves with innocent Mirth, treating one another according to Ability, but avoiding all Exceſs; not forcing any Brother to eat or drink beyond his own Inclination (according to the Old Regulation *-of King AHA-|¯¯¯¯¯¯¯¯¯¯¯¯¯¯ SHUERUS) nor hindering him from going home when he pleaſes: For tho' after *Lodge Hours* you are like other Men, yet the Blame of your Exceſs may be thrown upon the *Fraternity*, tho' unjuſtly.

* Page 24. Line 1.

3. 𝕭𝖊𝖍𝖆𝖛𝖎𝖔𝖚𝖗 *at meeting without* Strangers, *but not in a* Formed *Lodge.*

You are to ſalute one another as you have been or ſhall be inſtructed, freely communicating Hints of Knowledge, but without diſcloſing *Secrets*, unleſs to thoſe that have given long Proof of their Taciturnity and Honour; and without derogating from the Reſpect due to any Brother, were he not a Maſon: For tho' all *Brothers* and *Fellows* are upon the *Level*, yet *Maſonry* diveſts no Man of the Honour due to him before he was made a *Maſon*, or that ſhall become his Due afterwards; nay rather, it adds to his Reſpect, teaching us *to give Honour to whom it is due,* eſpecially to a *Noble* or Eminent *Brother*, whom we ſhould diſtinguiſh from all of his Rank or Station, and ſerve him readily, according to our Ability.

U 2   4. 𝕭𝖊𝖍𝖆𝖛𝖎𝖔𝖚𝖗

4. 𝕭𝖊𝖍𝖆𝖛𝖎𝖔𝖚𝖗 *in Presence of Strangers not* Masons.

You must be cautious in your Words, Carriage and Motions; that so the most penetrating Stranger may not be able to discover what is not proper to be intimated : and the impertinent or insnaring Questions, or ignorant Discourse of Strangers must be prudently manag'd by *Free-Masons*.

5. 𝕭𝖊𝖍𝖆𝖛𝖎𝖔𝖚𝖗 *at* Home *and in your Neighbourhood.*

Masons ought to be Moral Men, as above charged; consequently good Husbands, good Parents, good Sons, and good Neighbours, not staying too long from Home and avoiding all Excess; yet wise Men too, for certain Reasons known to them.

6. 𝕭𝖊𝖍𝖆𝖛𝖎𝖔𝖚𝖗 *towards a* foreign Brother *or* Stranger.

You are cautiously to examine him, as Prudence shall direct you; that you may not be imposed upon by a *Pretender*, whom you are to reject with Derision, and beware of giving him any Hints. But if you discover him to be true and faithful, you are to respect him as a *Brother*; and if in want, you are to relieve him, if you can; or else to direct him how he may be reliev'd: you must employ him, if you can; or else recommend him to be employ'd; but you are not charg'd to do beyond Ability.

7. 𝕭𝖊𝖍𝖆𝖛𝖎𝖔𝖚𝖗 *behind a Brother's* Back *as well as before his* Face.

Free and Accepted *Masons* have been ever charged to avoid all Slandering and Backbiting of a true and faithful Brother, or talking disrespectfully of his Person or Performances; and all Malice or unjust Resentment: Nay you must not suffer any others to reproach an honest Brother, but shall defend his Character as far as is consistent with Honour, Safety and Prudence; tho' no farther.

VII. CHARGE.

VII. CHARGE. Concerning Law-Suits.

IF a Brother do you Injury, apply firſt to your own or his *Lodge* ; and if you are not ſatisfy'd, you may appeal to the *Grand Lodge* ; but you muſt never take a legal Courſe till the Cauſe cannot be otherwiſe decided: For if the Affair is only between *Maſons* and about *Maſonry*, Law-Suits ought to be prevented by the good Advice of prudent Brethren, who are the beſt Referees of ſuch Differences.

But if that Reference is either impracticable or unſuccesful, and the Affair muſt be brought into the Courts of *Law* or *Equity* ; yet ſtill you muſt avoid all Wrath, Malice and Rancour in carrying on the Suit, not ſaving nor doing any Thing that may hinder either the Continuance or the Renewal of Brotherly Love and Friendſhip, which is the *Glory* and *Cement* of this antient *Fraternity* ; that we may ſhew to all the World the benign Influence of *Maſonry*, as all wiſe, *true* and *faithful*, Brothers have done from the Beginning of Time, and will do till *Architecture* ſhall be diſſolved in the general Conflagration.

A M E N ! So mote it be !

All theſe *Charges* you are to obſerve, and alſo Thoſe that ſhall be communicated unto you in a Way that cannot be written.

The *Antient* Manner of Conſtituting a *Lodge*,

A New Lodge, for avoiding many Irregularities, ſhould be ſolemnly *Conſtituted* by the *Grand Maſter* with his *Deputy* and *Wardens* : Or in the G. *Maſter's* Abſence, the Deputy acts for his *Worſhip*, the Senior G. Warden as *Deputy*, the *Junior* G. Warden as the *Senior*, and a preſent *Maſter of a Lodge* as the *Junior*.

Or if the *Deputy* is alſo abſent, the *Grand Maſter* may depute either of his G. Wardens, who can appoint Others to be G. *Officers* pro tempore.

The

The Lodge being open'd, and the *Candidates*, or the *New Master* and *Wardens* being yet among the *Fellow Crafts*, the G. Master shall afk his *Deputy*, if he has examin'd them, and finds the *Candidate Mafter* well fkill'd in the Noble *Science* and the Royal *Art*, and duly inftructed in our *Myfteries*? &c.

The Deputy anfwering in the Affirmative, shall (by the G. *Mafter's* Order) take the *Candidate* from among his *Fellows* and prefent him to the G. *Mafter*, faying, *Right Worfhipful* GRAND MASTER, *the Brethren here defire to be form'd into a* Lodge; *and I prefent my worthy Brother A. B. to be their* Mafter, *whom I know to be of good Morals and great Skill, true and trufty, and a Lover of the whole* Fraternity *wherefoever difpers'd over the Face of the Earth.*

Then the Grand Mafter placing the Candidate on his Left Hand, having afk'd and obtain'd the unanimous Confent of the Brethren, shall fay, *I conftitute and form thefe good Brethren into a* New Lodge, *and appoint you Brother A. B. the* Mafter *of it, not doubting of your Capacity and Care to preferve the* Cement *of the* Lodge, &c. with fome other Expreffions that are proper and ufual on that Occafion, but not proper to be written.

Upon this the *Deputy* shall rehearfe the *Charges* of a *Mafter*; and the Grand Mafter shall afk the *Candidate*, faying, *Do you fubmit to thefe Charges, as Mafters have done in all Ages?* And the *New* Mafter fignifying his Cordial Submiffion thereunto,

The Grand Mafter shall by certain fignificant Ceremonies and antient Ufages, inftal him and prefent him with the *Book* of *Conftitutions*, the *Lodge-Book* and the *Inftruments* of his Office; not altogether, but one after another; and after each of 'em the G. *Mafter* or his *Deputy* shall rehearfe the fhort and pithy Charge that is fuitable to the Thing prefented.

Next, the *Members* of this NEW LODGE, bowing all together to the G. *Mafter*, shall return his Worfhip their Thanks; and shall immediately do *Homage* to their *New Mafter*, and fignify their Promife of Subjection and Obedience to him by the ufual Congratulation.

The

The *Deputy* and *G. Wardens* and any other Brethren prefent that are not Members of this *New Lodge*, fhall next congratulate the NEW MASTER, and he fhall return his becoming Acknowledgments to the *G. Mafter* firft, and to the Reft in their Order.

Then the 𝕲𝖗𝖆𝖓𝖉 𝕸𝖆𝖘𝖙𝖊𝖗 orders the *New Mafter* to enter immediately upon the Exercife of his Office, *viz.* in chufing his *Wardens*: And calling forth two *Fellow-Crafts (Mafter-Mafons)* prefents them to the *G. Mafter* for his Approbation, and to the *New Lodge* for their Confent. Upon which

The *Senior* or *Junior* G. 𝕿𝖆𝖗𝖉𝖊𝖓, or fome Brother for him, fhall rehearfe the Charges of each *Warden* of a private Lodge: And they fignifying their cordial Submiffion thereunto,

The NEW MASTER fhall prefent them fingly with the feveral *Inftruments* of their Office, and in due Form inftal them in their proper Places: And the Brethren of this *New Lodge* fhall fignify their Obedience to thofe NEW WARDENS by the ufual Congratulation.

Then the *G. Mafter* gives all the Brethren Joy of their *New Mafter* and *Wardens*, and recommends Harmony; hoping their only Contention will be a laudable Emulation in cultivating the Royal *Art* and the Social *Virtues.*

Upon which all the *New Lodge* bow together in returning Thanks for the Honour of this CONSTITUTION.

The 𝕲𝖗𝖆𝖓𝖉 𝕸𝖆𝖘𝖙𝖊𝖗 alfo orders the *Secretary* to regifter this *New Lodge* in the *Grand Lodge Book*, and to notify the fame to the other particular *Lodges*; and after the *Mafter's Song* he orders the *G. Warden* to clofe the *Lodge.*

This is the Sum, but not the whole *Ceremonial* by far;. which the *Grand Officers* can extend or abridge at Pleafure, explaining Things that are not fit to be written : tho' none but Thofe that have acted as *Grand Officers* can accurately go through all the feveral Parts and Ufages of a new Conftitution in the juft Solemnity.

THE

The General REGULATIONS

OF THE

FREE and *Accepted* MASONS.

Compiled firſt by Brother GEORGE PAYNE, Eſq; when *Grand Maſter*, A. D. 1720. and approv'd by the General *Aſſembly* at *Stationers-Hall* on 24 *June* 1721. Next by Order of the *Duke* of MONTAGU when *Grand Maſter*, the Author James Anderſon compared them with the antient Records of the *Fraternity*, and digeſted them into this Method with proper Additions and Explications from the ſaid *Records* ; and the *Grand Lodge* having revis'd and approv'd them, order'd 'em to be printed in the *Book* of *Conſtitutions* on 25 *March* 1722.

To which are now added, in a diſtinct oppoſite Column.

The New REGULATIONS, or the Alterations, Improvements and Explica-tions of the Old, made by ſeveral *Grand Lodges*, ſince the *firſt* Edition.

OLD REGULATIONS.

New REGULATIONS.

I. THE G. *Maſter* or *Deputy* has full Authority and Right, not only to be preſent, but alſo to preſide in every Lodge, with the *Maſter* of the Lodge on his Left Hand ;

I. * THAT is, only when the G. WARDENS are abſent : For the G. *Maſter* cannot deprive 'em of their Office, without ſhewing Cauſe fairly appearing to the G. *Lodge* ac-cording to the *Old Regulation* XVIII. ſo that if they are preſent in a *particular Lodge*

Hand ; and to order his *Grand Wardens* to attend him, who are not to act as *Wardens* of *particular Lodges* but in his Prefence and at his Command: For the *G. Mafter*, while in a *particular Lodge*, may command the *Wardens* of *that Lodge*, or any Other *Mafter-Mafons*, to act there as his *Wardens* pro tempore. *

II. The MASTER of a *particular* Lodge has the Right and Authority of congregating the *Members* of his Lodge into a *Chapter* upon any Emergency or Occurrence ; as well as to appoint the Time and Place of their ufual *Forming :* And in Cafe of Death or Sicknefs, or neceffary Abfence of the *Mafter*, the SENIOR WARDEN fhall act as *Mafter* pro tempore, if no Brother is prefent who has been *Mafter* of that *Lodge* before : For the *Abfent Mafter's* Authority reverts to the *laft Mafter prefent*, tho' he cannot act till the *Senior Warden* has congregated the *Lodge.*

III. The

Lodge with the *Grand Mafter*, they muft act as WARDENS there.

On 17 *March* 173⁰⁄₁.

The *Grand Lodge*, to cure fome Irregularities, order'd, that None but the *G. Mafter*, his *Deputy* and *Wardens* (who are the only *Grand Officers*) fhall wear their *Jewels* in *Gold* pendant to *Blue Ribbons* about their Necks, and *White Leather* Aprons with *Blue Silk* ; which Sort of *Aprons* may be alfo worn by *former G. Officers.*

II. On 25 *Nov.* 1723.

It was agreed, that if a *Mafter* of a particular *Lodge* is depofed or demits, the *Senior Warden* fhall forthwith fill the the *Mafter's* Chair till the next Time of chufing ; and ever fince, in the *Mafter's* Abfence, he fills the Chair, even tho' a *former Mafter* be prefent.

> But was neglected to be recorded.

On 17 *March* 173⁰⁄₁.

Mafters and *Wardens* of *particular* Lodges may line their *white* Leather *Aprons* with white Silk, and may hang their *Jewels* at *white* Ribbons about their Necks.

III. In

X

Old Regulations.

III. The *Master* of each particular *Lodge,* or one of the *Wardens,* or some Other Brother by Appointment of the *Master,* shall keep a Book containing their *By-Laws,* the *Names* of their Members, and a List of all the *Lodges* in Town ; with the usual Times and Places of their forming : And also all the Transactions of their own Lodge that are proper to be written.

IV. No *Lodge* shall make more than *Five New* Brothers at one and the same Time without an urgent Necessity ; nor any Man under the Age of 25 Years (who must be also his own Master) unless by a *Dispensation* from the G. *Master.*

V. No Man can be accepted a *Member* of a *particular* Lodge without previous Notice *one Month* before given to the *Lodge* ; in order to make due Enquiry into the Reputation and Capacity of the Candidate, unless by a *Dispensation.* VI. But

New Regulations.

III. In the Mastership of DALKEITH, a List of *all* the *Lodges* was engraven by Brother *John Pyne* in a very small Volume ; which is usually reprinted on the Commencement of every *New Grand Master,* and dispersed among the Brethren.

On 21 *Nov.* 1724.

If a *particular* Lodge remove to a *New Place* for their stated Meeting, the *Officers* shall immediately signify the same to the *Secretary.*

On 27 *Dec.* 1727.

The *Precedency* of *Lodges* is grounded on the Seniority of their *Constitution.*

On 27 *Dec.* 1729.

Every *New Lodge,* for the Future, shall pay two *Guineas* for their *Constitution* to the General *Charity.*

IV. On 19 *Feb.* 172¾. No Brother shall belong to more than *one Lodge* within the Bills of Mortality (tho' he may visit them all) except the Members of a *foreign* Lodge.

But this *Regulation* is neglected for several Reasons, and now obsolete.

V. The *Secretary* can direct the Petitioners in the *Form* for a *Dispensation,* if wanted. But if they know the Candidate, they don't require a Dispensation. VI. On

Old REGULATIONS.

VI. But no Man can be enter'd a *Brother* in any *particular* Lodge, or admitted a *Member* thereof, without the *unanimous Consent* of *all* the Members of that *Lodge* then present when the *Candidate* is proposed, and when their Consent is formally asked by the *Master*. They are to give their Consent in their own prudent Way, either virtually or in Form, but with *Unanimity*. Nor is this inherent Privilege subject to a *Dispensation*; because the Members of a *particular* Lodge are the best Judges of it; and because if a *turbulent* Member should be imposed on them, it might spoil their Harmony or hinder the Freedom of their Communication, or even break and disperse the *Lodge*, which ought to be avoided by *all True* and *Faithful*.

VII. Every *New* Brother, at his *Entry*, is decently to *clothe the Lodge*, that is, all the Brethren present; and to deposite something for the Relief of indigent and decay'd Brethren, as the *Candidate* shall think fit to bestow, over and above the small Allowance that may be stated in the *By-Laws* of that *particular* Lodge: Which *Charity* shall be kept by the Cashier. *

Also the *Candidate* shall solemnly promise to submit to the *Constitutions* and other good Usages, that shall be intimated to him in Time and Place convenient.

New REGULATIONS.

VI. On 19 *Feb.* 172¾. No *Visitor*, however skill'd in Masonry, shall be admitted into a *Lodge*, unless he is personally known to, or well vouched and recommended by one of that Lodge present.

But it was found inconvenient to insist upon *Unanimity* in several Cases: And therefore the *Grand Masters* have allow'd the *Lodges* to admit a Member, if not above 3 *Ballots* are against him; though some *Lodges* desire no such *Allowance*.

VII. * See this explain'd in the Account of the *Constitution* of the *General Charity* below.

Only *particular* Lodges are not limited, but may take their own Method for *Charity*.

Old Regulations.

VIII. No Set or Number of Brethren shall withdraw or separate themselves from the *Lodge* in which they were made, or were afterwards admitted Members, unless the *Lodge* become too numerous; nor even then without a *Dispensation* from the G. Master or *Deputy*: And when thus separated, they must either immediately join themselves to such other *Lodges* that they shall like best, or else obtain the G. Master's *Warrant* to join in forming a *New Lodge* to be regularly constituted in good Time.

If any Set or Number of *Masons* shall take upon themselves to *form a Lodge*, without the G. Master's Warrant, the *regular* Lodges are not to countenance them, nor own them as *fair Brethren* duly formed, nor approve of their Acts and Deeds; but must treat them as *Rebels* until they humble themselves, as the G. Master shall in his Prudence direct

New Regulations.

VIII. On 25 *April* 1723.
Every Brother concern'd in making *Masons* clandestinely, shall not be allow'd to visit *any Lodge* till he has made due Submission, even tho' the Brothers so made may be allow'd.

On 19 *Feb.* 1724.
None who form a *Stated Lodge* without the G. *Master's* Leave shall be admitted into *regular* Lodges, till they make Submission and obtain Grace.

On 21 *Nov.* 1724.
If any Brethren *form a Lodge* without Leave, and shall irregularly make *New* Brothers, they shall not be admitted into any *regular* Lodge, no not as *Visitors*, till they render a good Reason or make due Submission.

On 24 *Feb.* 173⅘.
If any *Lodge* within the Bills of Mortality shall cease to meet regularly during 12 Months successive, its *Name* and *Place* shall be erazed or blotted out of the *Grand Lodge* Book and Engraven *List*: And if they petition to be again inserted and own'd as a *regular Lodge*, it must lose its former Place and Rank of *Precedency*, and submit to a *New* Constitution.

On 31 *March* 1735.
Seeing that some *extraneous* Brothers have been made lately in a clandestine Manner, that is, in no *regular* Lodge nor by any Authority or Dispensation from the G. *Master*, and upon

direct, and until he approve of them by his *Warrant* fignified to the *Other Lodges* ; as the Cuftom is when a *New Lodge* is to be regifter'd in the *Grand Lodge Book.*

IX. But if any *Brother* fo far mifbehave himfelf as to render his *Lodge* uneafy, he fhall be thrice duly admonifh'd by the *Mafter* and *Wardens* in a *Lodge formed:* And if he will not refrain his Imprudence, nor obediently fubmit to the Advice of his Brethren, he fhall be dealt with according to the *By-Laws* of that *particular* Lodge, or elfe in fuch a Manner as the *Quarterly*

---

upon fmall and unworthy Confiderations, to the Difhonour of the *Craft* ;

The *Grand Lodge* decreed, that no Perfon fo made, nor any concern'd in making him, fhall be a *Grand Officer*, nor an *Officer* of a *particular* Lodge, nor fhall any fuch partake of the General *Charity*, if they fhould come to want it.

IX. On 25 *Jan.* 173¾. The *Grand Lodge* made the following REGULATION.

Whereas Difputes have arifen about the *Removal* of *Lodges* from One Houfe to Another, and it has been queftion'd in whom that Power is vefted ; it is hereby declar'd,

That *no Lodge* fhall be removed without the *Mafter's* Knowledge ; that no Motion be made for removing in the *Mafter's* Abfence ; and that if the Motion be *feconded* or *thirded*, the *Mafter* fhall order Summons to every individual Member, fpecifying the Bufinefs, and appointing a Day for Hearing and Determining the Affair, at leaft Ten Days before : and that the Determination fhall be made by the *Majority*, provided the *Mafter* be one of *that* Majority : but if he be of the *Minority* againft Removing, the *Lodge* fhall not be removed unlefs the *Majority* confifts of full *Two Thirds* of the Members prefent.

But if the *Mafter* fhall refufe to direct fuch Summons, either of the *Wardens* may do it : and if the *Mafter* neglects to attend on the Day fix'd, the *Warden* may prefide in determining the Affair in the Manner prefcribed ; but they
fhall

Quarterly Communication shall in their great Prudence think fit; for which a *New Regulation* may be afterwards made.

shall not in the *Master's* Absence, enter upon any other Cause but what is particularly mention'd in the *Summons:* and if the *Lodge* is thus regularly order'd to be removed, the *Master* or *Warden* shall send Notice thereof to the *Secretary* of the *G. Lodge* for publishing the same at the next *Quarterly* Communication.

X. The *Majority* of every *particular* Lodge, when congregated (not else) shall have the Privilege of giving Instructions to their *Master* and *Wardens* before the meeting of the *Grand Chapter* or Quarterly *Communication*; because the said *Officers* are their Representatives, and are supposed to speak the Sentiments of their Brethren at the said *G. Lodge*.

X. Upon a sudden Emergency the *Grand Lodge* has allow'd a private Brother to be present, and with Leave ask'd and given to signify his Mind, if it was about what concern'd *Masonry*.

XI. All *particular* Lodges are to observe the same *Usages* as much as possible: in order to which, and also for cultivating a good Understanding among *Free-Masons*, some Members of every *Lodge* shall be deputed to visit the other *Lodges* as often as shall be thought convenient.

XI. The same *Usages*, for Substance, are actually observed in *every Lodge*; which is much owing to *visiting* Brothers who compare the *Usages*.

XII. The G R A N D L O D G E consists of, and is formed by, the *Masters* and *Wardens* of all the *particular* Lodges upon Record, with the G R A N D M A S T E R at their Head, the D E P U T Y on his Left Hand, and the G R A N D

XII. On 25 *Nov.* 1723.
No *New* Lodge is own'd, nor their *Officers* admitted into the *G. Lodge*, unless it be regularly constituted and register'd.

On 21 *Nov.* 1724.
All who have been or shall be *Grand Masters*, shall be Members of and vote in all *G. Lodges*.

On

Old Regulations.

Grand Wardens in their proper Places.

These muſt have 3 *Quarterly Communications*, before the *Grand Feaſt*, in ſome convenient Place, as the *Grand Maſter* ſhall appoint ; where none are to be preſent but it's own proper Members, without Leave aſked and given : And while ſuch a Stranger (tho' a *Brother*) ſtays, he is not allow'd to vote, nor even to ſpeak to any Queſtion without Leave of the *Grand Lodge* ; or unleſs he is deſir'd to give his Opinion.

All Matters in the *Grand Lodge* are to be determin'd by a *Majority* of Votes, each Member having *one Vote*, and the Grand Maſter *two Votes*; unleſs the *Lodge* leave any particular Thing to the Determination of the *Grand Maſter* for the Sake of Expedition.

XIII. At the *G. Lodge* in *Quarterly* Communication, all Matters that concern the *Fraternity* in *general*, or *particular*,

New Regulations.

On 28 *Feb.* 172⅚.

All who have been or ſhall be *D. Grand Maſters* ſhall be Members of and Vote in all *G. Lodges.*

On 10 *May* 1727.

All who have been or ſhall be *Grand Wardens* ſhall be Members of and Vote in all *G. Lodges.*

On 25 *June* 1728.

Maſters and *Wardens* of *Lodges* ſhall never attend the *G. Lodge* without their *Jewels* and *Clothing.*

On 26 *Nov.* 1728.

One of the 3 *Officers* of a *Lodge* was admitted into the *G. Lodge* without his *Jewel*, becauſe the *Jewels* were in the Cuſtody of the *Officer* abſent.

If any Officer cannot attend, he may ſend a *Brother* of that *Lodge* (but not a mere *Enter'd Prentice*) with his *Jewel*, to ſupply his Room and ſupport the Honour of his *Lodge.*

On 24 *Feb.* 173⅚.

Upon a Motion made by the former *Grand Officers*, it was reſolv'd that the *Grand Officers* preſent and former, each of 'em who ſhall attend the Grand *Lodge* in Communication (except on the *Feaſt* Day) ſhall pay *Half a Crown* towards the Charge of ſuch *Communication* when he attends.

XIII. On 13 *Dec.* 1733.

1. What Buſineſs cannot be tranſacted at *one Lodge*

particular Lodges, or *single* Brothers, are sedately and maturely to be discours'd of, 1.

Apprentices must be admitted *Fellow Crafts* and *Masters* only here, unless by a *Dispensation* from the *Grand Master*. 2.

Here also all Differences that cannot be made up or accommodated privately, nor by a *particular* Lodge, are to be seriously consider'd and decided: and if any Brother thinks himself aggrieved by the *Decision*, he may appeal to the *Annual Grand Lodge* next ensuing, and leave his *Appeal* in Writing with the G. *Master*, the *Deputy* or G. *Wardens*. 3.

Hither also all the *Officers* of *particular* Lodges shall bring a *List* of such Members as have been made, or even admitted by them since the last *Grand Lodge*.

There shall be a Book kept by the G. *Master* or *Deputy*, or rather by some Brother appointed *Secretary* of the *Grand Lodge*; wherein shall be recorded *all the Lodges*, with the usual Times and Places of their *Forming* and the *Names* of all the Members of Each *Lodge*: also all the Affairs of the G. *Lodge* that are proper to be written. 4.

The G. *Lodge* shall consider of the most prudent and effectual Method of collecting and disposing of what Money shall be lodged with them in *Charity*, towards the Relief only of any *true Brother* fallen into Poverty and Decay, but of none else.

But each *particular* Lodge may dispose of their *own Charity* for poor Brothers according

Lodge, may be referr'd to the *Committee* of *Charity*, and by them reported to the *next Grand Lodge*.

2. On 22. *Nov.* 1725.

The *Master* of a Lodge with his *Wardens* and a competent *Number* of the Lodge assembled in due Form, can make *Masters* and *Fellows* at Discretion.

3. On 25 *Nov.* 1723.

It was agreed (tho' forgotten to be recorded in the *Grand Lodge Book*) that no Petitions and Appeals shall be heard on the *Feast-Day* or *Annual* Grand *Lodge*, nor shall any Business be transacted that tends to interrupt the *Harmony* of the *Assembly*, but shall be all referr'd to the next G. *Lodge*.

4. On 24 *June* 1723.

The G. *Lodge* chose *William Cowper*, Esq; to

𝕺𝖑𝖉 Regulations.

according to their own *By-Laws* ; until it be agreed by all the *Lodges* (in a New Regulation) to carry in the *Charity* collected by them to the *G. Lodge* at the *Quarterly* or *Annual* Communication ; in order to make a *Common Stock* for the more handsome Relief of poor Brethren.

They shall also appoint a 𝕿𝖗𝖊𝖆𝖘𝖚𝖗𝖊𝖗, a Brother of good Worldly Substance, who shall be a Member of the *G. Lodge* by Virtue of his Office, and shall be always present, and have a Power to move to the *G. Lodge* any Thing that concerns his *Office.*

To him shall be committed all Money rais'd for the General *Charity*, or for any other Use of the *G. Lodge* ; which he shall write down in a *Book* with the respective Ends and Uses for which the several Sums are intended, and shall expend or disburse the same by such a certain *Order* sign'd, as the *G. Lodge* shall hereafter agree to in a *New Regulation.* 5.

But by Vertue of his Office as *Treasurer*, without any other Qualification, he shall not vote in chusing a *New G. Master* and *Wardens* ; tho' in every other Transaction.

In like Manner the 𝕾𝖊𝖈𝖗𝖊𝖙𝖆𝖗𝖞 shall be a Member of the *G. Lodge* by Vertue of his *Office*, and shall vote in every Thing except in chusing *Grand Officers.*

The *Treasurer* and *Secretary* may have each a *Clerk* or Assistant, if they think fit, who must be a Brother and a *Master-Mason* ; but must never be a *Member* of the *G. Lodge*, nor speak without being allow'd or commanded.

The Grand Master or 𝕯𝖊𝖕𝖚𝖙𝖞 have Authority always to command the *Treasurer* and *Secretary* to attend him with their *Clerks* and *Books* ; in order to see how Matters go on, and to know what is expedient to be done upon any Emergency.

Another Brother and *Master-Mason* should be appointed the *Tyler*, to look after the Door ; but he must be no Member of the *G. Lodge.*

Y

𝕹𝖊𝖜 Regulations.

to be their *Secretary.* But ever since then, the *New G. M.* upon his Commencement appoints the *Secretary*, or continues him by returning him the Books. His *Badge* is of *two Golden Pens* across on his *Left* Breast. And On 19 *Feb.* 172$\frac{3}{4}$. The *Officers* of particular *Lodges* shall bring to the *G. Lodge* the *Lists* of all the Members of their respective *Lodges* to be inserted in the *G. Lodge Book.*

But 5. See

Old Regulations.

But thefe Offices may be farther explain'd by a *New Regulation*, when the Neceffity or the Expediency of 'em may more appear, than at prefent, to the *Fraternity*.

XIV. If at any G. LODGE, ftated or Occafional, Quarterly or Annual, the *Grand Mafter* and *Deputy* fhould both be abfent; then the prefent *Mafter* of a *Lodge*, that has been longeft a *Free-Mafon*, fhall take the Chair and prefide as *Grand Mafter* pro tempore, and fhall be vefted with all his Honour and Power for the Time being; provided there is no Brother prefent that has been *Grand Mafter* or *Deputy* formerly; for the laft former *Grand Mafter* or *Deputy* in Company takes place, of Right, in the Abfence of the prefent *G. Mafter* or *Deputy*.

XV. In the G. Lodge none can act as *Wardens* but the *prefent* G. WARDENS if in Com-

New Regulations.

5. See *This* at large in the *Conftitution* of the *Committee* of *Charity*, Below.

XIV. In the *firft* Edition, the Right of the G. WARDENS was omitted in this *Regulation*; and it has been fince found that the *Old Lodges* never put into the Chair the *Mafter* of a *particular Lodge*, but when there was no *Grand Warden* in Company, *prefent* nor *former*, and that in fuch a Cafe a *Grand Officer* always took place of any *Mafter* of a *Lodge* that has not been a *G. Officer*.

Therefore in Cafe of the Abfence of all *G. Mafters* and *Deputies*, the prefent *Sen.* G. WARDEN fills the Chair, and in his Abfence the prefent *Jun.* G. WARDEN, and in his Abfence the *oldeft* former G. WARDEN in Company; and if no *former G. Officer* be found, then the *oldeft Free-Mafon* who is now the *Mafter* of a *Lodge*.

But to avoid Difputes, the *G. Mafter* ufually gives a particular Commiffion under his Hand and Seal of Office, counterfign'd by the *Secretary*, to the *Senior G. Warden*, or in his Abfence, to the *Junior*, to act as *D. G. Mafter* when the *Deputy* is not in Town.

XV. Soon after the *firft* Edition of the *Book of Conftitutions*, the GRAND LODGE finding it was always the antient Ufage that the oldeft *former* G WARDENS

Old REGULATIONS.

Company ; and if abfent, the *G. Mafter* fhall order private *Wardens* to act as *G. Wardens* pro tempore; whofe Places are to be fupplied by two *Fellow-Crafts,* or *Mafter-Mafons* of the fame *Lodge,* call'd forth to act or fent thither by the *Mafter* thereof; or if by him omitted, the G. MASTER, or *He* that prefides, fhall call 'em forth to act; that fo the *G. Lodge* may be always compleat.

XVI. The *Grand Wardens,* or any Others, are firft to advife with the *Deputy* about the Affairs of the *Lodges* or of private fingle Brothers ; and are not to apply to the *G. Mafter* without the Knowledge of the *Deputy,* unlefs he refufe his Concurrence. **1.**

In which Cafe, or in Cafe of any Difference of Sentiment between the *Deputy* and *G. Wardens* or other Brothers, both Parties are to go to the *G. Mafter* by Confent ; who, by Vertue of his great Authority and Power, can eafily decide the Controverfy and make up the Difference. **2.**

The G. Mafter fhould not receive any private Intimations of Bufinefs concerning Mafons and Mafonry but from his *Deputy* firft, except in fuch Cafes as his *Worfhip* can eafily judge of: And if the Application to the *G. Mafter* be *irregular,* his Worfhip can order the *G. Wardens,* or any Other fo applying, to wait upon the *Deputy,*

New REGULATIONS.

G. WARDENS fupplied the Places of thofe of the Year when abfent, the *G. Mafter* ever fince has order'd them to take place immediately and act as *G. Wardens* pro tempore; which they have always done in the Abfence of the *G. Wardens* for the Year, except when they have waved their Privilege for that Time, to honour fome Brother whom they thought more fit for the prefent Service.

But if no *former Grand Wardens* are in Company, the GRAND MASTER, or *He* that *prefides,* calls forth whom he pleafes to act as *Grand Wardens* pro tempore.

XVI. 1. This was intended for the Eafe of the *G. Mafter,* and for the Honour of the *Deputy.*

2. No fuch Cafe has happened in our Time; and all *Grand Mafters* have govern'd more by Love than Power.

3. No irregular Applications have been made to the G. *Mafter*

Y 2   who

Old REGULATIONS.

who is speedily to prepare the Business, and to
lay it orderly before his *Worship*. 3.

XVII. No G. *Master*, D. G. *Master*, G. *Warden*, *Treasurer*, *Secretary*, or whoever acts for them or in their Stead *pro tempore*, can, at the same Time, act as the *Master* or *Warden* of a *particular Lodge*; but as soon as any of 'em has discharg'd his publick *Office*, he returns to that Post or Station in his particular *Lodge* from which he was call'd to officiate.

XVIII. If the DEPUTY be sick or necessarily absent, the G. *Master* can chuse any Brother he pleases to act as his *Deputy* pro tempore. 1.

But he that is chosen DEPUTY at the *Annual* Feast, and also the G. WARDENS, cannot be discharg'd, unless the Cause fairly appear to the G. *Lodge*: For the G. MASTER, if he is uneasy, may call a G. *Lodge* on Purpose, to lay the Cause before 'em, for their Advice and Concurrence. 2.

And if the Members of the G. *Lodge* cannot reconcile the G. *Master* with his *Deputy* or *Wardens*, they are to allow the G. *Master* to discharge his *Deputy* or *Wardens*, and to chuse another *Deputy* immediately; and the same G. *Lodge*, in that Case, shall forthwith chuse other G. *Wardens*; that so Harmony and Peace may be preserved. 3.

XIX. If

New REGULATIONS.

Master in our Time.

XVII. *Old G. Officers* are now, some of 'em, *Officers* of *particular Lodges*; but are not thereby depriv'd of their Privilege in the *G. Lodge* to sit and vote there as *old G. Officers*: Only he deputes one of his particular *Lodge* to act *pro tempore* as the *Officer* of *that Lodge* at the *Quarterly* Communication.

XVIII. 1. The *Senior* G. WARDEN now ever supplie the DEPUTY's Place, the *Junior* acts as the SENIOR, the *oldest* former G. *Warden* a the JUNIOR, all the *oldest Mason* a above.

2. This was never done in our Time. See *New Regulation* I.

3. Should this Case ever happen, the G. MASTER appoints his G. *Officers*, as at first. See *Old Regulation* XXXV.

XIX. The

Old REGULATIONS.

New REGULATIONS.

XIX. If the G. MASTER fhould abufe his great Power, and render himfelf unworthy of the Obedience and Subjection of the *Lodges*, he fhall be treated in a Way and Manner to be agreed upon in a *New Regulation*: Becaufe hitherto the antient *Fraternity* have had no Occafion for it.

XIX. The *Free-Mafons* firmly hope that there never will be any Occafion for fuch a *New Regulation*.

XX. The G. MASTER with his *Deputy*, G. *Wardens* and *Secretary*, fhall, at leaft *once*, go round and vifit *all the Lodges* about Town during his *Mafterfhip*.

XX. Or elfe he fhall fend his G. *Officers* to vifit the *Lodges*. This old and laudable Practice often renders a *Deputy* neceffary: And when he vifits them, the *Senior* G. WARDEN acts as *Deputy* the *Junior* as the SENIOR, as above: Or if both or any of 'em be abfent, the DEPUTY, or *he* that *prefides* for him, may appoint whom he pleafes in their Stead *pro tempore*.

For when both the G. *Mafters* are abfent, the *Senior* or the *Junior* G. *Warden* may prefide as *Deputy* in vifiting the *Lodges*, or in the *Conftitution* of a *New Lodge*; neither of which can be done without, at leaft, *one* of the *prefent G. Officers*.

XXI. If the G. MASTER die during his *Mafterfhip*, or by Sicknefs, or by being beyond'Sea, or any other Way fhould be render'd uncapable of difcharging his Office, the *Deputy*, or in his Abfence the *Senior* G. WARDEN, or in his Abfence the *Junior* G. WARDEN, or in his Abfence any 3 prefent *Mafters* of *Lodges*, fhall affemble the G. *Lodge* immediately; in order to advife together upon that Emergency, and to fend two of their Number to invite the *laft* G. MASTER to refume his Office, which now of Courfe reverts to him: And if he refufe to act, then the *next Laft*, and fo backward.

XXI. Upon fuch a Vacancy, if no *former* G. MASTER nor *former* DEPUTY be found, the prefent *Senior* G. WARDEN fills the Chair, or in his Abfence the *Junior* till a *N. G. Mafter* is chofen: And if no prefent nor former G. *Warden* be found, then the *Oldeft Free-Mafon* who

Old Regulations.   **New** Regulations.

ward. But if no *former* G. Master be found, the who is now *present* Deputy shall act as Principal till a *New* the *Master* of G. *Master* is chosen: Or if there be no *Deputy*, then a *Lodge.* the *oldest Mason* the present *Master* of a *Lodge.*

XXII. The *Brethren* of *all the Lodges* in and about *London* and *Westminster*, shall meet *annually* in some convenient Place or publick Hall. **1.**

They shall assemble either on St. John *Evangelist's* Day or St. John *Baptist's* Day, as the G. *Lodge* shall think fit by a *New Regulation*; having of late Years met on St. John *Baptist's* Day. **2.**

Provided the *Majority* of the G. *Lodge*, about *Three* Months before, shall agree that there shall be a *Feast* and a general *Communication* of *all the Brethren:* For if they are against it, others must forbear it at that Time.

But whether there shall be a *Feast* or not for all the Brethren, yet the G. *Lodge* must meet in some convenient Place on St. John's Day; or if it be a *Sunday*, then on the next Day, in order to chuse or recognize every Year a *New* G. *Master*, *Deputy* and *Wardens.*

XXII. **1.** Or any *Brethren* round the Globe, who are *True* and *Faithful*, at the Place appointed, till they have built a Place of their own.

2. The *annual Feast* has been held on both the St. John's Days, as the G. *Master* thought fit. And

On 25 *Nov.* 1723. it was ordain'd that one of the *Quarterly Communications* shall be held on St. John *Evangelist's* Day, and another on St. John *Baptist's* Day every Year, whether there be a *Feast* or not, unless the G. *Master* find it inconvenient for the Good of the *Craft*, which is more to be regarded than Days.

But of late Years, most of the *Eminent* Brethren being out of Town on both the St. John's Days, the G. *Master* has appointed the *Feast* on such a Day as appeared most convenient to the *Fraternity.*

On 29 *January* 173⁰⁄₁.

It was ordain'd that no *particular Lodge* shall have a *separate Feast* on the Day of the General *Feast.*

XXIII. If.   XXIII. The

Old REGULATIONS.

XXIII. If the G. MASTER and *Lodge* fhall think it expedient to hold the *Annual General Affembly* and *Feaft*, according to the antient and laudable Cuftom of *Mafons*; then the G. WARDENS fhall have the Care of preparing *Tickets* feal'd with the G. *Mafter's Seal* of *Office*, of difpofing the *Tickets*, of buying the Materials of the *Feaft*, of finding out a proper and convenient Place to feaft in, and of every other Thing that concerns the Entertainment.

But that the Work may not be too burdenfome to the *Two Grand Wardens*, and that all Matters may be expeditioufly and fafely

New REGULATIONS

XXIII. The GRAND WARDENS were antiently affifted by a certain Number of *Stewards* at every Feaft, or by fome general Undertaker of the Whole.

On 28 *April* 1724. the G. Lodge ordain'd, that at the Feaft, the *Stewards* fhall open no Wine till Dinner be laid on the Tables; that the *Members* of *each Lodge* fhall fit together as much as poffible: That after *Eight a Clock* at Night, the *Stewards* fhall not be oblig'd to furnifh any Wine or other Liquors; and that either the *Money* or *Tickets* fhail be return'd to the *Stewards*.

On 26 *November* 1728. The *Office* of STEWARDS, that had been difufed at 3 preceding *Feafts*, was revived by the G. *Lodge*, and their Number to be always 12. who, together with the G. WARDENS, fhall prepare the *Feaft*.

On 17 *March* 173⁹⁄₁₀. The STEWARDS for the Year were allow'd to have *Jewels* of Silver (tho' not guilded) pendent to *Red* Ribbons about their Necks, to bear *White* Rods, and to line their *White* Leather *Aprons* with *Red* Silk.

Former Stewards were alfo allow'd to wear the fame Sort of Aprons, *White* and *Red*.

On 2d *March* 173½. The G. Lodge allow'd each of the acting STEWARDS for the future, at the *Feaft*, the Privilege of Naming his Succeffor in that Office for the Year enfuing.

On 24 *June* 1735. Upon an Addrefs from Thofe that have been STEWARDS, the G. *Lodge*, in Confideration of their paft Service and future Ufefulnefs, ordain'd,

1. That

Old Regulations.

safely managed, the *G. Master* or his *Deputy* shall have Power to nominate and appoint a certain Number of Stewards, as his *Worship* shall think fit, to act in Concert with the *two* G Wardens: And all Things relating to the *Feast* shall be decided amongst 'em by a *Majority* of Votes; except the *G. Master* or his *Deputy* interpose by a particular Direction or Appointment.

New Regulations.

1. That they should be constituted a *Lodge* of *Masters*, to be call'd the Stewards Lodge, to be register'd as such in the *Grand Lodge Books* and printed *List*, with the Times and Place of their Meetings.

2. That the Stewards Lodge shall have the Privilege of sending a Deputation of 12 to every *G. Lodge*, viz. the *Master*, *Two Wardens* and *Nine* more, and *Each* of the 12 shall vote there, and *Each* of 'em that attends shall pay *Half a Crown*, towards the Expence of the *G. Lodge*.

3. That no Brother who has not been a *Steward* shall wear the same Sort of *Aprons* and *Ribbons*.

4. That each of the 12 *Deputies* from the *Stewards Lodge* shall, in the *G. Lodge*, wear a peculiar *Jewel* suspended in the *Red* Ribbon; the Pattern of which was then approved.

5. That the 12 Stewards of the current Year shall always attend the *G. Lodge* in their proper *Clothing* and *Jewels*, paying at the Rate of 4 *Lodges* towards the Expence of the *Communication:* But they are not to vote, nor even to speak, except when desired, or else of what relates to the ensuing *Feast* only.

XXIV. The G. Wardens and Stewards shall in due Time wait upon the G. *Master* or *Deputy* for Directions and Orders about the Premises: But if both their *Worships* are sick or necessarily absent, they may call together the *Masters* and *Wardens* of Lodges, on Purpose for their Advice and Orders: Or else they may take the whole Affair upon themselves and do the best they can.

XXIV. The Stewards now take the whole Affair upon themselves and do the best they can.

Nor are their Accounts now audited

The

Old REGULATIONS.　　**New** REGULATIONS.

The G. *Wardens* and *Stewards* are to account for all the Money they receive or expend, after Dinner, to the G. *Lodge*, or when the *Lodge* shall think fit to audite their Accounts.

audited by the G. *Lodge*; for that generally the *Stewards* are out of Pocket.

XXV. The MASTERS of *Lodges* shall each appoint one experienced and discreet Brother of his *Lodge*, to compose a Committee consisting of *One* from *every Lodge*, who shall meet in a convenient Apartment to receive every Person that brings a *Ticket*; and shall have Power to discourse him, if they think fit, in order to admit or debar him, as they shall see Cause. Provided

They send no Man away before they have acquainted all the Brethren *within Doors* with the Reasons thereof; that so no *true* Brother may be debarr'd, nor a *false* Brother or a mere *Pretender* admitted. This *Committee* must meet very early on St. JOHN's Day at the Place, before any Persons come with Tickets.

XXV. On 25 *Jan.* 1723. The G. *Lodge* order'd that the *Committee* of *Enquiry* and the *Stewards* with Others, shall be early at the Place of the *Feaſt* for thoſe Purpoſes mention'd in this *Old Regulation*, and the *Order* was confirm'd by the G. *Lodge*, viz. on 17 *Nov.* 1725.

XXVI. The G. MASTER shall appoint *Two* or more true and truſty Brothers to be *Porters* and *Door-Keepers*, who are alſo to be early at the Place for ſome good Reaſons; and who are to be at the Command of the ſaid *Committee*.

XXVI. The *Tylers* and other Servants, within or without Doors, are now appointed only by the *Stewards*.

XXVII. The G. WARDENS or the STEWARDS shall before-hand, appoint ſuch a Number of Brethren to ſerve at *Table* as they think fit: and they may adviſe with the *Officers* of *Lodges* about the moſt proper Perſons, if they pleaſe, or may retain

XXVII. Now only the STEWARDS appoint the *Attenders* at Table; who are

Z

Old Regulations.

retain such by their Recommendation: For none are to serve that Day but *Free and Accepted Masons*; that the Communication may be free and harmonious.

XXVIII. All the Members of the G. Lodge must be at the *Place* of the *Feast* long before Dinner, with the G. Master or his Deputy at their Head ; who shall retire and form themselves. And this in order,

1. To receive any *Appeals* duly lodged as above regulated; that the *Appellant* and *Respondent* may both be heard, and the Affair may be amicably decided before Dinner, if possible.

But if it cannot, it must be delay'd till after the *New G. Master* takes the Chair.

And if it cannot be decided after Dinner, the G. *Master* must refer it to a special *Committee*, that shall quickly adjust it and make Report to the next G. *Lodge* ; that so brotherly Love may be preserved.

2. To prevent any Difference or Disgust which may be fear'd to arise that Day ; that so no Interruption may be given to the Harmony and Pleasure of the *General Assembly* and *Grand Feast*.

3. To consult about whatever concerns the Decency and Decorum of

New Regulations.

are the more necessary if the *Cooks* and *Butlers* are not *Brothers*.

XXVIII. No *Petitions* or *Appeals* on the Day of the General *Assembly* and *Feast*. See *New Regulation* XIII. at 25 *Nov.* 1723.

In antient Times the *Master*, *Wardens* and *Fellows* on St. John's Day met either in a *Monastery*, or on the *Top* of the highest *Hill* near them, by Peep of Day: And having there chosen their *New G. Officers*, they descended walking in due Form to the *Place* of the *Feast*, either a *Monastery*, or the House of an *Eminent Mason*, or some large House of Entertainment as they thought best tyled.

But of late they go in *Coaches*, as described in the *March* of Norfolk, Part III. Pag. 125.

Sometimes the *Masters* and *Wardens* of particular *Lodges* have met the G. Master and his Retinue at the Door or Gate, and have attended him into the *Lodge-Room*: And sometimes he with his Retinue has gone in first, and sent his *Wardens* for the said *Masters* and *Wardens*. But

Old Regulations.

of the *Grand Assembly*, and to prevent ill Manners ; the Assembly being promiscuous, that is, of all Sorts of *Free-Masons*.

XXIX. After these Things are discuss'd, the G. Master, the Deputy, the G. Wardens, the Stewards, the Treasurer, the Secretary, the *Clerks* and every other Person, shall withdraw and leave the *Masters* and *Wardens* of particular *Lodges* alone ; in order to their amicable Consulting about the Election of a *New G. Master*, or the Continuing of the *Present* another Year ; if the said *Masters* and *Wardens* have not met and done it the Day before.

And if they agree by a *Majority* to continue the *present* G. Master, his *Worship* shall be call'd in ; and, after Thanks, shall be humbly desir'd to do the *Fraternity* the *Honour* of ruling them another Year. And after Dinner, it will be known whether he accepts of it or not ; for it should not be discover'd till then.

XXX. Then the *Masters* and *Wardens*, and all the Brethren may converse promiscuously, or as they please to sort together

New Regulations.

But it is equal : for the G. Lodge must be formed before *Dinner*.

XXIX. This old Regulation was found inconvenient : Therefore at the *Assembly* on 27 *Dec.* 1720. (Page 111.) it was agreed that the *New G. Master* should by the *Present* be propos'd to the G. Lodge at their Communication, some time before the Day of the *Annual Feast* ; and that if he was approv'd then, or no Objection made, he was to be forthwith saluted G. Master *Elect*, if there ; or if absent, his Health was to be toasted as such ; and that as such he was to march to the *Feast* on the *present* G. Master's Left Hand.

Thus on *Lady-day* 1721. P.111.

Payne G. *Master* proposed the Duke of Montagu : and All have since been so proposed. Therefore

Now, before Dinner, there is no *Election*, but only a *Recognizing* of the former Approbation of the *New G. Master*, which is soon done.

XXX. The G. Master may say Grace himself, or employ some Brother who is a *Clergyman*, or else the *Secretary*,

Z 2   to

ther until the *Dinner* is coming in, when every Brother takes his Seat at Table.

XXXI. Some Time after *Dinner* the G. Lodge is form'd, not in Retirement, but in Presence of all the Brethren, who yet are not Members of it; and none of those that are not, must speak, until they are desir'd and allow'd.

XXXII. If the G. Master of last Year has consented with the *Masters* and *Wardens* in private before Dinner to continue for the Year ensuing, then *One* of the G. Lodge, deputed for that Purpose, shall represent to all the Brethren *his Worship's good Government*, &c. and turning to him, shall in the Name of the G. *Lodge*, humbly request him to do the *Fraternity* the *great Honour* (if nobly born, if not) the great *Kindness* of continuing to be their G. Master for the Year ensuing: And his *Worship* declaring his Consent by a Bow or a Speech, as he pleases, the said deputed Member of the G. Lodge shall proclaim him aloud

GRAND MASTER of Masons!

All the Members of the G. *Lodge* shall salute him in due Form; and all the Brethren shall, for a few Minutes, have leave to declare their Satisfaction, Pleasure and Congratulation.

XXXIII. But if either the *Masters* and *Wardens* have not in private this Day before Dinner,

to say Grace, both before and after Dinner.

XXXI. This *old* Method was found inconvenient: Therefore as the whole *Assembly* sit together at Dinner in the Form of a *Grand Lodge*, there is no Alteration, but the *Members* of the G. *Lodge* continue promiscuous in their Seats.

XXXII. There has been no Occasion yet in our Time of putting this *Old Regulation* in Practice; because the *New* Grand Master is proposed by the *present* Grand Master, and approved by the G. *Lodge*, some Time before the Feast; as in the *New Regulation* XXIX. and because no G. *Master* has been yet requested to continue a 2d Year.

XXXIII. There has been no Occasion

Dinner, nor the Day before, defir'd the *laſt* G. *Maſter* to continue in his Maſterſhip another Year; or if He, when deſir'd, has not conſented, Then;

The *preſent* G. MASTER ſhall nominate his Succeſſor for the Year enſuing, who, if unanimouſly approv'd by the *Grand Lodge*, and there preſent, ſhall be proclaim'd, ſaluted and congratulated the *New* G. MASTER, as above hinted, and immediately inſtall'd by the laſt G. *Maſter* according to Uſage. *

XXXIV. But if that *Nomination* is not unanimouſly approv'd, the *New* G. MASTER ſhall be choſen immediately by *Ballot*; every *Maſter* and *Warden* writing his Man's Name, and the *laſt* G. *Maſter* writing his Man's Name too; and the Man whoſe Name the *laſt* G. *Maſter* ſhall firſt take out caſually or by Chance, ſhall be

GRAND MASTER *of* MASONS

for the Year enſuing; and if preſent, he ſhall be proclaim'd, ſaluted and congratulated, as above hinted, and forthwith inſtall'd by the *laſt* G. *Maſter* according to Uſage.

XXXV. The *laſt* G. MASTER thus continued, or the *New* G. MASTER thus inſtall'd, ſhall next nominate and appoint his *Deputy* G. MASTER, either the *Laſt* or a *New One*, who ſhall be alſo proclaim'd, ſaluted and congratulated in due Form.

The *New* G. MASTER ſhall alſo nominate

caſion yet for putting this *Old Regulation* in Practice; becauſe no *Grand Maſter* has been requeſted in our Time to continue a 2d Year. * See the Manner of *Inſtalment* at RICHMOND, Part III. Page 117.

XXXIV. There has been no Occaſion in our Time for this *old Regulation*, nor can be now; for that there muſt be no *Balloting* nor any *Controverſy* on the *Feaſt-Day*, according to Agreement. See *New Regulation* XIII. at 25 *Nov.* 1723.

XXXV. A DEPUTY was always needful when the G. MASTER was *nobly born:* And in our Time, the G. MASTER *Elect* has not publickly ſignified before Hand the

nominate his *New* G. WARDENS; and if unanimously approv'd by the *G. Lodge*, they shall be forthwith pro claim'd, saluted and congratulated in due Form.

But if not, they shall be chosen by *Ballot* in the same Way as the *G. Master* was chosen, and as *Wardens* of *private* Lodges are chosen when the Members do not approve of their *Master's* Nomination.

XXXVI. But if the Brother whom the *present* G. MASTER shall nominate for his Successor, or whom the *G. Lodge* shall chuse by *Ballot*, as above, is by Sickness, or other necessary Occasion, absent, he cannot be proclaim'd G. MASTER; unless the *old G. Master*, or some of the *Masters* and *Wardens* of *Lodges*, can vouch upon the *Honour* of a *Brother*, that the said Person, so nominated or chosen, will readily accept of the *Office*. In which Case the *old G. Master* shall act as *Proxy*, and in his Name shall nominate the *Deputy* and *Wardens*; and in his Name shall receive the usual Honours, Homage and Congratulations.

XXXVII. Then the G. MASTER shall allow any Brother, a *Fellow-Craft*, or *Enter'd Prentice*, to speak, directing his Discourse to his *Worship* in the Chair; or to make any Motion for the Good of the *Fraternity*, which shall

the Names of his intended *Deputy* and *Wardens*, nor till he is first install'd in *Solomon's* Chair.

For then *first* he calls them forth by Name, and appoints them to officiate instantly, as soon as they are install'd.

XXXVI. The 𝔓𝔯𝔬𝔵𝔶 must be either the *last* or a *former* G. MASTER; as the Duke of *Richmond* was for Lord *Paisley*, Page 119. or else a very reputable Brother; as Lord *Southwell* was for the Earl of *Strathmore*, Page 130.

But the *New Deputy* and G. *Wardens* are not allow'd *Proxies* when appointed.

XXXVII. This is not allow'd till the *New* G. MASTER has made the 2d *Procession* round

shall be either immediately consider'd, or else referr'd to the Consideration of the *Grand Lodge* at their next *Communication* stated or occasional. When that is over,

round the *Tables* ; as at RICHMOND, Page 118.

XXXVIII. The G. MASTER, or *Deputy*, or some other appointed by him, shall harangue all the Brethren and give them good Advice. And lastly,

After some other *Transactions* that cannot be written in any Language, the Brethren may stay longer or go away, as they please, when the *Lodge* is closed in good Time.

XXXVIII. After the *Oration*, the 5 publick *Healths* may be toasted ; and before or after each, a *Masons Song* with the best Instruments of Musick.

Other Things relating to the *Charges*, &c. of the G. MASTER, are best known to the *Fraternity*.

XXXIX. Every *Annual* G. LODGE has an inherent Power and Authority to make *New Regulations*, or to alter *These* for the real Benefit of this antient *Fraternity*, provided always that the *Old Land Marks* be carefully preserved, and that such *New Regulations* and Alterations be proposed and agreed to at the 3d *Quarterly* Communication preceding the *Annual* Grand *Feast* ; and that they be offer'd to the Perusal of *all the Brethren* before Dinner in writing, even of the youngest *Enter'd Prentice* ; the Approbation and Consent of the *Majority* of *all the Brethren* present being absolutely necessary to make

XXXIX. On 24 *June* 1723. at the *Feast*, the G. LODGE before Dinner made this RESOLUTION, that *it is not in the Power of any Man or Body of Men to make any Alteration or Innovation in the Body of Masonry, without the Consent first obtain'd of the* G. LODGE. And on 25 *Nov.* 1723. the G. LODGE in *Ample Form* resolved, that *any G. Lodge duly met has a Power to amend or explain any of the printed Regulations in the Book of Constitutions, while they break not in upon the antient Rules of the Fraternity.*

But that no Alterations shall be made in this printed Book of Constitutions

Old Regulations.

make the same Binding and Obligatory; which must therefore after Dinner, and after the *New G. Master* is install'd, be solemnly desir'd; as it was desir'd and obtain'd for these *Old Regulations*, when proposed by the G. Lodge to about 150 Brethren at *Stationers-Hall* on St. John *Baptist's* Day 1721.

The End of the **Old Regulations.**

New Regulations.

Constitutions without Leave of the G. Lodge.

Accordingly,
All the *Alterations* or New Regulations above written are only for amending or explaining the Old Regulations for the Good of *Masonry*, without breaking in upon the antient *Rules* of the *Fraternity*, still preserv-

ing the *Old Land Marks*; and were made at several Times, as Occasion offer'd, by the Grand Lodge; who have an inherent Power of amending what may be thought inconvenient, and ample Authority of making New Regulations for the Good of *Masonry*, without the Consent of *All the Brethren* at the *Grand* Annual Feast; which has not been disputed since the said 24 *June* 1721. for the *Members* of the G. Lodge are truly the Representatives of *All the Fraternity*, according to Old Regulation X.

And so on 6 *April* 1736.

John Ward, Esq; *D. Grand Master* in the Chair, proposed a *New Regulation* of 10 Rules for explaining what concern'd the *Decency* of *Assemblies* and *Communications*; which was agreed to by that *Grand Lodge*, viz.

XL. 1. That no *Brothers* be admitted into the G. Lodge but those that are the known *Members* thereof; viz. The *four present* and all *former* G. Officers, the *Treasurer* and *Secretary*, the *Masters* and *Wardens* of all *regular Lodges*, the *Masters* and *Wardens* and *Nine* more of the *Stewards Lodge*: except a Brother who is a Petitioner or a Witness in some Case, or one call'd in by a Motion.

2. That at the 3d *Stroke* of the G. Master's Hammer (always to be repeated by the *Senior Grand Warden)* there shall be a general Silence; and that he who breaks Silence without Leave from the Chair shall be publickly reprimanded. 3. That

3. That under the same Penalty, every Brother shall take his Seat and keep strict Silence whenever the G. MASTER or *Deputy* shall think fit to rise from the Chair and call to order.

4. That in the G. LODGE every Member shall keep in his Seat, and not move about from Place to Place, during the *Communication*; except the G. WARDENS, as having more immediately the Care of the *Lodge*.

5. That according to the Order of the G. LODGE on 21 *April* 1730. (as in the *Lodge-Book*) no Brother is to speak but *once* to the same Affair; unless to explain himself, or when call'd by the *Chair* to speak.

6. Every one that speaks shall rise and keep standing, addressing himself to the *Chair*: Nor shall any presume to interrupt him, under the foresaid Penalty; unless the G. MASTER, finding him wandering from the Point in Hand, shall think fit to reduce him to Order; for then the said *Speaker* shall sit down: But after he has been set right, he may again proceed, if he pleases.

7. If in the G. LODGE any Member is twice call'd to *Order*, at one *Assembly*, for transgressing these Rules, and is guilty of a 3d *Offence* of the same Nature, the *Chair* shall peremptorily command him to quit the *Lodge-Room* for that Night.

8. That whoever shall be so rude as to *hiss at a Brother*, or at what another says or has said, he shall be forthwith solemnly excluded the *Communication*, and declared incapable of ever being a *Member of any Grand Lodge* for the Future, till another Time he publickly owns his Fault and his Grace be granted.

9. No Motion for a *New Regulation*, or for the Alteration of an *Old One*, shall be made, till it is first handed up in *writing* to the CHAIR: And after it has been perused by the G. MASTER at least about Ten Minutes, the Thing may be moved publickly; and then it shall be audibly read by the *Secretary*: And if *he* be seconded and thirded, it must be immediately committed to the Consideration of the *whole Assembly*, that their Sense may be fully heard about it: After which the G. MASTER shall put the Question *pro* and *con*.

A a

10. The

10. The Opinions or *Votes* of the *Members* are always to be signified by each holding up *one of his Hands:* Which uplifted *Hands* the G. WARDENS are to count; unless the *Numbers of Hands* be so unequal as to render the Counting useless. Nor should any other Kind of *Division* be ever admitted among MASONS. The End of the 𝔑𝔢𝔴 REGULATIONS.

The CONSTITUTION of the COMMITTEE of *Masons* 𝕮𝖍𝖆𝖗𝖎𝖙𝖞 first proposed at the *Grand Lodge* on 21 *Nov.* 1724.

CHARLES LENNOS Duke of *Richmond* and *Lennox* (and now also Duke *d'Aubigny*) being *Grand Master*; 𝔐𝔞𝔯𝔱𝔦𝔫 𝔉𝔬𝔩𝔨𝔢𝔰, Esq; *Deputy* Grand 𝔊𝔢𝔬𝔯𝔤𝔢 𝔓𝔞𝔶𝔫𝔢, Esq; Grand with several *Master,* 𝔉𝔯𝔞𝔫𝔠𝔦𝔰 𝔖𝔬𝔯𝔢𝔩𝔩, Esq; *Wardens,* noble Brothers, and the Officers of 45 Lodges.

Brother FRANCIS SCOT Earl of *Dalkeith* (now Duke of *Buckleugh*) the last Grand *Master,* proposed, in Pursuance of the *Old Regulation XIII. That in Order to promote the charitable Disposition of* FREE-MASONS, *and to render it more extensively beneficial to the Society,* each Lodge *may make a certain Collection, according to Ability, to be put into a* Joint-Stock, *lodged in the Hands of a* Treasurer *at every* Quarterly Communication, *for the Relief of distress'd Brethren that shall be recommended by the* Contributing Lodges *to the* Grand Officers *from Time to Time.*

The Motion being readily agreed to,

RICHMOND *Grand Master* desir'd all present to come prepar'd to give their Opinion of it, at next 𝔊𝔯𝔞𝔫𝔡 𝔏𝔬𝔡𝔤𝔢; which was held in *Ample* Form on 17 *March* 172⅘ When

At the *Lodge's* Desire, G. M. RICHMOND named a *Committee* for considering of the best Methods to regulate the said *Masons*

General

General *Charity:* They met and chofe for Chairman 𝔚𝔦𝔩𝔩𝔦𝔞𝔪 𝔠𝔬𝔴𝔭𝔢𝔯, Efq; Clerk of the Parliament, who drew up the *Report.*

But the Affair requiring great Deliberation, the *Report* was not made till the 𝔊𝔯𝔞𝔫𝔡 𝔏𝔬𝔡𝔤𝔢 met in *Ample* Form on 27 *Nov.* 1725. when RICHMOND G. M. order'd the *Report* to be read. It was well approved and recorded in the Book of the *Grand Lodge* ; for which that Committee receiv'd publick Thanks, and Copies of it were order'd to be fent to the particular *Lodges.*

Yet no 𝔗𝔯𝔢𝔞𝔣𝔲𝔯𝔢𝔯 was found, till at the *Grand Lodge* in *Ample* Form on 24 *June* 1727, INCHIQUIN G. M. requefted Brother 𝔑𝔞𝔱𝔥𝔞𝔫𝔦𝔢𝔩 𝔅𝔩𝔞𝔨𝔢𝔯𝔟𝔶, Efq; to accept of that Officer, which he very kindly undertook.

Then alfo it was refolv'd, that the 4 *Grand Officers* for the Time being, together with Brother *Martin Folkes, Francis Sorell* and *George Payne,* Efqs; as a COMMITTEE of 7, fhould, upon due Recommendations, difpofe of the intended Charity ; and frefh Copies of the *Report* were fent to the *Lodges.*

At laft this good Work of 𝔠𝔥𝔞𝔯𝔦𝔱𝔶 was begun at the *Grand Lodge* on 25 *Nov.* 1729. KINGSTON being *Grand Mafter,* and in his Abfence D. G. Mafter 𝔅𝔩𝔞𝔨𝔢𝔯𝔟𝔶, the *Treafurer,* in the Chair; who after a warm Exhortation, order'd the *Lodges* to be call'd over a fecond Time, when fome *Officers* gave in the Benevolence of their refpective *Lodges* ; for which they were thank'd, and their *Charity* being forthwith recorded, was put into the Hands of the *Treafurer,* as an hopeful Beginning : and other *Lodges* following the good Example,

At the 𝔊𝔯𝔞𝔫𝔡 𝔏𝔬𝔡𝔤𝔢 in *Due* Form on 27 *Dec.* 1729. D. G. M. 𝔅𝔩𝔞𝔨𝔢𝔯𝔟𝔶 the *Treafurer,* in the Chair, had the Honour to thank many *Officers* of *Lodges,* for bringing their liberal *Charity* : When by a Motion of Brother *Thomas Batfon* Counfellor at Law, the *Grand Lodge* ordain'd *that every* new Lodge, *for their* Conftitution, *fhall pay two Guineas towards this General* Charity *of* Mafons.

And ever fince, the *Lodges,* according to their Ability, have, by their Officers, fent their Benevolence to every Grand Lodge, except on the Grand *Feaft* Day : And feveral diftrefs'd Brothers have been handfomely reliev'd.

But

But finding the forefaid *Committee* of *Seven* too few for the good Work, the 𝕲𝖗𝖆𝖓𝖉 𝕷𝖔𝖉𝖌𝖊 in *Due* Form on 28 *Aug.* 1730. NORFOLK being *Grand Mafter*, and in his Abfence D. G. M. 𝕭𝖑𝖆𝖐𝖊𝖗𝖇𝖞, the *Treafurer*, in the Chair, refolv'd, *That the* COM-MITTEE *of* Charity *fhall have added to 'em* 12 𝕸𝖆𝖘𝖙𝖊𝖗𝖘 *of contributing Lodges*; *that the firft* 12 *in the* printed Lift *fhall be fucceeded by the next* 12, *and fo on*: *And that for Difpatch, any* 5 *of 'em fhall be a* Quorum, *provided one of the* 5 *is a prefent* Grand Officer. Accordingly,

The COMMITTEE of *Charity* met the *Treafurer* 𝕭𝖑𝖆𝖐𝖊𝖗𝖇𝖞 the firft Time in the *Maftership* of NORFOLK.

On 13 *Nov.* 1730. When

They confider'd the Petitions of fome poor Brethren, whom they reliev'd, not exceeding 3 Pounds to each Petitioner: And ever fince they have adjourn'd, from Time to Time, for fupplying the Diftrefs'd according to their Powers; or elfe have recommended 'em to the greater Favour of the *Grand Lodge*.

Yet the COMMITTEE had not all their Powers at once: For at the 𝕲𝖗𝖆𝖓𝖉 𝕷𝖔𝖉𝖌𝖊 on 15 *Dec.* 1730. NORFOLK being *Grand Mafter*, and in his Abfence the *Deputy* 𝕭𝖑𝖆𝖐𝖊𝖗𝖇𝖞 in the Chair, it was ordain'd, *That for Difpatch, all Complaints and Informations about* Charity, *fhall be referred, for the future, to the* COM-MITTEE *of* Charity; *and that they fhall appoint a Day for hearing the fame, fhall enter their Proceedings in their own Book, and fhall report their Opinion to the* Grand Lodge.

And now hence forward, the *Minutes* of the COMMITTEE of *Charity* are read and confider'd at every *G. Lodge*, except on the *G. Feaft* Day.

At the COMMITTEE of Charity 16 *March* 173⁰⁄₁. it was agreed *that no Petition fhall be read, if the Petitioner don't attend the Committee in Perfon*; *except in the Cafes of Sicknefs, Lamenefs or Imprifonment*.

At the 𝕲𝖗𝖆𝖓𝖉 𝕷𝖔𝖉𝖌𝖊 on 14 *May* 1731. upon the Motion of LOVEL *Grand Mafter* it was refolv'd, 1. *That all former Grand Mafters and Deputies fhall be Members of the* Committee of Charity.

2. That

2. *That the* COMMITTEE *shall have a Power to give* 5 *Pounds, as casual* Charity, *to a poor Brother, but no more, till the* Grand Lodge *assemble.*

At the COMMITTEE of *Charity* on 18 *June* 1731. it was agreed, *that no poor Brother, that has been once assisted, shall, a second Time, present a Petition, without some new Allegation well attested.*

At the **Grand Lodge** on 8 *June* 1732. *Viscount* MONTAGU being *G. Master,* and in his Absence D. G. M. **Batson** in the Chair, having signified, That notwithstanding the *General Charity,* some poor Brothers had molested Noblemen and Others (being *Masons*) with private Applications for Charity, to the Scandal of the *Craft;* it was resolv'd, *that any Brother who makes such private Applications for the future, shall be for ever debarr'd from any Relief from the* Committee of Charity, *the* Grand Lodge, *or any Assemblies of* Masons.

At the COMMITTEE of *Charity* on 5 *July* 1732. it was agreed *that no Brother shall be reliev'd, unless his Petition be attested by* 3 *Brothers of the Lodge to which he does, or did once, belong.*

At the **Grand Lodge** on 21 *Nov.* 1732. *Viscount* MONTAGU being *G. Master,* and in his Absence *Deputy* **Batson** in the Chair, it was resolv'd, *that all former and present Grand Officers,* viz. *G. Masters, Deputies* and *Wardens,* with 20 **Masters** *of contributing* Lodges *in a Rotation, according to the printed List, shall be Members of the* Committee of Charity. And

At the **Grand Lodge** on 13 *Dec.* 1733. upon the Motion of SRATHMORE *G .Master* in the Chair, it was resolv'd,

1. *That all* Masters *of regular* Lodges, *that have contributed to the Charity within* 12 *Months past, shall be Members of the* COMMITTEE, *together with all former and present* Grand Officers.

2. *That considering the usual Business of a Quarterly Communication was too much for one Time; whatever Business cannot be dispatched here, shall be referr'd to the* COMMITTEE of *Charity, and their Opinion reported to the next* Grand Lodge.

3. *That*

3. *That all Questions debated at the said Committee shall be decided by a Majority of those present.*

4. *That all Petitions for Charity presented to the Grand Lodge shall be referred to the said Committee, who are to report their Opinion to the next Grand Lodge, viz. Whether or not the Case of any distress'd Brother deserves more Relief than is in the Power of the Committee to give?*

5. *That the said Committee shall twice give publick Notice, in some publick News Paper, of the Time and Place of their Meetings.*

At the **Grand Lodge** on 24 *Feb.* 173$\frac{4}{5}$. CRAUFURD G. *Master* in the Chair, it was recommended by the *Committee*, and now resolv'd here,

1. *That no* Master *of a* Lodge *shall be a* Member *of the said* Committee, *whose* Lodge *has not contributed to the* General Charity *during* 12 *Months past.*

2. *That one of the Brethren, signing and certifying a poor Brother's Petition, shall attend the Committee to attest it.*

At the **Grand Lodge** on 31 *March* 1735. Upon the Motion of CRAUFURD *Grand Master* in the Chair, it was resolv'd,

1. *That no extraneous Brothers, that is, not regularly made, but clandestinely, or only with a View to partake of the Charity; nor any assisting at such irregular Makings, shall be ever qualified to partake of the Masons general Charity.*

2. *That the Brothers attesting a Petition for Charity shall be able to certify, that the Petitioner has been formerly in reputable, at least, in tolerable Circumstances.*

3. *That every Petition receiv'd shall be sign'd or certified by the Majority of the Lodge to which the Petitioner does, or did, belong.*

4. *That the Name and Calling of the Petitioner be expresly mention'd.*

At the **Grand Lodge** on 6 *April* 1736. WEYMOUTH being *Grand Master*, and in his Absence, D. G. *Master* WARD in the Chair; upon the Motion of the COMMITTEE of *Charity*, it was resolv'd, *That no* Petition *for* Charity *shall be receiv'd which*

has

has not been offer'd first to the Secretary *and laid in his Hands Ten Days, at least, before the Meeting of the* Committee *of Charity, that he may have Time to be inform'd of its Allegations, if they are dubious.*

Thus the COMMITTEE of *Charity* has been eftablifh'd among the FREE and Accepted MASONS of *England,* who have very handfomely contributed to their *General* Fund, and do ftill perfevere in the Good Work.

The COMMITTEE regularly meets and has reliev'd many diftrefs'd Brothers with fmall Sums, not exceeding 5 *l.* to each: And the 𝕲𝖗𝖆𝖓𝖉 𝕷𝖔𝖉𝖌𝖊 have order'd the *Treafurer* to pay more to fome Petitioners, according to Exigence; fometimes 10, or 15, or 20 Pounds, as they thought the Cafe requir'd: So that the *Diftrefs'd* have found far greater Relief from this *General Charity,* than can be expected from particular *Lodges*; and the Contributions, being paid by the Lodges in *Parcels,* at various Times, have not been burdenfome.

The 𝕿𝖗𝖊𝖆𝖘𝖚𝖗𝖊𝖗'𝖘 *Accounts* have been audited and ballanced at every *Grand Lodge*; whereby all know the Stock in Hand, and how every Parcel of the *Charity* has been difpos'd of; every Thing being duly recorded in the Grand *Lodge-Book,* and in *that* of the COMMITTEE, of which every *Mafter* of a *contributing Lodge* is a Member.

The *Treafurer* 𝕭𝖑𝖆𝖐𝖊𝖗𝖇𝖞 has not employ'd a Clerk or Affi-ftant for faving Charges; being hitherto affifted only by the *Se-cretary* of the *Grand Lodge:* And when the *Treafurer* is call'd abroad, he leaves Money with the *Secretary* REVIS to pay what is drawn upon him; and for all his generous Cares and good Conduct, the 𝕿𝖗𝖊𝖆𝖘𝖚𝖗𝖊𝖗 is publickly and folemnly thank'd by every *Grand Lodge.*

At laft on 6 *April* 1738. at the 𝕲𝖗𝖆𝖓𝖉 𝕷𝖔𝖉𝖌𝖊, the *Treafurer* 𝕭𝖑𝖆𝖐𝖊𝖗𝖇𝖞, having juftly cleared his Accounts, and ftated the Ballance, thought fit to demit or lay down his Office. Upon which the *Secretary* 𝕽𝖊𝖛𝖎𝖘 was appointed *Treafurer.* But

At

At the GENERAL ASSEMBLY on 27 *April* 1738. Mr *John Revis* the 𝕾𝖊𝖈𝖗𝖊𝖙𝖆𝖗𝖕 declin'd the Office of *Treasurer*; for that both those Offices should not be reposed in one Man, the One being a Check to the Other: Yet the *Grand Master* CAERNARVON and the Brethren, desir'd Brother *Revis* to act as *Treasurer* till one is appointed.

May this good Work of CHARITY abound, as one of the happy Effects of the Love and Friendship of *true Masons*, till Time and Architecture shall be no more!

A LIST of the LODGES in and about *London* and *Westminster*.

MANY *Lodges* have by Accidents broken up, or are partition'd, or else removed to new Places for their Conveniency, and so, if subsisting, they are called and known by those new Places or their *Signs*.

But the *subsisting Lodges*, whose *Officers* have attended the 𝕲𝖗𝖆𝖓𝖉 𝕷𝖔𝖉𝖌𝖊 or *Quarterly Communication*, and brought their Benevolence to the General *Charity* within 12 Months past, are here set down according to their Seniority of *Constitution*, as in the *Grand Lodge-Books* and the *Engraven List*.

Signs of the Houses.	Dates of Constitution.	Days of *Forming.*
Thus the LODGES at 1. KING's-ARMS Tavern in St. *Paul's Church-Yard*, removed from the GOOSE and GRIDIRON, meet in Form.	- - - - -	Every first *Tuesday* in the Month.
This is the *Senior Lodge*, whose *Constitution* is immemorial.		

2. HORN

Signs of the Houses.	Dates of Constitution.	Days of Forming.
2 HORN Tavern in *New Palace-Yard*, *Weftminfter*, the *Old Lodge* removed from the RUMMER and GRAPES, *Channel Row*, whofe *Conftitution* is alfo immemorial, it being one of the *four Lodges* mention'd Page 109.	- - - - -	2d *Thurfday.*
3. SHAKESPEAR's-HEAD in *Marleborough-ftreet*.	17 *Jan.* 172⁰⁄₁.	2d *Monday.*
4. BELL in *Nickolas-Lane* near *Lombard-ftreet*.	11 *July* 1721.	2d *Wednefday.*
5. BRAUND's-HEAD Tavern in *New Bond-ftreet*.	19 *Jan.* 172½.	2d and 4th *Tuefday.*
6. RUMMER Tavern in *Queen-ftreet, Cheapfide*.	28 *Jan.* 172½.	2d and 4th *Thurfday.*
7. DANIEL's *Coffee-houfe* within *Temple-Bar*.	25 *April* 1722.	1ft *Monday.*
8. RED-CROSS in *Barbican* ———	*May* 1722.	1ft *Wednefday.*
9. KING's-ARMS Tavern in *New Bond ftreet*.	25 *Nov.* 1722.	Laft *Thurfday.*
10. QUEEN's-HEAD in *Knave's-Acre*. This was one of the *four Lodges* mention'd Page 109. *viz* the APPLE-TREE *Tavern* in *Charles-ftreet*, *Covent-Garden*, whofe *Conftitution* is immemorial : But after they removed to the QUEEN's Head, upon fome Difference, the Members that met there came under a *new Conftitution*, tho' they wanted it not, and it is therefore placed at this Number. *N. B.* The CROWN in *Parker's-Lane*, the Other of the *four* old *Lodges*, is now extinct.	27 *Feb.* 172⅓.	1ft and 3d *Wednefday.*
11. CASTLE Tavern in *Drury-Lane*.——	*March* 172⅔.	1ft and 3d *Wednefday.*
12. BURY's *Coffee-houfe* in *Bridges-ftreet*, where there is alfo a *Mafters-Lodge*.	28 *March* 1723.	2d and 4th *Tuefday.*
13. QUEEN's-HEAD Tavern in Great *Queen-ftreet*.	30 *March* 1723	1ft and 3d *Monday.*

14. BULL's-

Signs of the Houses.	Dates of Constitution.	Days of Forming.
14. BULL's-HEAD Tavern in Southwark	1 April 1723.	2d Monday.
15. LE GUERRE Tavern in St. Martin's-Lane.	3 April 1723.	1st and 3d Wednesday.
16. SUN Tavern in Lower Holbourn.—	5 May 1723.	1st and 3d Friday.
17. MOURNING BUSH Tavern at Aldersgate	- - - 1723.	2d and 4th Friday.
18. SWAN Tavern in Long-Acre, a French Lodge.	12 June 1723.	1st and 3d Monday.
19. ANCHOR and Baptist's Head Tavern Chancery Lane.	4 Aug. 1723.	2d and last Thursday.
20. DOG Tavern Billingsgate.——	11 Sept. 1723.	1st Wednesday.
21. HALF-MOON Tavern Cheapside.——	18 Sept. 1723.	1st and 3d Tuesday.
22. SWAN and COCOA-TREE in White-cross-street.	- - - 1723.	1st Friday.
23. WHITE HORSE in Wheeler's-street, Spittlefields.	24 Dec. 1723.	2d Monday.
24. FORREST's Coffee-house Charing-Cross, the old Lodge.	27 March 1724.	2d and last Monday.
25 The SASH and COCOA-TREE in Moor-Fields.	July 1724.	1st and 3d Thursday.
26. SUN in Hooper's Square, Goodman's-Fields.	- - - 1724	1st and 3d Monday.
27. SUN Tavern in St. Paul's Church-Yard.	April 1725.	4th Monday.
28. ANGEL and CROWN Tavern White-Chappel.	- - - 1725.	1st and 3d Wednesday.
29. KING's-ARMS Tavern Strand.——	25 May 1725.	1st Monday.
30. SWAN Tavern in Long-Acre, an English Lodge.	Sept. 1725.	2d and last Wednesday.
31. SWAN and RUMMER Tavern in Finch-Lane, where there is also a Masters Lodge.	2 Feb. 17$\frac{25}{26}$.	2d and 4th Wednesday.
32. MOUNT Coffee-house in Grovenor-street	12 Jan. 172$\frac{6}{7}$.	1st Thursday.
33. GLOBE Tavern in Fleet-street. ——	9 Aug. 1727.	1st and 3d Friday.
34. FISHER's Coffee-house in Burlington-Gardens.	31 Jan. 172$\frac{7}{8}$	2d and 4th Friday.
35. HOOP and GRIFFIN Tavern in Leaden-hall-street.	- - - 1728.	2d and 4th Monday.
36. ROYAL-OAK in great Earl-street, Seven Dials.	- - - 1728.	1st and 3d Friday.

37. OLD-MAN's

Signs of the Houses.	Dates of Constitution.	Days of Forming.
37. OLD-MAN's Coffee-House, Charing-Cross.	- - - 1728.	1ſt and 3d *Friday.*
38. ANCHOR and CROWN in King-ſtreet, Seven Dials.	- - - 1728.	1ſt and 3d *Thurſday.*
39. STAR and GARTER in St. Martin's-Lane.	15 *April* 1728.	2d and 4th *Wedneſday.*
40. St. GEORGE in St. *Mary-Axe.*——	22 *Jan.* 172$\frac{8}{9}$.	2d and 4th *Wedneſday.*
41. FOUNTAIN Tavern on *Snow-hill.*	24 *Jan.* 173$\frac{0}{1}$.	1ſt and 3d *Thurſday.*
42. BACCHUS in *Greville ſtreet,* Hatton Garden.	- - - 1730	1ſt and 3d *Friday.*
43. VINE Tavern in *Long-Acre,* where there is alſo a *Maſters Lodge.*	28 *April* 1730.	2d and 4th *Wedneſday*
44. BACCHUS in *Bloomsbury* Market. —	22 *May* 1730.	2d and 4th *Monday.*
45. GLOBE Tavern in *Old-Jury.*——	26 *June* 1730.	1ſt and 3d *Monday.*
46. RAINBOW *Coffee houſe* in *York-*Buildings.	17 *July* 1730.	2d and 4th *Thurſday.*
47. QUEEN's-HEAD in *Old Bailey,* where there is alſo a *Maſter's-Lodge.*	- - - 1730	2d and 4th *Monday.*
48. BLACK-LION in *Jockey Fields.*—	11 *Jan.* 173$\frac{30}{31}$.	1ſt and 3d *Monday.*
49. Two ANGELS and CROWN in *Little St. Martin's-Lane.*	- - - 1731.	2d and 4th *Friday.*
50. THREE TONS Tavern in *Newgate-*ſtreet.	21 *Oct.* 1731.	2d and laſt *Monday.*
51. THREE TONS Tavern in *Smith field.*	17 *Dec.* 1731.	2d and 4th *Wedneſday.*
52. OLD ANTWERP Tavern *Threadneedle-ſtreet.*	13 *Nov.* 1731.	1ſt *Tueſday.*
53. FOUNTAIN Tavern in the *Burrough, Southwark.*	24 *Jan.* 173$\frac{1}{2}$.	1ſt and 3d *Tueſday.*
54. KING's-ARMS Tavern on St. *Margaret's-Hill, Southwark.*	2 *Feb.* 173$\frac{1}{2}$.	3d *Monday.*
55. HORSESHOE and RUMMER Tavern in *Drury-Lane.*	11 *April* 1732.	2d and 4th *Tueſday.*
56. SUN Tavern in *Fleet-ſtret* ———	12 *April* 1732.	2d and laſt *Tueſday.*
57. KING's-HEAD in *Tower-ſtreet.* ——	25 *May* 1732.	2d and 4th *Friday.*
58. KING and QUEEN in *Roſemary-*Lane.	21 *June* 1732.	2d and 4th *Monday.*
59. OXFORD-ARMS Tavern in *Ludgate-ſtreet.*	29 *June* 1732.	2d and 4th *Thurſday.*
60. KING's-ARMS Tavern in *Dorſet-*ſtreet, *Spittle-Fields.*	12 *July* 1732.	2d and 4th *Thurſday.*

61. KING's-

Signs of the Houses.	Dates of Constitution.	Days of Forming.
61. KING's-ARMS Tavern in Piccadilly.	17 Aug. 1732.	2d and last Thursday.
62. HOOP and GRIFFIN Tavern in Leadenhall street, another Lodge.	18 Aug. 1732.	1st and 3d Friday.
63. CROWN in Upper Moor Fields. ——	29 Aug. 1732.	2d Tuesday.
64 ROYAL VINEYARD Tavern in St. James's-Park.	5 Sept. 1732.	1st and 3d Saturday.
65. ROYAL STANDARD Tavern in Leicester Square.	8 Sept. 1732.	1st and 3d Tuesday.
66. SALMON and BALL in Wheeler-street, Spittle-Fields	15 Nov. 1732.	1st and 3d Tuesday.
67. TURK's-HEAD Tavern in Greek-street, Soho.	12 Dec. 1732.	3d Thursday.
68. SHIP Coffee-house near the Hermitage Bridge.	2 Feb. 173$\frac{2}{3}$.	1st and 3d Thursday.
69. THEATRE Tavern in Goodman's-Fields.	17 Feb. 173$\frac{2}{3}$.	4th Monday.
70. KING's-ARMS in Tower-street near the Seven-Dials.	3 March 173$\frac{2}{3}$.	1st and 3d Tuesday.
71. FOUNTAIN Tavern in Katharine-street, Strand.	23 March 1733.	2d and 4th Thursday.
72. CROWN in Fleet-Market ————	27 Dec 1733.	1st and 3d Monday.
73. FORREST's Coffee-house Charing-Cross, another Lodge.	- 173$\frac{3}{4}$.	2d Wednesday.
74. KING's-ARMS Tavern in Wild-street, where there is also a Master's Lodge.	- - - 1734.	1st and 3d Tuesday.
75. MARLEBOROUGH's-HEAD in Petticoat-Lane, White-Chappel.	5 Nov. 1734.	2d and 4th Friday.
76. BELL in Nicholas-Lane near Lombard-street, another Lodge, where there is also a Masters Lodge.	11 June 1735.	2d and 4th Tuesday.
77. STEWARDS LODGE at Shake-spear's-Head, Covent-Garden, in January April, July and October.	25 June 1735.	3d Wednesday.
78. BEAR Tavern in the Strand. ——	26 Aug. 1735.	2d and 4th Tuesday.
79. ANCHOR in Cock-Lane on Snow Hill.	30 Oct. 1735.	1st and 3d Tuesday.
80. ASHLEY's London Punch-house on Ludgate-Hill.	1 March 173$\frac{5}{6}$.	1st and 3d Thursday.
81. GREYHOUND in Lamb-street, Spittle-Fields.	11 June 1736.	1st and 3d Tuesday.

82. SUN

Signs of the Houses.	Dates of Con- stitution.	Days of Forming.
82. SUN Tavern on *Fish-street-Hill* —	16 *Aug.* 1736.	1ft and 3d *Monday*.
83. YORKSHIRE-GREY in *Beer-Lane, Thames-ftreet*, where there is alfo a *Mafters Lodge*.	2 *Sept.* 1736.	2d and 4th *Wednefday*.
84. BLACK-DOG in *Caftle-ftreet, Seven Dials*, where there is alfo a *Mafters Lodge*.	21 *Dec.* 1736.	2d and 4th *Tuefday*.
85. BLOSSOM'S-INN in *Laurence-Lane, Cheapfide*, where there is a *Mafters Lodge*.	31 *Dec.* 1736.	1ft and 3d *Thurfday*.
86. CITY OF DURHAM in *Swallow-ftreet, St. James's*.	24 *Jan.* 163⁶⁄₇.	1ft *Thurfday*.
87. CROWN Tavern in *Smithfield* —	14 *Feb.* 173⁶⁄₇.	1ft and 3d *Wednefday*.
88. KING'S-ARMS Tavern in *Cateaton-ftreet*.	22 *Feb.* 173⁶⁄₇.	1ft and 3d *Wednefday*.
89. THREE TONS Tavern in *Wood ftreet*.	22 *March* 173⁶⁄₇.	1ft *Monday*.
90. At the Sign of WESTMINSTER-HALL in *Dunning's-Alley, Bifhopf-gate-ftreet*.	30 *March* 1737.	1ft and 3d *Wednefday*.
91. *Whitechapel* COURT-HOUSE in *Whitechapel*.	18 *April* 1737.	2d and 4th *Friday*.
92. THREE TONS Tavern on *Snow-Hill*.	20 *April* 1737.	2d and 4th *Thurfday*.
93. KING'S-HEAD in *Old Jewry* —	10 *May* 1737.	2d and 4th *Wednefday*.
94. GUN Tavern in *Jermyn ftreet, St. James's*.	24 *Aug.* 1737.	2d and 4th *Wednefday*.
95. BLACK-POSTS in *Maiden-Lane*, where there is alfo a *Mafter's Lodge*.	21 *Sept.* 1737.	1ft 2d and 3d *Thurfday*.
96. KING'S-HEAD Tavern in *St. John's-ftreet*.	8 *Dec.* 1737.	2d and 4th *Tuefday*.
97. FOUNTAIN Tavern in *Bartholo-mew-Lane* near the *Exchange*.	27 *Jan* 173⅞.	1ft and 3d *Monday*.
98. BACCHUS Tavern in little *Bufh-Lane, Canon ftreet*, where there is alfo a *Mafters Lodge*.	17 *Feb.* 173⅞.	3d *Wednefday*.
99. KATHARINE-WHEEL in *Windmill-ftreet*.	27 *March* 1738.	1ft and 3d *Tuefday*.

100. ANGEL

Signs of the Houses.	Dates of Constitution.	Days of Forming.
100. ANGEL in *Crispin-street, Spittle-Fields*.	- - - 1738.	1ſt and 3d *Tueſday*.
101. GORDON's *Punch-houſe* in the *Strand*.	16 *May* 1738.	1ſt and 3d *Friday*.
102. BELL and DRAGON in *King-ſtreet*, St. *James's*.	- - - 1738.	laſt *Wedneſday*.
103. SWAN Tavern upon *Fiſh-ſtreet-Hill*.	- - - 1738.	1ſt and 3d *Thurſday*.
104. CHECKER *Charing-Croſs* have petition'd to be Conſtituted.	- - - - -	2d and 4th *Monday*.
105. CAMERON's Coffee-Houſe in *Bury-ſtreet*, St. *James's*.	- - - - -	1ſt and 3d *Friday*.
106. KEY and GARTER Tavern in *Pall-Mall*.	- - - - -	1ſt and 4th *Friday*.

DEPUTATIONS

Of ſeveral *Grand Maſters*,

To WALES, the *Country* of ENGLAND, and *foreign Parts*.

I. TO WALES. The Learned of that old Principality can beſt deduce their own *Hiſtory* of *Maſonry* from the noble antient *Briton* CADWAN the firſt King of *Wales*, A. D. 589. down to King RODERIC MAWR, who partition'd his Kingdom into 3 *Principalities* among his 3 Sons, which again cemented into one *Principality*, till EDWARD I. King of *England* over-ran
Wales,

Wales, A. D. 1283. When, their *Princes* being flain without Iffue, their Nobles and Gentry willingly fubmitted to the Crown of *England*, till King Henry VIII. united *Wales* to *England*, A. D. 1536. and fo down to thefe Times.

For in *Wales* there are many venerable Remains of moft antient religious Houfes, and many ftately Ruins of the ftrongeft Caftles in the 𝕲𝖔𝖙𝖍𝖎𝖈 Stile. See Part II. Ch. 2.

But now the Augustan *Stile* is as well efteem'd *in Wales* as in *England*, and there alfo the Brethren of the *Royal Art* have coalefced into *Lodges*, as Branches of our Fraternity under our Grand Master.

Thus on 10 *May* 1727.

Inchiquin *Grand Mafter* granted a 𝕯𝖊𝖕𝖚𝖙𝖆𝖙𝖎𝖔𝖓 to Hugh Warburton, Efq; to be 𝕻𝖗𝖔𝖛𝖎𝖓𝖈𝖎𝖆𝖑 *Grand Mafter* of *North-Wales* at *Chefter*.

— And another on 24 *June* 1727. to Sir Edward Mansel, Bart. to be 𝕻𝖗𝖔𝖛𝖎𝖓𝖈𝖎𝖆𝖑 *Grand Mafter* of *South-Wales* at *Caermarthen*.

II. DEPUTATIONS have been requefted from and fent to feveral Countries, Cities and Towns of *England*.

Thus,

—Lovel *Grand Mafter* granted a 𝕯𝖊𝖕𝖚𝖙𝖆𝖙𝖎𝖔𝖓 to Sir Edward Matthews, to be 𝕻𝖗𝖔𝖛𝖎𝖓𝖈𝖎𝖆𝖑 *Grand Mafter* of *Shropfhire*.

—Craufurd *Grand Mafter* granted a 𝕯𝖊𝖕𝖚𝖙𝖆𝖙𝖎𝖔𝖓 to Edward Entwizle, Efq; to be 𝕻𝖗𝖔𝖛𝖎𝖓𝖈𝖎𝖆𝖑 *Grand Mafter* of *Lancafhire*.

— Another to Joseph Laycock, Efq; to be 𝕻𝖗𝖔𝖛𝖎𝖓𝖈𝖎𝖆𝖑 *Grand Mafter* of *Durham*.

— Another to Matthew Ridley, Efq; to be 𝕻𝖗𝖔𝖛𝖎𝖓𝖈𝖎𝖆𝖑 *Grand Mafter* of *Northumberland*.

Thefe

These and other *Grand Masters* have also granted 𝕯𝖊𝖕𝖚𝖙𝖆𝖙𝖎𝖔𝖓𝖘. at the Request of some good Brothers in Cities and Towns throughout *England*, for *Constituting* the following *Lodges*, as recorded in the *Grand Lodge-Books*, and in the engraven *List*, who have their *Rank* of *Seniority* at the *Grand Lodge*, according to the *Date* of their CONSTITUTION, viz.

The LODGES at

— NORWICH at the 3 Tons, constituted *A. D.* 1724. and meet every Month on the 1st *Thursday.*

— CHICHESTER, at the *White Horse,* constitutrd 17 *July* 1724. and meet 3d *Friday.*

— CHESTER at the *Spread-Eagle,* constituted *A. D.* 1724. and meet 1st *Tuesday.*

— DITTO at the *Crown* and *Mitre,* constituted *A. D.* 1724. and meet 1st *Thursday*

— CAERMARTHEN at the *Bunch* of *Grapes,* constituted *A. D.* 1724.

— PORTSMOUTH at the *Vine,* constituted *A. D.* 1724 and meet 1st and 2d *Friday.*

— CONGLTON in *Cheshire,* at the *Red-Lion,* constituted *A. D.* 1724.

— SALFORD near *Manchester,* at the *King's-Head,* constituted *A. D.* 1727. and meet 1st *Monday.*

— WARWICK, at the *Woolpack,* constituted 22 *April* 1728. and meet 1st and 3d *Friday.*

— SCARBOROUGH, at *Vipont's* Long Room constituted 27 *Aug.* 1729. and meet 1st *Wednesday.*

— LYN REGIS, *Norfolk,* at the *Lion,* constituted 1 *Oct* 1729. and meet 1st *Friday.*

— NORTHAMPTON, at the *George,* constituted 16 *Jan.* 17$\frac{29}{30}$. and meet 1st *Saturday.*

— St. ROOK's-HILL near *Chichester,* constituted *A. D.* 1730. and meet once in the Year, viz. on *Tuesday* in *Easter* Week.

— CANTERBURY, at the *Red-Lion.* constituted 3 *April* 1730 and meet 1st and 3d *Tuesday.*

— LINCOLN, at the *Saracen's-Head,* constituted 7 *Sept.* 1730. and meet 1st *Tuesday.*

— LEIGH in *Lancashire,* at the *King's-Arms,* constituted 22 *Feb.* 173$\frac{0}{1}$.

— BURY St. EDMUND's, at the *Fountain,* constituted *A. D.* 1731. meet 2v and 4th *Tuesday.*

— MACCLESFIESD in *Cheshire,* at the *Angel,* constituted *A. D.* 1731. meet

BURY St. EDMUND's, at the *Fleece,* constituted 1 *Nov.* 1731. meet 1st and 3d *Thursday.*

— WOOLVERHAMPTON in *Staffordshire,* at the *Bell* and *Raven,* constituted 28 *March* 1732. and meet 1st *Monday.*

— IPSWICH, at the *White Horse,* constituted *A D.* 1732 and meet 2d and 4th *Thursday.*

— EXETER, at the *New-Inn,* constituted *A. D.* 1732. and meet 1st and 3d *Wednesday.*

— DARBY, at the *Virgin's-Inn,* constituted 14 *Sept.* 1732. and meet

— BOLTON

— BOLTON LEE MOORS in Lancashire, at a private Room, constituted 9 Nov. 1732. and meet after every Full Moon, 1st Wednesday.

— BURY St. EDMUND'S, at the Seven Stars, constituted 15 Dec. 1732. and meet 2d and 4th Thursday.

— SALISBURY, at the Ram, constituted 27 Dec. 1732. and meet 1st and 3d Wednesday.

— BATH, at the Bear, constituted 18 March 173$\frac{2}{3}$. and meet 1st and 3d Friday.

— BURY in Lancashire, at the Red Lion, constituted 26 July 1733. and meet after every Full Moon, 1st Thursday.

— STOURBRIDGE in Worcestershire, at the Dog, constituted 1 Aug. 1733. meet each Wednesday.

— BIRMINGHAM, at the Swan, constituted A. D. 1733. and meet last Monday.

— PLYMOUTH, at the Mason's Arms, constituted A. D. 1734. and meet 1st and 3d Friday.

— NEWCASTLE upon Tyne, at the Fencers, constituted A. D. 1735. meet 1st Monday.

— WARMINSTER in Wiltshire, at Lord Weymouth's-Arms, constituted A. D. 1735. meet 1st Thursday.

— BRISTOL, at the Rummer, constituted 12 Nov. 1735, and meet 1st and 3d Friday.

— COLCHESTER, at the 3 Cups, constituted A. D. 1735. and meet 1st and 3d Monday.

— GATES-HEAD in the Bishoprick of Durham, at the Fountain, constituted 8 March 173$\frac{4}{5}$. meet

— SHREWSBURY, at the Fountain, constituted 16 April 1736. and meet 1st Monday.

— WEYMOUTH and MELCOMB REGIS in Dorsetshire, at the 3 Crowns, constituted A. D. 1736. meet

— NORWICH, at the King's-Head, constituted A. D. 1736. meet

— LIVERPOOL, at the George, constituted 25 June 1736. and meet 1st Wednesday.

— BIRMINGHAM, at the King's-Arms and Horshoe, constituted A. D. 1736. and meet 2d and last Tuesday.

— BRAINTREE in Essex, at the Horse, constituted 17 March, 173$\frac{6}{7}$. meet on 1st and 3d Tuesday.

— SHIPTON MALLET in Somersetshire, at - - - constituted 12 Dec. 1737. and meet

— LINCOLN Above-Hill in the Baily Wyke, at the Angel, constituted 23 Dec. 1737. and meet 1st and 3d Monday.

— HEREFORD, at the Swan and Falcon, constituted 16 Jan. 173$\frac{7}{7}$. 1st and 3d Monday.

— GLOUCESTER, at the Wheat-Sheaf, constituted 28 March 1738. meet

— HALLIFAX in Yorkshire, at the Black-Bull, constituted 1st Aug. 1738.

III. DEPU-

III. DEPUTATIONS sent beyond Sea.

Thus

— INCHIQUIN *Grand Master* granted a **Deputation** to some Brothers in *Spain*, for constituting a *Lodge* at **Gibraltar**.

— COLERANE *Grand Master* granted one for constituting a *Lodge* at **Madrid**.

— KINGSTON *Grand Master* granted one to Brother GEORGE POMFRET to constitute a *Lodge* at **Bengal** in *East India*, that had been requested by some Brethren residing there.

— NORFOLK *Grand Master* granted one to Captain RALPH FAR WINTER, to be **Provincial** *Grand Master* of EAST-INDIA at *Bengal*.

—Another to *Monsieur* DU THOM to be **Provincial** *Grand Master* of the *Circle* of Lower SAXONY.

— Another to Mr. DANIEL COX to be **Provincial** *G. Master* of NEW JERSEY in *America*.

— LOVEL *Grand Master* granted one to noble Brother CHESTERFIELD Lord *Ambassador* at the *Hague*, for holding a *Lodge* there, that made his *Royal* Highness FRANCIS Duke of *Lorrain* (now *Grand* Duke of *Tuscany*) an *Enter'd Prentice* and *Fellow Craft*.

— Another to Capt. JOHN PHILIPS to be **Provincial** *G. M.* of RUSSIA.

— Another to Capt. JAMES CUMMERFORD to be **Provincial** *G. M.* of ANDALOUSIA in *Spain*.

— VISCOUNT MONTAGU *Grand Master* granted one for constituting a *Lodge* at **Valenciennes**.

—Another for constituting a *Lodge* at the *Hotel de Bussy* in PARIS.

— STRATHMORE *Grand Master* granted one to eleven *German* Gentlemen, good Brothers, for constituti a *Lodge* at **Hamburg**.

-- **Weymouth**

--- WEYMOUTH *Grand Master* granted one to noble Brother RICHMOND for holding a *Lodge* at his Castle 𝔡'𝔄𝔲𝔟𝔦𝔤𝔫𝔶 in *France.*

--- Another to RANDOLPH TOOKE, Esq; to be 𝔓𝔯𝔬𝔳𝔦𝔫𝔠𝔦𝔞𝔩 *G. M.* of SOUTH-AMERICA.

--- Another to Brother GEORGE GORDON for constituting a *Lodge* at 𝔏𝔦𝔰𝔟𝔬𝔫 in *Portugal.*

--- Another to Mr. ROGER LACY, Merchant, for constituting a *Lodge* at 𝔖𝔞𝔳𝔞𝔫𝔫𝔞𝔥 of *Georgia* in *America.*

--- Another to RICHARD HULL, Esq; to be 𝔓𝔯𝔬𝔳𝔦𝔫𝔠𝔦𝔞𝔩 *G. M.* at GAMBAY in *West Africa.*

--- LOUDOUN *G. M.* granted one to ROBERT TOM-LINSON, Esq; to be 𝔓𝔯𝔬𝔳𝔦𝔫𝔠𝔦𝔞𝔩 *G. M.* of NEW-ENGLAND in *America.*

--- Another to JOHN HAMMERTON, Esq; to be 𝔓𝔯𝔬𝔳𝔦𝔫𝔠𝔦𝔞𝔩 *G. Master* of SOUTH-CAROLINA in *America.*

--- Another to DAVID CREIGHTON, M. D. to be P. G. M. at CAPE-COAST-CASTLE in *Africa.*

--- DARNLEY *G. M.* granted one to JAMES WATSON, Esq; to be 𝔓𝔯𝔬𝔳𝔦𝔫𝔠𝔦𝔞𝔩 *G. M.* of the Island of MONTSERRAT in *America.*

--- Another to GEORGE HAMMILTON, Esq; to be 𝔓𝔯𝔬𝔳𝔦𝔫𝔠𝔦𝔞𝔩 *G. M.* of 𝔊𝔢𝔫𝔢𝔳𝔞.

--- Another to HENRY WILLIAM MARSHALCH, Esq; Hereditary *Mareschal* of *Thuringia*, to be 𝔓𝔯𝔬𝔳𝔦𝔫𝔠𝔦𝔞𝔩 *G. M.* of the *Circle* of UPPER SAXONY.

--- Another to Capt. WILLIAM DOUGLAS to be 𝔓𝔯𝔬𝔳𝔦𝔫𝔠𝔦𝔞𝔩 *G. M.* on the *Coast* of AFRICA and in the *Islands* of AMERICA; excepting such Places where a 𝔓𝔯𝔬𝔳𝔦𝔫𝔠𝔦𝔞𝔩 *G. M.* is already deputed.

--- Another to Capt. RICHARD RIGGS to be 𝔓𝔯𝔬𝔳𝔦𝔫𝔠𝔦𝔞𝔩 *G. M.* of NEW-YORK.

--- CAERNARVON the present *G. M.* has granted a 𝔇𝔢𝔭𝔲𝔱𝔞𝔱𝔦𝔬𝔫 to his Excellency WILLIAM MATTHEWS, Esq; Captain-General and Governor in Chief of his Majesty's *Leeward*

Caribbee

Caribbee Iſlands, Vice-Admiral and Chancellor of the ſame, to be P<small>ROVINCIAL</small> G. M. there.

All theſe foreign Lodges are under the Patronage of our 𝕲𝖗𝖆𝖓𝖉 𝕸𝖆𝖘𝖙𝖊𝖗 of *England*.

But the *old Lodge* at Y<small>ORK</small> City, and the *Lodges* of S<small>COT-</small> <small>LAND</small>, I<small>RELAND</small>, F<small>RANCE</small> and I<small>TALY</small>, affecting Independen-cy, are under their own *Grand Maſters*, tho' they have the ſame *Conſtitutions, Charges, Regulations*, &c. for Subſtance, with their Brethren of *England*, and are equally zealous for the *Auguſtan Stile*, and the *Secrets* of the antient and honourable *Fraternity*.

Thoſe inquiſitive *Europeans* who travel and traffick in A<small>FRICA</small> and *Weſtern* A<small>SIA</small>, have there diſcover'd ſuch beautiful *Remains* of old magnificent *Colonading*, as give much Cauſe to lament the horrid Devaſtations made by the *Mahometans*, and heartily to wiſh for the *Revival* of the *Arts* of *Deſigning* in thoſe Parts, that good *old Maſonry* may alſo be revived there.

The antient Nations of *Eaſtern* A<small>SIA</small>, the *Mogulliſtans, Chineſe, Japoneſe, Siameſe*, &c. are ſhy of communicating their Hiſtories and Antiquities to the *Europeans*; yet the *Miſſionaries* and *Mer-chants* have there diſcover'd many wonderful Monuments of the old Architecture.

We know not much of the A<small>MERICANS</small> before the *Spaniards* came there *A. D.* 1593. and till the *Spaniards* gave us a few Accounts of the two old Empires of M<small>EXICO</small> and P<small>ERU</small>; where the *Aborigines* had built Cities and Caſtles after their own Manner. But in the *European* Colonies of *America*, true *Maſonry* has flou-riſh'd, and will do more and more, along with Commerce and Learning.

But in E<small>UROPE</small>, even after the Devaſtations made by the 𝕲𝖔𝖙𝖍𝖘, and in the darkeſt Ages, while other Parts of *Learning* were lock'd up in *Monaſtries*, A<small>RCHITECTURE</small> appear'd abroad, tho' in the 𝕲𝖔𝖙𝖍𝖎𝖈𝖐 *Stile*, till the A<small>UGUSTAN</small> *Stila* was revived in *Italy*. *See* Part I. Chap. VII.

Nay, in Proceſs of Time, the *Orders* or Fraternities of the *Warlike Knights* (and ſome of the *Religious* too) borrow'd many ſolemn Uſages from our *more antient* F<small>RATERNITY</small> that has

exiſted

exifted from the Beginning: For each *Order* of *Knights* have their GRAND MASTER, or one like him, and other *Grand Officers*, with their *Conftitutions*, *Charges*, *Regulations*, their peculiar *Jewels*, *Badges* and *Clothings*, their Forms of *Entrance*, *Promotion* and *Affembling*, of their *Seffions* and *Proceffions*, their *Communications* and *Secrets*, with many other fuch Cuftoms, &c. and as they were difperfed over *Chriftendom*, each *Fraternity* had in divers Places their feveral Meetings, or particular *Chapters*, or *Lodges* with proper Officers, accountable to the *Grand Chapter* of their refpective GRAND MASTER, who was often a *King*, or a Sovereign *Prince*, or fome *Nobleman* (as the Prince's *Deputy* 𝕲𝖗𝖆𝖓𝖉 𝕸𝖆𝖘𝖙𝖊𝖗) refiding at a certain Place in great State and Magnificence, and who govern'd the *Fraternity* wherever they were difpers'd, fupported them in their Undertakings, and protected them in their Privileges, Rights and Poffeffions, &c. as plainly appears from the Hiftories of thofe *Knightly Societies*, and from thofe of 'em that exift in Splendor to this Day.

From the Whole, it muft be own'd

That *no other* ART has been fo much encouraged by the better Sort of Mankind from the Beginning in every Part of the Earth ; as indeed *none other* is fo extenfively ufeful : And the MASONS thus countenanced by their *Royal*, *Princely*, *noble* and *learned* Brothers and Fellows, did ever feparate themfelves from the common Croud of *Artizans* and *Mechanicks* in their *well-form'd Lodges* under their proper Officers.

And now the *Freeborn* BRITISH Nations, difengaged from Wars, and enjoying the good Fruits of *Liberty* and *Peace*, the Brothers of the *Royal Art* have much indulged their bright Genius for true antient *Mafonry*, in many *particular* Lodges, *quarterly* Communications and *annual* ASSEMBLIES ; wherein their *Secrets* and *Ufages* are wifely preferved and propagated, the *Science* and the *Art* are duly cultivated, and the CEMENT of the *Lodge* is made fo firm, that the *whole Body* refembles a *well-built* ARCH of the beautiful *Auguftan Stile*.

Nay

Nay some ROYAL Perſons, with many NOBLEMEN, many eminent *Gentlemen, Citizens, Clergymen* and *Scholars* of moſt Profeſſions and Denominations, have join'd this amicable *Fraternity,* have ſtrengthen'd and adorn'd the *Lodge,* and have frankly ſubmitted to the *Charges* and wore the *Badges* of a FREE and 𝕬𝖈𝖈𝖊𝖕𝖙𝖊𝖉 MASON ; eſpecially from the Time of

𝕲𝖗𝖆𝖓𝖉 𝕸𝖆𝖘𝖙𝖊𝖗 the *Duke* of *MONTAGU,* to our preſent 𝕲𝖗𝖆𝖓𝖉 𝕸𝖆𝖘𝖙𝖊𝖗 the *Marquis* of *CAERNARVON.*

The

The APPROBATION of this BOOK of the CONSTITUTIONS.

WHEREAS at the Grand Lodge *on 24th* February 173¾. *the* Earl *of* CRAUFURD Grand Master *being in the Chair, the Author* James Anderson, *D. D. having represented that a* New *Book of* CONSTITUTIONS *was become necessary, and that he had prepar'd Materials for it; the* GRAND MASTER *and the* Lodge *order'd him to lay the same before the present and former* Grand-Officers, *as in the Grand* Lodge-Book.

And our said Brother Anderson *having submitted his Manuscript to the Perusal of some* former *Grand* Officers, *particularly our noble Brother* RICHMOND, *and our Brothers* Desaguliers, Cowper, Payne, *and others, who, after making some Corrections, have signify'd their* Approbation.

And having next, according to the foresaid Order, committed his Manuscript to the Perusal of the present *Grand* Officers, *who having also review'd and corrected it, have declared their* Approbation *of it to the* Grand Lodge *assembled in* ample *Form on the 25th* January 173⅞.

This GRAND LODGE *then agreed to order our said Brother* Anderson *to print and publish the said Manuscript or* New Book *of* CONSTITUTIONS. And it is hereby approved and recommended as the *only Book* of CONSTITUTIONS, *for the Use of the* Lodges, *of the* FREE *and* Accepted MASONS, *by the said* GRAND LODGE *on the said 25th* January 173⅞. in the Vulgar Year of *Masonry* 573⅞.

DARNLEY, Grand Master,
JOHN WARD, *Deputy* Grand Master,
ROBERT LAWLEY, } Grand
WILLIAM GRÆME, } Wardens.

John Revis
Secretary.

Some

Some of the usual *Free-Masons* Songs.

The 𝔐asters Song, by the *Author* of this Book.

In the first Book it is in 5 Parts, comprehending the History of *Masonry ; but being too long, the 3d Part is only printed here.*

I.

WE sing of Masons antient Fame !
    Lo, *Eighty Thousand* Craftsmen rise
Under the Masters of great Name,
    More than *Three Thousand* Just and Wise.
Employ'd by *SOLOMON* the Sire,
    And Gen'ral Master *Mason* too,
As Hiram was in stately *Tyre*,
    Like *Salem* built by *Mason*'s true.

2.

The *Royal* Art was then *Divine*,
    The *Craftsmen* counsell'd from above,
The *Temple* was the Grand Design,
    The wond'ring World did All approve.
Ingenious Men from every Place
    Came to survey the glorious *Pile* ;
And when return'd, began to trace
    And imitate its *lofty Stile*.

3.

At length the Grecians came to know
    Geometry, and learn'd the *Art*
Pythagoras was rais'd to show,
    And glorious Euclid to impart:
Great Archimedes too appear'd,
    And *Carthaginian* Masters bright ;
Till *Roman* Citizens uprear'd
    The Art with Wisdom and Delight.

5. They

4.

But when proud *Afia* they had quell'd,
    And *Greece* and *Egypt* overcome,
In Architecture they excell'd,
    And brought the Learning all to *Rome:*
Where wife VITRUVIUS *Warden* prime,
    Of Architects the *Art* improv'd
In great *AUGUSTUS*' peaceful Time,
    When *Arts* and *Artifts* were belov'd.

5.

They brought the Knowledge from the *Eaft*,
    And as they made the Nations yield,
They fpread it thro' the *North* and *Weft*,
    And taught the World the Art to build.
Witnefs their *Citadels* and *Tow'rs*
    To fortify their Legions fine,
Their *Temples*, *Palaces* and *Bow'rs*
    That fpoke the Mafons GRAND DESIGN.

6.

Thus mighty *Eaftern* Kings and fome
    Of ABRAM's Race, and Monarch's good
Of *Egypt*, *Syria*, *Greece* and *Rome*,
    True ARCHITECTURE underftood.
No wonder then if *Mafons* join
    To celebrate thofe MASON-KINGS,
With folemn Note and flowing Wine,
    Whilft every Brother jointly fings.

Chorus.

Who can unfold the *Royal Art*,
    Or fhew its *Secrets* in a Song?
They're fafely kept in *Mafon*'s Heart,
    And to the antient *Lodge* belong!
        To the KING and the CRAFT.
            D d   II. The

II. The 𝕮𝖆𝖗𝖉𝖊𝖓𝖘 Song, also by the *Author* of this *Book*.

In the firſt Book it was of 13 *Verſes*, too long : But this laſt *Verſe* and *Chorus* is thought enough to be ſung.

FROM henceforth ever ſing
The *Craftſman* and the *King*,
With Poetry and Muſick ſweet
Reſound their Harmony compleat,
And with *Geometry* in ſkilful Hand
Due Homage pay,
Without Delay,
To great CAERNARVON now our MASTER GRAND.
He rules the Freeborn *Sons* of *Art*
By Love and Friendſhip, Hand and Heart.

𝕮𝖍𝖔𝖗𝖚𝖘 of the 𝕮𝖆𝖗𝖉𝖊𝖓𝖘 Song.

Who can rehearſe the Praiſe
In ſoft Poetick Lays,
Or ſolid Proſe, of *Maſons* true,
Whoſe Art tranſcends the common View?
Their *Secrets* ne'er to Strangers yet expos'd,
Preſerv'd ſhall be
By *Maſons Free*,
And only to the *antient Lodge* diſclos'd ;
Becauſe they're kept in *Maſons Heart*
By Brethren of the *Royal Art*.

To the GRAND MASTER.

III. The

III. The Fellow Craft's Song, by Brother CHARLES DE LA FAY, Esq; in the First Book.

1.

HAIL MASONRY! Thou *Craft* divine!
 Glory of Earth! from Heaven reveal'd!
Which doth with *Jewels* precious shine,
 From all but *Masons* Eyes conceal'd.

Chorus.

Thy Praises *due who can rehearse,*
In nervous Prose *or flowing* Verse?

2.

As Men from Brutes distinguish'd are,
 A *Mason* other Men excels;
For what's in Knowledge choice and rare
 But in his Breast securely dwells?

Chorus.

His silent Breast *and faithful* Heart
Preserve the Secrets *of the* Art.

3.

From scorching Heat and piercing Cold,
 From Beasts whose Roar the Forest rends,
From the Assaults of Warriors bold
 The *Masons* ART Mankind defends.

Chorus.

Be to this Art *due Honour paid.*
From which Mankind receives such Aid.

4.

Ensigns of State that feed our Pride,
 Distinctions troublesome and vain,
By *Masons true* are laid aside,
 Arts *Freeborn Sons* such Toys disdain.

Chorus.

Innobled by the Name *they bear,*
Distinguish'd by the Badge *they wear.*

5. Sweet

5.

Sweet *Fellowſhip* from Envy free,
 Friendly Converſe of *Brotherhood*
The *Lodge's* laſting CEMENT be,
 Which has for Ages firmly ſtood.

Chorus.

A LODGE *thus built for Ages paſt*
Has laſted, and ſhall ever laſt.

6.

Then in our *Songs* be Juſtice done
 To thoſe who have inrich'd the *Art,*
From ADAM to CAERNARVON down,
 And let each Brother bear a Part.

Chorus.

Let noble Maſons *Healths go round,*
Their Praiſe in Lofty Lodge *reſound.*

To the Deputy GRAND MASTER and Grand Wardens.

IV. The *Enter'd* Prentice's SONG, by Brother
 Matthew Birkhead, deceas'd, in the firſt Book.
  To be ſung after grave Buſineſs is over.

1.

COME let us prepare,
 We Brothers that are,
Aſſembled on merry Occaſion;
 Let's drink, laugh and ſing,
 Our Wine has a Spring,
Here's an Health to an *Accepted Maſon.*
  All Charged.

2.

 The World is in Pain
 Our Secrets to gain,
And ſtill let them wonder and gaze on;
 Till they're ſhorn the Light,
 They'll ne're know the right
Word or Sign of an *Accepted Maſon.*   3. 'Tis

3.

Tis *This* and 'tis *That*,
They cannot tell *what*,
Why so many great Men of the Nation,
Should Aprons put on
To make themselves one,
With a *Free* and an *Accepted Mason*.

4.

Great Kings, Dukes and Lords
Have laid by their Swords,
Our Myst'ry to put a good Grace on,
And ne're been asham'd
To hear themselves nam'd
With a *Free* and an *Accepted Mason*.

5.

Antiquity's Pride
We have on our Side,
And it maketh Men just in their Station;
There's nought but what's good
To be understood
By a *Free* and an *Accepted Mason*.

6.

We're true and sincere
And just to the *Fair*;
They'll trust us on any Occasion:
No Mortal can more
The Ladies adore,
Than a *Free* and an *Accepted Mason*.

7

Then join Hand in Hand,
By each Brother firm stand,
Let's be merry and put a bright Face on:
What Mortal can boast
So noble a Toast,
As a *Free* and an *Accepted Mason*?

Chorus.

Chorus.

No Mortal can boaſt
So noble a Toaſt,
As a FREE *and an* ACCEPTED MASON.
Thrice repeated in due Form,
To all the *Fraternity* round the *Globe*.

The following SONGS are not in the *firſt Book*, but being
uſually ſung, they are now printed.

I. The *Deputy Grand Maſter's* SONG.

N. B. *Every two* laſt Lines *of each Verſe is the* Chorus.

I.

ON, on, my dear *Brethren*, purſue your great *Lecture*,
  And refine on the Rules of old *Architecture* :
High Honour to *Maſons* the *Craft* daily brings,
To thoſe Brothers of *Princes* and Fellows of *Kings*.

2.

We drove the rude Vandals and Goths off the Stage,
Reviving the *Art* of AUGUSTUS' fam'd Age :
And *Veſpaſian* deſtroy'd the *vaſt* TEMPLE in vain,
Since ſo many now riſe in CAERNARVON's mild Reign.

3.

The noble *five Orders* compos'd with ſuch Art,
Will amaze the fixt Eye, and engage the whole Heart :
Proportion's ſweet Harmony gracing the Whole,
Gives our *Work*, like the glorious *Creation*, a Soul.

4.

Then *Maſter* and *Brethren*, preſerve your great Name,
This LODGE ſo majeſtick will purchaſe you Fame ;
Rever'd it ſhall ſtand till *all Nature* expire,
And it's Glories ne're fade till the *World* is on Fire.

5. See

5.

See, see, behold here, what rewards all our Toil,
Infpires our Genius, and bids Labour fmile :
To our *noble* GRAND MASTER let a Bumper be crown'd,
To *all* 𝕸𝖆𝖋𝖔𝖓𝖘 a Bumper, fo let it go round.

6.

Again, my lov'd *Brethren*, again let it pafs,
Our antient firm *Union* cements with the Glafs ;
And all the Contention 'mongft *Mafons* fhall be,
Who better can work, or who better agree.

Additional Stanza *by Brother* Gofton, *at the Time when the* PRINCE
was made a Mafon, *and while the* PRINCESS *was pregnant.*

7.

Again let it pafs to the ROYAL lov'd NAME,
Whofe glorious Admiffion has crown'd all our Fame:
May a LEWIS be born, whom the World fhall admire,
Serene as his *Mother*, Auguft as his *Sire*.

Chorus.

Now a LEWIS is born, whom the World fhall admire,
Serene as his MOTHER, *Auguft* as his SIRE.

To our Brother FREDERICK, his *Royal* Highnefs the Prince of *Wales*.
To our Brother FRANCIS, his *Royal* Highnefs the *Grand* Duke of *Tufcany*.
To the 𝕷𝖊𝖜𝖎𝖘.

II. The 𝕲𝖗𝖆𝖓𝖉 𝖂𝖆𝖗𝖉𝖊𝖓𝖘 SONG.   By Brother *Oates*.

I.

LET *Mafonry* be now my Theme,
   Throughout the Globe to fpread it's Fame,
And eternize each worthy Brother's Name.
      Your Praife fhall to the Skies refound,
      In lafting Happinefs abound,
And with fweet *Union* All your noble Deeds } Repeat
   be crown'd.   } this Line.

Chorus.

Chorus.

Sing then, my Muse, to Mason's *Glory,*
Your Names are so rever'd in Story,
That all th' admiring World do now adore ye !

2.

Let Harmony divine inspire
Your Souls with Love and gen'rous Fire,
To copy well wise SOLOMON your SIRE.
Knowledge sublime shall fill each Heart,
The Rules of *G'ometry* t'impart,
While *Wisdom, Strength* and *Beauty* crown the } Repeat
glorious *Art.* this Line.

Chorus. *Sing then my Muse,* &c.

3.

All Charged.

Let Great CAERNARVON's Health go round,
In swelling Cups all Cares be drown'd,
And Hearts united 'mongst the *Craft* be found.
May everlasting Scenes of Joy
His peaceful Hours of Bliss employ,
Which Time's all-conquering Hand shall ne'er, shall } Repeat
ne'er destroy. this Line.

Chorus. *Sing then my Muse,* &c.

4.

My Brethren, thus all Cares resign,
Your Hearts let glow with Thoughts divine,
And Veneration shew to SOLOMON's *Shrine.*
Our annual Tribute thus we'll pay,
That late Posterity shall say,
We've crown'd with Joy this glorious, *Happy,* } All Sing.
Happy Day.

Chorus.

Sing then my Muse *to* Masons *Glory,*
Your Names are so rever'd in Story,
That all th' admiring World do now adore ye.
To all the *noble* LORDS that have been GRAND MASTERS.

The

III. The Treasurer's SONG.

N. B. The two *last Lines* of each Verse is a Chorus.

1.

GRANT me, kind Heaven, what I request ;
In *Masonry* let me blest ;
Direct me to that happy Place
Where *Friendship* smiles in every Face ;
 Where *Freedom* and sweet *Innocence*
 Enlarge the Mind and cheer the Sense.

2.

Where scepter'd *Reason* from her Throne
Surveys the LODGE and makes us one ;
And *Harmony*'s delightful Sway
For ever sheds Ambrosial Day ;
 Where we blest *Eden*'s Pleasure taste,
 Whilst balmy Joys are our Repast.

3.

Our LODGE the social *Virtues* grace,
And *Wisdom*'s Rules we fondly trace ;
Whole *Nature*, open to our View,
Points out the Paths we should pursue.
 Let us subsist in lasting Peace,
 And may our Happiness increase.

4.

No *prying Eye* can view us here,
No *Fool* or *Knave* disturb our Cheer ;
Our well-form'd *Laws* set Mankind free,
And give Relief to *Misery* :
 The POOR oppress'd with Woe and Grief,
 Gain from our bounteous Hands *Relief.*

To all *Charitable* MASONS.

E e   The

IV. The Secretary's SONG.

N. B. The two *last Lines* of each Verse is the Chorus.

1.

YE *Brethren* of the antient *Craft*,
　Ye fav'rite Sons of Fame,
Let Bumpers cheerfully be quaff'd
　To great CAERNARVON's Name.
Happy, long happy may he be,
Who loves and honours *Masonry*.
　With a Fa, la, la, la, la.

2.

In vain would *Danvers* with his Wit *
　Our flow Resentment raise;
What He and all Mankind have writ
　But celebrates our Praise.
His Wit this only *Truth* imparts,
That MASONS have firm *faithful Hearts*.
　With a Fa, &c.

* That those who hang'd Capt. *Porteous* at *Edinburgh* were all *Free Masons*, because they kept their own Secrets. See *Craftsman*, 16 *April* 1736. Nº. 563.

3.

Ye *British* FAIR, for Beauty fam'd,
　Your Slaves we wish to be ;
Let none for Charms like yours be nam'd
　That love not *Masonry*.
This Maxim *D'Anvers* proves full well,
That MASONS *never kiss and tell*.
　With a Fa, la, &c.

4.

True *Masons !* no Offences give,
　Let Fame your Worth declare,
Within your *Compass* wisely live,
　And act upon the *Square :*
May *Peace* and *Friendship* e'er abound,
And *Great* CAERNARVON's Health go round.
　With a Fa, la, la, la, la, &c.

To All True and Faithful.

V. The

V. The Sword bearer's Song.

N. B. The laft *two Lines* of each Verfe is the Chorus.

1.

TO all who *Mafonry* defpife
  This Counfel I beftow:
Don't ridicule, if you are wife,
  A *Secret* you don't know.
Yourfelves you banter, but not it,
You fhew your *Spleen*, but not your *Wit*.
  With a Fa, la, la, la, la.

2.

Infpiring *Virtue* by our Rules,
  And in ourfelves fecure,
We have Compaffion for thofe Fools
  Who think our *Acts* impure:
We know from *Ignorance* proceeds
Such mean Opinion of our *Deeds*.
  With a Fa, &c.

3.

If *Union* and *Sincerity*
  Have a Pretence to pleafe,
We *Brothers* of the MASONRY
  Lay juftly Claim to thefe:
To *State-Difputes* we ne'er give Birth,
Our Motto *Friendfhip* is, and *Mirth*.
  With a Fa, &c.

E e 2   4. Then

4.

Then let us laugh, fince we've impos'd
  On thofe who make a Pother,
And cry, the *Secret* is difclos'd
  By fome falfe-hearted Brother :
The *mighty* SECRET's gain'd, they boaft,
From *Poft-Boy* and from *Flying-Boy.*
  With a Fa, la, la, la, la.

To all *Mafters* and *Wardens* of regular *Lodges.*

VI. An Ode to the FREE MASONS.

N. B. The two *laft Lines* of each Verfe is the Chorus.

1.

BY MASONS *Art* th' afpiring *Domes*
  In ftately *Columns* fhall arife ;
All Climates are their Native Homes,
  Their learned Actions reach the Skies,
Heroes and *Kings* revere their Name,
While *Poets* fing their lafting Fame.

2.

Great, Noble, *Gen'rous,* Good *and* Brave,
  Are Titles they moft juftly claim :
Their *Deeds* fhall live beyond the Grave,
  Which thofe unborn fhall loud proclaim.
Time fhall their glorious Acts enrol,
While Love and Friendfhip charm the Soul.

To the lafting *Honour* of the FREE MASONS.

VII. An

VII. An Ode on MASONRY, by Brother J. BANCKS.
N. B. The two *laſt Lines* of each Verſe is the Chorus.

1.

GENIUS of MASONRY deſcend,
  In myſtick Numbers while we ſing;
Enlarge our Souls, the *Craft* defend,
  And hither all thy Inſluence bring.
With ſocial Thoughts our Boſoms fill,
And give thy Turn to every Will.

2.

While yet Batavia's wealthy *Pow'rs*
  Neglect thy Beauties to explore;
And winding SEINE, adorn'd with Tow'rs,
  Laments thee wand'ring from his Shore;
Here ſpread thy Wings, and glad theſe Iſles,
Where *Arts* reſide, and *Freedom* ſmiles.

3.

Behold the LODGE riſe into View,
  The Work of *Induſtry* and *Art*;
'Tis Grand, and Regular, and True,
  For ſo is each good *Maſon's* Heart.
Friendſhip cements it from the Ground,
And *Secrecy* ſhall fence it round.

4.

A ſtately DOME o'erlooks our *Eaſt*,
  Like Orient *Phœbus* in the Morn;
And *two tall* PILLARS in the *Weſt*
  At once ſupport us and adorn.
Upholden thus the *Structure* ſtands,
Untouch'd by ſacrilegious Hands.

5. For

5

For *Concord* form'd, our Souls agree,
  Nor Fate this *Union* ſhall deſtroy :
Our Toils and Sports alike are free,
  And all is *Harmony* and Joy.
So S A L E M's 𝔗𝔢𝔪𝔭𝔩𝔢 roſe by Rule,
Without the Noiſe of noxious Tool.

6.

As when *Amphion* tun'd his Song,
  Ev'n rugged Rocks the Muſick knew ;
Smooth'd into Form, they glide along,
  And to a T H E B E S the *Deſart* grew:
So at the Sound of H I R A M's *Voice*
We riſe, we join, and we rejoice.

7.

Then may our Vows to *Virtue* move,
  To *Virtue* own'd in all her Parts :
Come *Candour*, *Innocence* and *Love*,
  Come and poſſeſs our faithful Hearts:
Mercy, who feeds the hungry *Poor*,
And *Silence*, Guardian of the Door.

8.

And thou A S T R Æ A (tho' from Earth,
  When Men on Men began to prey,
Thou fled'ſt to claim celeſtial Birth)
  Down from *Olympus* wing thy Way ;
And mindful of thy antient Seat,
Be preſent ſtill where M A S O N S meet.

9.

Immortal S C I E N C E too be near,
  (We own thy Empire o'er the Mind)
Dreſs'd in thy radiant Robes appear,
  With all thy beauteous Train behind ;
I N V E N T I O N young and blooming There,
Here G E O M E T R Y with *Rule* and *Square*.

10. In

10.

In *Egypt's* FABRICK * Learning dwelt,
 And *Roman* Breasts could Virtue hide :
But *Vulcan's* Rage the Building felt,
 And *Brutus*, last of *Romans*, dy'd :
Since when, dispers'd the *Sisters* rove,
Or fill paternal Thrones above.

        * The *Ptolemans* Library.

11.

But lost to half of human Race,
 With us the *Virtues* shall revive ;
And driv'n no more from Place to Place,
 Here SCIENCE shall be kept alive :
And manly *Taste*, the Child of *Sense*,
Shall banish Vice and Dulness hence.

12.

United thus, and for these Ends,
 Let *Scorn* deride, and *Envy* rail ;
From Age to Age the CRAFT descends,
 And what we build shall never fail :
Nor shall the World *our Works survey* ;
But every Brother *keeps the Key !*

To ARTS and SCIENCES.

A DEFENCE

A DEFENCE of MASONRY, publiſh'd *A. D.* 1730.
Occaſion'd by a *Pamphlet* call'd *Maſonry Diſſected.*

CHAP. I. AMONG the extraordinary Diſcoveries of the preſent Age, nothing
has been received with more Delight and Exultation, than a few
Sheets, written, it ſeems, *without Partiality,* call'd *Maſonry Diſſected.* The *Grand*
𝕾𝖊𝖈𝖗𝖊𝖙, which has long withſtood the Batteries of Temptation, that neither *Mo-*
ney, the Maſter Key of the Heart, nor *good Liquor,* that unlocks the very Soul,
nor *Hunger,* that breaks through Stone-Walls, nor Thirſt, a ſore Evil to a *Working*
Maſon, could bring to Light; has at laſt been diſgorged *upon Oath,* to the great
Eaſement of a tender Stomach, the eternal Scandal of the *Fraternity,* and the Good
of the *Publick* never to be forgotten! The Deſign was no leſs then to diſburthen a
loaded *Conſcience,* to acquaint the World, *That never did ſo ridiculous an Impoſition*
appear among Mankind; and to prevent ſo many innocent Perſons being drawn into ſo
pernicious a Society!

What could induce the *Diſſector* to take that Oath, or the *Magiſtrate* to admit it,
ſhall not at this Time be decided.

However, I muſt give the World Joy of ſo notable a Diſcovery, ſo honourable,
ſo circumſtantiated! a mighty Expectation was raiſed, and, without Doubt, is wonderfully gratified by this Courſe of Anatomy. *It muſt be this, it can be nothing elſe:*
It is as we always ſuppoſed, a whimſical Cheat *ſupported by great* Names *to ſeduce*
Fools, *who, once gull'd out of their Money, keep the Fraud ſecret to draw in*
others.

I confeſs, I cannot come into this Method of Arguing; nor is it, in my Opinion, a fair Way of treating a *Society,* to run implicitly with the Cry, without
examining whether theſe Reproaches are founded upon any Thing in the *Myſtery*
(as now repreſented) either *wicked* or *ridiculous.* For that ſtupid Imputation of
drawing in Fools for the Sake of their Money, can have no Weight in the preſent
Caſe; ſince the *Fraternity,* as it now ſtands, conſiſts principally of Members of
great Honour and Diſtinction, much ſuperior to Views ſo ſordid and ungenerous.

For once then, let this *Diſſection* contain *all* the *Secrets* of FREE MASONRY;
admit that every Word of it is *genuine* and literally *true,* and that the whole Scheme
conſiſts of no more nor no leſs: Yet under all theſe Conceſſions, under all the Diſ-
advantages and Prejudices whatever, I cannot but ſtill believe, *there have been Im-*
poſitions upon Mankind more ridiculous, and that many have been drawn into a Society
more pernicious.

I would

I would not be thought agitated upon this Occasion, as if I were any Way concern'd whether this *Diſſection* be true or falſe? or whether the Credit of *Free Maſonry* be affected by it or not? Theſe Conſiderations can give me no Trouble. My Deſign is to addreſs to the ſenſible and ſerious Part of Mankind, by making a few impartial Remarks upon this *Diſſection*, without contending for the Reputation of *Maſonry* on the one Hand, or reflecting upon the *Diſſector* on the other.

CHAP. II. THE formidable Objection which has given Offence to the better Part of Men, is the Copy of the *Oath* as it lies in the *Diſſection*. It has been a Matter of Admiration, that ſo many Perſons of great Piety, ſtrict Conſcience and unſpotted Character, ſhould lay themſelves under ſo ſolemn an Obligation, under Penalties ſo terrible and aſtoniſhing, upon a Subject ſo trifling and inſignificant.

To obviate this Objection, I obſerve; that the *End*, the *Moral* and *Purport* of MASONRY, as deſcribed in the *Diſſection*, is *to ſubdue our Paſſions, not to do our own Will; to make a daily Progreſs in a laudable Art; to promote Morality, Charity, good Fellowſhip, good Nature and Humanity*. This appears to be the *Subſtance*, let the *Form* or Vehicle be ever ſo unaccountable.

As for the Terms relating to *Architecture*, *Geometry* and *Mathematicks*, that are diſperſed throughout the *Diſſection*, it would be ſtrange if a Society of ſuch a Denomination, could ſubſiſt wholly without them; tho' they ſeem (to me at leaſt) to be rather *Technical* and *Formal* (yet deliver'd perhaps by long Tradition) than eſſentially attached to the *Grand* DESIGN.

Now where is the *Impiety*, where the *Immorality*, or *Folly*, for a Number of Men to form themſelves into a Society, whoſe main End is to improve in commendable Skill and Knowledge, and to promote univerſal Beneficence and the ſocial Virtues of human Life, under the ſolemn Obligation of an *Oath?* And This, in what *Form*, under what ſecret Reſtrictions, and with what innocent Ceremonies They think proper?

This Liberty all Incorporate Societies enjoy without Impeachment or Reflection: An *Apprentice* is bound to keep the Secrets of his *Maſter*, a *Freeman* is obliged to conſult the Intereſt of his Company, and not to proſtitute in common the *Myſteries* of his Trade: Secret *Committees* and Privy *Councils* are ſolemnly enjoin'd not to publiſh abroad their Debates and Reſolutions. There appears to be ſomething like *Maſonry* (as the *Diſſector* deſcribes it) in all regular Societies of whatever Denomination: They are *All* held together by a Sort of *Cement*, by Bonds and Laws that are peculiar to each of them, from the Higheſt to the little Clubs and Nightly Meetings of a private Neighbourhood. There are *Oaths* adminiſter'd, and ſometimes ſolemn Obligations to *Secrecy*: There are a MASTER, two Wardens, and a Number of *Aſſiſtants*, to make what the *Diſſector* may call (if he pleaſes) a *Perfect Lodge* in the City-Companies. There is the Degree of *Enter'd Prentices*, Maſter of his Trade, or *Fellow Craft*, and Maſter, or the *Maſter* of the Company There are *Conſtitutions* and Orders, and a ſucceſſive, a gradual Enjoyment of Offices, according to the ſeveral Rules and Limitations of Admiſſion.

But

But it is reply'd, that the general Design of *Masonry* may be commendable, or at least innocent, and yet be carried on to the same Advantage without the Solemnity of an *Oath*, especially pressed under such dreadful Penalties.

In answer, I observe, t at the *Question* is not whether the Purpose of *Masonry* may as well be served without an *Oath* ? But *whether an* Oath, *in the present Case, be lawful, and may be taken with a good Conscience ?* And to solve this Difficulty I shall introduce the Opinion of *Bishop* SANDERSON, the most judicious Casuist that ever treated upon the Subject of *Oaths*; who says, *When a Thing is not by any Precept or Interdict, Divine or Human, so determin'd; but every Man,* pro hic & nunc, *may at his Choice do or not do, as he sees expedient; Let him do what he will, he sinneth not,* 1 Cor. vii. 36. *As if* Caius *should swear to sell his Land to* Titius, *or to lend him an hundred Crowns: The Answer is brief, an Oath in this Case is both lawful and binding.*

De Obligatione Juramenti Prælect. 3. Sect. 15.

Now I would know what Precept, *Divine* or *Human,* has any way determin'd upon the Contents of the *Dissection?* And whether the general Design of *Masonry,* as there laid down, is not at least of equal Benefit and Importance to the Publick, with the lending of an hundred Crowns to a private Man ? The Answers to these Questions are obvious, and the Consequence is equally plain, that *an Oath upon the Subject of Masonry is at least justifiable and lawful.*

As for the Terror of the *Penalty,* the World, upon that Occasion, is commonly mistaken; for the *Solemnity* of the *Oath* does not in the least add to the Obligation; or, in other Words, the *Oath* is equally binding without any *Penalty* at all. The same Casuist has this Expression : *A* Solemn Oath *of itself, and in its own Nature, is not more obligatory than a* Simple One; *because the Obligation of an* Oath *ariseth precisely from* This, *that God is invoked, as a Witness and Revenger, no less in a* Simple Oath *than in the solemn and corporal; for the Invocation is made precisely by the Pronunciation of the Words (which is the same both in the* simple *and* solemn) *and not by any corporal Motion or concomitant Sign, in which the* Solemnity *of the* Oath *consists.*

Prælect. 5. Sect. 12.

I write to intelligent Readers, and therefore this Citation wants not to be explain'd.

But further, if the *Oath* in the *Dissection* be taken by *all Masons* upon their Admission, no Member of the *Fraternity,* upon any Pretence whatsoever, dares violate the Obligation of it, without incurring the Guilt of *Perjury;* even supposing that *Masonry* were more trifling and indifferent, than in the *Dissection* it may appear to be. And therefore if the Conduct of the *Dissector* has stagger'd the Conscience of any one of the Brotherhood, concerning the Observation of *that Oath;* and has induced him to trifle and play with the Force of it, I hope he will desist betimes, lest he becomes actually forsworn.

Prælect. 4. Sect. 11 This Case is thus determin'd by the same Casuist, *A Voluntary* Oath *is the more binding for being* Voluntary; *because there is no straiter Obligation than that which we take willingly upon ourselves.* And in another Place Prælect. 3. Sect. 15. the Casuist is more particular, *Where a Matter is so trivial*

that

that it is not worth the Deliberation of a wise Man, nor matters a Straw whether it be done or not done; as to reach up a Chip or to rub one's Beard; or for the Slightness of the Matter is not much to be esteem'd; as to give a Boy an Apple, or to lend a Pin; an Oath is binding in a Matter of the least Moment: Because weighty and trivial Things have a like Respect unto Truth and Falshood; And farther, because every Party swearing is bound to perform all he promised as far as he is able, and as far as it is lawful: But to give an Apple to a Boy is both possible and lawful; he is bound therefore to perform it, he ought to fulfil his Oath,

CHAP. III. HAVING taken off the Weight of the great Objection, the Design of this Chapter is to remove an Imputation, which has been often urged with great Confidence, *viz. The* Principles *and the whole Frame of* Free Masonry *is so very weak and ridiculous, that it reflects upon Men of the least Understanding to be concern'd in it!* And now, say the merry Gentlemen, it appears evidently to be so by the *Dissection*, which discovers nothing but an unintelligible Heap of Stuff and Jargon, without common Sense or Connection.

I confess I am of another Opinion; tho' the *Scheme of Masonry*, as reveal'd by the *Dissector*, seems liable to Exceptions: Nor is it so clear to me as to be fully understood at first View, by attending only to the *literal* Construction of the Words: And for aught I know, the *System*, as taught in the regular *Lodges*, may have some Redundancies or Defects, occasion'd by the Ignorance or Indolence of the old Members. And indeed, considering through what Obscurity and Darkness the *Mystery* has been deliver'd down; the many Centuries it has survived; the many Countries and Languages, and *Sects* and *Parties* it has run through; we are rather to wonder it ever arriv'd to the present Age, without more Imperfection. In short, I am apt to think that MASONRY (as it is now explain'd) has in some Circumstances declined from its *original Purity!* It has run long in muddy Streams, and as it were, under Ground: But notwithstanding the great Rust it may have contracted, and the forbidding Light it is placed in by the *Dissector*, there is (if I judge right) much of the *old Fabrick* still remaining; the essential Pillars of the Building may be discover'd through the Rubbish, tho' the Superstructure be over-run with Moss and Ivy, and the Stones, by Length of Time, be disjointed. And therefore, as the 𝕭usto of an *old* HERO is of great Value among the Curious, tho' it has lost an Eye, the Nose, or the Right Hand; so MASONRY with all its Blemishes and Misfortunes, instead of appearing ridiculous, ought (in my humble Opinion) to be receiv'd with some Candour and Esteem, from a Veneration to its *Antiquity*.

I was exceedingly pleas'd to find the *Dissector* lay the *Original* Scene of *Masonry* in the EAST, a Country always famous for *Symbolical* Learning supported by *Secrecy*; I could not avoid immediately thinking of the *old* EGYPTIANS, who conceal'd the chief *Mysteries* of their Religion under *Signs* and *Symbols*, call'd 𝕳ieroglyphics: and so great was their Regard for *Silence* and *Secrecy*, that they

F f 2   had

Vid. Imagines Deorum, | had a *Deity* call'd HARPOCRATES, whom they respected
a *Vincentio Chartario.* | with peculiar Honour and Veneration. A learned Author
has given us a Description of this *Idol*, thus; HARPOCRATES *the God of* Silence
was formed with his Right Hand *placed near the* Heart, *cover'd with a* Skin
before, full of Eyes *and* Ears; *to signify by this, that many Things are to be seen
and heard, but little to be spoken.* And among the same People, their great Goddess I IS (*the same as* MINERVA, *the Goddess of* Strength *and* Wisdom, *among
the* Greeks) *had always the* Image *of a* Sphinx *placed in the Entrance of her
Temples; because their Secrets should be preserved under* sacred *Coverings, that they
might be kept from the Knowledge of the* Vulgar, *as much as the* Riddles *of*
Sphinx!

PYTHAGORAS, by travelling into *Egypt*, became instructed in the *Mysteries* of
that Nation; and here he laid the Foundation of all his *Symbolical* Learning. The

Vid. JAMBLICHUS. Vit. Pythagoræ. | several Writers that have mention'd this *Phi-*
LAERTIUS, Vit. Pythagoræ. | *losopher*, and given an Account of his *Sect* and
PORPHYRIUS. CLEM. ALEX. Strom. | Institutions, have convinced me fully, that
FREE MASONRY, as publish'd by the *Dissector*, is very nearly allied to the old
Pythagorean Discipline; from whence, I am perswaded, it may, in some Circum-
stances, very justly claim its Descent. To mention a few,

Upon the Admission of a Disciple, he was bound by a *solemn Oath* to conceal
the *Mysteries* from the *Vulgar* and *Uninitiated.*

The principal and most efficacious of their Doctrines were (says JAMBLICHUS)
ever kept Secret *among themselves; they were continued* unwritten, *and preserved only
by* Memory *to their Successors, to whom they deliver'd them as* Mysteries *of the*
Gods.

They conversed with one another by Signs, *and had particular Words which they
received upon their Admission, and which were preserved with great Reverence, as the
Distinction of their Sect :* For (it is the judicious Remark of *LAERTIUS*) as Generals *use* Watch-Words *to distinguish their own Soldiers from Others, so it is proper to communicate to the Initiated, peculiar Signs and Words, as distinctive Marks of a*
Society.

The PYTHAGOREANS professed a great Regard for what the *Dissector* calls the
four Principles of MASONRY, *viz. A Point, a Line, a Superficies,* and *a Solid ;*
and particularly held that a SQUARE was a very proper Emblem of the *Divine*

Vid. PROCLUS in *Euclid.* | *Essence ; the Gods*, they say, *who are the Authors of every
Lib.* 11. Def. 2. & 34. | *Thing established in* Wisdom, Strength *and* Beauty, *are
not improperly represented by the Figure of a Square.*

Many more Instances might be produced, would the Limits of my Design admit;

CLEM. ALEXANDR. | I shall only observe, that there was a *FalseBrother*, one HIPPAR-
Strom. 5. | CHUS, of this Sect, who, out of Spleen and Disappointment,
broke through the *Bond* of his *Oath*, and committed the *Secrets* of the Society to
Writing, in Order to bring the Doctrine into Contempt : He was immediately expell'd the School, as a Person most infamous and abandon'd, as one dead to all

Sense

Senſe of Virtue and Goodneſs; and the *Pythagoreans*, according to their Cuſtom, made *a Tomb* for him, as if he had been actually Dead. The Shame and Diſgrace, that juſtly attended this *Violation* of his *Oath*, threw the poor Wretch into a Fit of Madneſs and Deſpair, ſo that *He cut his Throat* and periſh'd by his own Hands; and (which ſurprized me to find) his Memory was ſo abhorred after Death, that his Body lay *upon the Shore* of the Iſland of *Samos*, and had no other Burial than in the *Sands of the Sea!*

The ESSENES among the *Jews* were a Sort of *Pythagoreans*, and correſponded, in many Particulars, with the Practice of the *Fraternity*, as deliver'd in the *Diſ-ſection*. For Example.

When a Perſon deſired to be admitted into their Society, he was to paſs through *Two* Degrees of Probation, before he could be perfect Maſter of their *Myſteries*. When he was received into the Claſs of *Novices*, he was preſented with a *White Garment*; and when he had been long enough to give ſome competent Proofs of his *Secrecy* and *Virtue*, he was admitted to further Knowledge: But ſtill he went on with the Trial of his Integrity and good Manners, and then was fully taken into the Society.

But before he was received as an eſtabliſh'd Member, he was firſt to bind himſelf by ſolemn Obligations and Profeſſions, *To do Juſtice, to do no Wrong, to keep Fait with all Men, to embrace the Truth, to keep his Hands clear from Theft and fraudulent Dealing*; *not to conceal from his Fellow Profeſſors any of the* Myſteries, *nor communicate any of them to the Profane. tho' it ſhould be to ſave his Life; to deliver nothing but what he received, and to endeavour to preſerve the Principle that he profeſſes. They eat and drink at the ſame Common Table; and the* Fraternity *that come from any other Place are ſure to be received there. They meet together in an* Aſſembly, *and the* Right Hand *is laid upon the Part between the* Chin *and the* Breaſt, *while the* Left Hand *is let down ſtraight by their Side.*

Vid. PHILO de Vita Contemplativa. JOSEPHUS Antiq. lib. 8. cap. 2.

The CABALISTS, another *Sect*, dealt in hidden and myſterious Ceremonies. The *Jews* had a great Regard for this Science, and thought they made uncommon Diſcoveries by means of it. They divided their Knowledge into *Speculative* and *Operative*. DAVID and SOLOMON, they ſay, were exquiſitely ſkill'd in it; and no body at firſt preſumed to commit it to *Writing*: But (what ſeems moſt to the preſent Purpoſe) the Perfection of their Skill conſiſted in what the *Diſſector* calls *Lettering of it*, or by ordering the Letters of a Word in a particular Manner.

Vid. BASNAGE's Hiſt. of the *Jews*, on CABALA. COLLIER's Dictionary on the Word *Cabala*.

The laſt Inſtance I ſhall mention is That of the DRUIDS in our own Nation, who were the only *Prieſts* among the antient *Britons*. In their Solemnities they were clothed in *White*; and their Ceremonies always ended with a good *Feaſt*. POMPONIUS MELA relates of 'em, *that their* Science *was only an Effort of Memory; for they wrote down nothing, and they never fail'd to repeat many* Verſes, *which they*
received

Vid. CÆSARIS Comment. lib. 6. SAMMS's Hiſtory of *Britain*, Book I. Chap. 4.

received by Tradition. CÆSAR obferves, *that They had a* Head *or* CHIEF, *who had fovereign Power :* This Prefident *exercifed a Sort of Excommunication, attended with dreadful* Penalties, *upon fuch as either divulged or profaned their Myſteries.*

Thus, with reafonable Allowance for Diſtance of Time, Place, and other inter-mediate Accidents, the preceding *Collections* diſcover ſomething, at leaſt, like *Ma-ſonry,* if the *Diſſection* contains any ſuch Thing.

CHAP. IV. WHatever *Reflections* may attend the few Remarks that follow in this Chapter, ariſing either from an Overflow of Wit, or ill Nature, I ſhall be unconcern'd, and leave them wholly to the Mercy of the ſerious Reader ; only deſiring them to remember that no more ought in any Caſe to be expected, than what the Nature of it will reaſonably admit. I own freely, I received a great Pleaſure in collecting, and was frequently ſurpriz'd at the Diſco-veries that muſt evidently occur to an obſerving Eye.

The Conformity between the *Rites* and Principles of *Maſonry* (if the *Diſſection* be true) and the many Cuſtoms and *Ceremonies* of the *Antients,* muſt give Delight to a Perſon of any Taſte and Curioſity ; to find any Remains of *Antique* Uſage and Learning preſerved by a *Society* for many Ages, without Books or *Writing,* by *oral Tradition* only.

I. The *Number* THREE is frequently mention'd in the *Diſſection*; and I find that the Antients, both *Greeks* and *Latins,* profeſſed a great Veneration for that | *Idyll.* B. | Number. THEOCRITUS thus introduces a Perſon who dealt in ſecret Arts.

ʼΕς τρὶς ἀποσπένδω κ̀ τρὶς τάδε πότνια Θωρῶ !

Thrice, Thrice I pour, and thrice repeat my Charms !

| *Ovid.* Metam. lib. 7. | Verbaque Ter dixit : *Thrice he repeats the Words.*

| *Virg.* Ecl. 8. | Necte tribus Nodis ternos, Amarille, colores. *Three Colours in Three Knots unite.*

Whether this Fancy owes its Original to the *Number* THREE, becauſe containing a *Beginning, Middle* and *End,* it ſeems to ſignify *All* Things in the World ; or whether to the Eſteem the *Pythagoreans* and other *Philoſophers* had for it, on Ac-count of their TRIAD or TRINITY ; or laſtly (to mention no more Opinions) to its Aptneſs to ſignify the *Power of all the Gods,* who were divided into *Three Claſſes, Celeſtial, Terreſtrial* and *Infernal*; I ſhall leave to be determin'd by Others.

The *Gods* had a particular Eſteem for this Number, as *Virgil* aſſerts.

| Eclog. 8. | Numero Deus impare gaudet. *Unequal Numbers pleaſe the Gods.*

We find THREE *fatal Siſters,* THREE *Furies,* THREE *Names* and Appearances of *Diana.* Tria Virginis Ora Dianæ, *Three different Forms does chaſte Diana bear.* Virgil. Æneid. lib. 4.

The

The Sons of *Saturn*, among whom the Empire of the World was divided, were THREE : And for the same Reason we read of JUPITER's *Fulmen Trifidum* or *Three-forked Thunderbolt* ; and of NEPTUNE's *Trident*, with several other Tokens of the Veneration they bore to this particular Number.

II. A particular Ceremony belonging to the *Oath* (as declared by the *Diſſector*) bears a near Relation to a Form of Swearing among the *Antients* mention'd by a learned Author *The Perſon who took the Oath, was to be* upon his bare Knees *with a naked Sword pointed to his Throat, invoking the* Sun, Moon *and* Stars *to be Witneſſes to the Truth of what he ſwore.* | Alexander ab Alexandro Lib. V cap. 10.

III. A Part of the MASONS *Catechiſm* has given Occaſion to a great deal of idle Mirth and Ridicule, as the moſt trifling and deſpicable Sort of Jargon that Men of common Senſe ever ſubmitted to. The *Bone Box* and the *Tow Line* has given wonderful Diverſion: I think there are ſome Verſes in the laſt Chapter of the Book of *Eccleſiaſtes*, which in ſome Manner reſemble this Form of Expreſſion: I ſhall tranſcribe them with the Opinion of the Learned upon them, without making any particular Application, *viz.*

In the Day when the Keepers of the Houſe ſhall tremble ; and the Grinders ceaſe, becauſe they are few ; and thoſe that look out at the Windows be darkned ; and the Doors ſhall be ſhut in the Streets ; when the Sound of the Grinding is low ; and he ſhall riſe up at the Voice of the Bird ; and all the Daughters of Muſick ſhall be brought low : Or ever the Silver Cord be looſed ; or the Golden Bowl be broken ; or the Pitcher be broken at the Fountain ; or the Wheel broken at the Ciſtern! | Eccl. xii. ver. 3, 4, 6.

The Expoſitors upon theſe Verſes are almoſt unanimous in their Opinion, that they ought to be thus explain'd, *viz.* The 𝕶eepers of the Houſe are the *Shoulders*, *Arms* and *Hands* of an human Body ; the 𝕲rinders are the *Teeth* ; thoſe that look out at the 𝖂indows are the two *Eyes* ; the 𝕯oors are the *Lips* ; the 𝕾treets are the *Mouth* ; the 𝕾ound of the 𝕲rinding is the *Noiſe* of the *Voice* ; the 𝖁oice of the 𝕭ird is the *Crowing* of the *Cock* ; the 𝕯aughters of 𝕸uſick are the *two Ears* ; the 𝕾ilver 𝕮ord is the *String* of the *Tongue* ; the 𝕲olden 𝕭owl is the *Pia Mater* ; the 𝕻itcher at the 𝕱ountain is the *Heart*, the *Fountain of Life* ; the 𝖂heel is the *Great Artery* ; and the 𝕮iſtern is the *Left Ventricle* of the *Heart!* | Biſh. *Patrick,* Doctor *Smith,* *Forſterus,* *Melanchton,* in locum, &c.

IV. There could not poſſibly have been deviſed a more ſignificant Token of Love, Friendſhip, Integrity and Honeſty, than the *Joining* of the RIGHT HANDS, a Ceremony made uſe of by all civilized Nations, as a Token of a faithful and true Heart. FIDES or *Fidelity* was a *Deity* among the Antients, of which a learned Writer has given us this Deſcription, *viz. The proper Reſidence of* Faith *or* Fidelity *was thought to be* | Chartarius in lib. ut ſupra. *in the* Right Hand, *and therefore this* Deity *ſometimes was repreſented by* Two Right Hands Joined together ; *ſometimes by* two little Images ſhaking each the Other's Right Hand ; ſo that the *Right Hand was by the Antients eſteemed as a* Thing Sacred. And agreeable to this are thoſe Expreſſions in *Virgil*, Æneid. IV.

E t

En Dextra Fidesque ! as if shaking by the Right Hand was an inseparable Token of an honest Heart. And Æneid. I.

——————— cur Dextræ jungere Dextram
Non datur, & veras audire & reddere Voces ?

that is, *Why should we not join* Right Hand *to* Right Hand, *and bear and speak the Truth.*

Vol. I. pag. 251.| *In all Contracts and Agreements* (says Archbishop POTTER, in his Antiquities of Greece) *it was usual to take Each Other by the* Right Hand, *That being the Manner of plighting Faith.* And this was done either out of Respect to the Number *Ten,* as some say, there being *Ten Fingers* on the Two Hands; or because such a Conjunction was a Token of *Amity* and *Concord*; whence at all friendly Meetings they join Hands, as a Sign of the *Union* of their Souls.

It was one of the Cautions of PYTHAGORAS to his Disciples, *Take heed to whom*
In Vit. Pythagr.| *you offer your* Right Hand *!* which is thus explain'd by **Jamblichus.** *Take no One by the* Right Hand *but the Initiated, that is, in the Mystical Form; for the* Vulgar *and the* Profane *are altogether unworthy of the* Mystery *!*

V. The *Dissector* frequently taking Notice of the Number SEVEN, I instantly
Pignorius in Mens.| recurred to the old *Egyptians*, who held the Number *Seven* to be *Sacred*; more especially they believ'd that whilst their Feast of *Seven Days* lasted, the *Crocodiles* lost their inbred Cruelty : And **Leo Afer,** in his Description of *Africa*, Lib. VIII. says, *that even in his Time, the Custom of Feasting* Seven Days *and* Nights, *was still used for the happy Overflowing of the* Nile. The *Greeks* and *Latins* professed the same Regard for that Number, which might be proved by many Examples.

VI. The Accident, by which the Body of *Master* HIRAM was found after his Death, seems to allude, in some Circumstances, to a beautiful Passage in the 6th Book of *Virgil's* Æneids. **Anchises** had been dead for some Time ; and ÆNEAS his Son professed so much Duty to his departed Father, that he consulted with the *Cumæan Sibyl*, whether it were possible for him to descend into the *Shades below,* in Order to speak with him. The Prophetess encouraged him to go; but told him he could not succeed, unless he went into a certain Place and pluck'd a *golden Bough* or *Shrub*, which he should carry in his Hand, and by that means obtain Directions where he should find his Father. The Words are well translated by *Dryden*, viz.

——————— *In the neighbouring Grove*
There stands a Tree; the Queen of Stygian JOVE
Claims it her own : Thick Woods and gloomy Night
Conceal the happy Plant from mortal Sight !
One Bough it bears, but wondrous to behold,
The ductile Rind and Leaves of Radiant Gold;

This

This from the vulgar Branches muſt be torn,
And to fair PROSERPINE *the Preſent born,*
Ere Leave be given to tempt the nether Skies;
The firſt thus rent, a ſecond will ariſe,
And the ſame Metal *the ſame Room ſupplies.*
The willing Metal *will obey thy Hand,*
Following with Eaſe.——

ANCHISES, the great Preſerver of the *Trojan Name*, could not have been diſcover'd but by the Help of a *Bough*, which was pluck'd with great Eaſe from the *Tree*; nor, it ſeems, could HIRAM, the *Grand 𝕸aſter* of MASONRY, have been found but by the Direction of a *Shrub*, which (ſays the *Diſſector*) *came eaſily up.* The principal Cauſe of ÆNEAS's Deſcent into the *Shades*, was to enquire of his Father the *Secrets* of the *Fates*, which ſhould ſometime be fulfill'd among his Poſterity: The Occaſion of the *Brethrens* ſearching ſo diligently for their *Maſter* was, it ſeems, to receive from him the *ſecret Word* of *Maſonry*, which ſhould be deliver'd down to their *Fraternity* in After-Ages. This remarkable Verſe follows,

> Præterea jacet exanimum tibi corpus amici,
> Heu neſcis!
> *The Body of your Friend lies near you dead,*
> *Alas, you know not how!*—————— This was

MISENUS, that was murder'd and buried *Monte ſub Aerio, under an high Hill*; as (ſays the *Diſſector*) Maſter HIRAM was.

But there is another Story in *Virgil*, that ſtands in a nearer Relation to the Caſe of HIRAM, and the Accident by which he is ſaid to have been diſcover'd; which is this: PRIAMUS King of *Troy*, in the Beginning of the *Trojan* War, committed his Son 𝕻olydorus to the Care of *Polymneſtor* King of *Thrace*, and ſent with him a great Sum of Money: But after *Troy* was taken, the *Thracian*, for the Sake of the Money, kill'd the young Prince and privately buried him; ÆNEAS coming into that Country, and accidentally plucking up a *Shrub* that was near him on the *Side* of an *Hill*, diſcover'd the murder'd Body of 𝕻olydorus, *Æneid.* III. By *Dryden.*

> *Not far, a riſing* Hillock *ſtood in View,*
> *Sharp Myrtles on the Sides and Cornels grew;*
> *There while I went to crop the Sylvan Scenes,*
> *And ſhade our Altar with the leafy Greens,*
> *I pull'd a* Plant: *With Horror I relate*
> *A Prodigy ſo ſtrange and full of Fate!*
> *Scarce dare I tell the Sequel! From the Womb*
> *Of wounded Earth, and Caverns of the Tomb,*
> *A Groan, as of a troubled Ghoſt, renew'd*
> *My Fright; and then theſe dreadful Words enſued:*
> *Why doſt thou thus my buried Body rend?*
> *O ſpare the Corps of thy unhappy Friend!*

The Agreement between theſe two Relations is ſo exact, that there wants no further Illuſtration.

VII. We are told that a *Sprig* of *Caffia* was placed by the *Brethren* at the Head of HIRAM's *Grave*; which refers to an old Cuftom of thofe *Eaftern* Countries of Embalming the Dead, in which Operation CASSIA was always ufed, efpecially in preparing the *Head* and drying up the *Brain*; as *Herodotus* more particularly explains. The Sweet-Wood, Perfumes and Flowers, ufed about the *Graves* of the *Dead*, occur fo frequently in the old *Poets*, that it would he tedious to mention them. *Ovid* thus defcribes the Death of the P H O E N I X.

Metam. lib. 15.

> Upon a fhady Tree fhe takes her Reft,
> And on the higheft Bough her funeral Neft
> Her Beak and Talons build; then ftrews thereon
> Balm, CASSIA, Spikenard, Myrrh and Cinamon:
> Laft on the fragrant Pile herfelf fhe lays,
> And in confuming Odours ends her Days!

Brother EUCLID's *Letter* to the *Author* Againft unjuft Cavils.

BRother ANDERSON, after Thanks for printing the clever DEFENCE, by the Advice of our Brethren, I fend you this Epiftle, to anfwer fome lying Cavils. But firft we would acknowledge, that

Indeed, the *Free Mafons* are much obliged to the generous Intention of the unbiafs'd *Author* of the above *Defence*: Tho' had he been a *Free-Mafon*, he had in Time perceived many valuable Things fuitable to his extended Views of Antiquity, which could not come to the *Diffector's* Knowledge; for that They are not intrufted with any Brothers till after due Probation: And therefore fome think the ingenious DEFENDER has fpent too much fine Learning and Reafoning upon the foolifh *Diffection*, that is juftly defpifed by the Fraternity, as much as the other pretended Difcoveries of their Secrets in publick *News-Papers* and *Pafquils*, all of a Sort; for all of 'em put together don't difcover the profound and fublime Things of *old Mafonry*; nor can any Man, not a Mafon, make ufe of thofe incoherent Smatterings (interfpers'd with ignorant Nonfenfe and grofs Falfities) among bright Brothers, for any Purpofe but to he laught at; our *Communications* being of a quite different Sort. Next, it is well known,

That the Antiquity and Decorum of our Worfhipful *Fraternity* have been envied by fome, who, very lately, have coalefced into Societies, in Imitation of the *Free-Mafons*, and fome in Oppofition to them, tho' in vain; as the Gozmagons, who foon difappear'd, and Others are going.

But

But tho' we envy not the Prosperity of any Society, nor meddle with their Transactions and Characters, we have not met with such fair Treatment from Others; nay, even Those that never had an Opportunity of obtaining any certain Knowledge of us, have run implicitly with the Cry, and without Fear or Wit, have vented their Spleen in accusing and condemning us unheard, untry'd; while we, innocent and secure within, laugh only at their gross Ignorance and impotent Malice.

Have not People in former Ages, as well as now, alledged that the *Free Masons* in their *Lodges* raise the Devil in a *Circle*, and when they have done with him, that they lay him again with a *Noise* or a *Hush* as they please?

How have some diverted themselves with the wild Story of *an old Woman between the Rounds of a Ladder?* Only they should allow the *Free-Masons* to laugh too in their Turn.

Others will swear to the Cook's *red hot Iron* or Salamander, *for making the Indelible Character on the new made Mason, in order to give him the Faculty of Taciturnity!* Sure such Blades will beware of coming through the Fingers of the *Free-Masons.*

Some have basely calumniated the *Fraternity* as the *Enemies* of the FAIR SEX, in Terms not fit to be rehears'd, and unworthy of a Reply: But tho' in *Lodge Hours* Masons don't allow of *Womens* Company (like many other Societies of Men) yet they make as good Husbands as any other Men, according to their laudable Charges.

Others wonder *at their admitting Men of all Professions, Religions and Denominations:* But they don't consider that *Masons* are true Noachidæ, and require no other Denominations, (all other Distinctions being of Yesterday) if the new Brother is a *good Man and True:* For Those of 'em that don't study *Architecture,* are often capable of encouraging the *Craft,* and help to support the poor decay'd Brethren.

Have not some rigid People been displeas'd *at the Admission of some worthless Men?* But if the *Free-Masons* are sometimes deceiv'd about Mens Characters, they are not the only Persons so deceiv'd: Yet when a Brother is obnoxious to Censure, if they don't expel him, they endeavour to reform him. However, the *Grand Lodge* has taken due Care of That.

Others complain *that the* Masons *continue too long in the Lodge, spending their Money to the Hurt of their Families, and come home too late, nay sometimes intoxicated with Liquor!* But they have no Occasion to drink much in *Lodge Hours,* which are not long; and when the *Lodge* is closed (always in good Time) any Brother may go home when he pleases: So that if any stay longer and get intoxicated, it is at their own Cost, not as *Masons,* but as other imprudent Men may do; for which the *Fraternity* is not accountable: And the Expence of a *Lodge* is not so great as That of many a private *Club.*

Some observing *that* Masons *are not more religious, nor more knowing, than other Men, are astonish'd at what they can be conversant about in Lodge Hours!* But tho' a *Lodge* is not a School of Divinity, the Brethren are taught the great Lessons of their *old* Religion, *Morality, Humanity* and *Friendship,* to abhor *Persecution,* and to be *peaceable* Subjects under the Civil Government wherever they reside: And as for *other Knowledge,* they claim as large a Share of it, as other Men in their Situation. G g 2 Indeed

Indeed, the *antient Lodges* were fo many Schools or *Academies* for teaching and improving the *Arts* of *Defigning*, efpecially *Architecture*; and the prefent *Lodges* are often employ'd that Way in *Lodge-Hours*, or elfe in other agreeable Converfation, tho' without Politicks or Party Caufes; and none of them are ill employ'd, have no Tranfactions unworthy of an honeft Man or a Gentleman, no perfonal Piques, no Quarrels, no Curfing and Swearing, no cruel Mockings, no obfcene Talk, nor ill Manners: For the *noble* and eminent *Brethren* are affable to the *Meaneft*; and *Thefe* are duly refpectful to their Betters in *Harmony* and *Proportion*; and tho' on the *Level*, yet always within *Compafs*, and according to the *Square* and *Plumb*.

Nor can it be denied, that a *Fraternity* fo ftrongly cemented, is more eligible and fafe than moft Others; efpecially that there is no Fear of betraying Converfation: and that fince *Mafonry* has been fo much countenanced by Great Men, there have been more fine *Architects* and more expert *Fellow Crafts* in *Britain*, than, perhaps, in all *Europe* befides

This appears by the ftately and regular *Buildings* throughout thefe *Iflands*, from the firft Days of the *Great* 𝕴𝖓𝖎𝖌𝖔 𝕵𝖔𝖓𝖊𝖘, the *Englifh* PALLADIO; nor is the fine Tafte abated in this prefent Reign of *King* GEORGE II. but is rather improved; witnefs the curious Houfe for the *Bank* of *England*, the *South-Sea* Houfe, the *Front* of the *Eaft-India* Houfe, the *Lord Talbot's* fine Houfe in *Lincoln's-Inn-Fields*, the many ftately *Fabricks* in the Parifhes of St. *George Hanover* and *St. Mary la Bonne*, and many more in and about *London* and *Weftminfter*, and other Towns and Cities, befides Country-Seats, raifed in the *good old* AUGUSTAN 𝕾𝖙𝖎𝖑𝖊; and fome alfo defign'd only, or begun, as the *Lord* MAYOR of *London's* New Palace, the admirable New *Bridge* at *Weftminfter* crofs the *Thames*, &c. all which difcover the *Englifh* MASONS *Grand Defign* of rivalling fair *Italy* in *Architecture*, even thofe eminent *Revivers* of the AUGUSTAN 𝕾𝖙𝖎𝖑𝖊 mentioned Part I. Chap. VII.

May the ROYAL ART go on and profper, and fpread itfelf from *Pole* to *Pole*, from *Eaft* to *Weft*! As it certainly now does in all polite Nations, in fpite of the Ignorant and Malicious. I am

From our *old Lodge*, the HORN, in New *Palace-Yard*, *Weftminfter*, this 2d *Thurfday*, or 9th *Nov.* in the *Vulgar* Year of MASONRY 5738.

Your true and faithful Brother

𝕰𝖚𝖈𝖑𝖎𝖉.

While the BOOK was in the PRESS,

The *Author* was kindly encouraged by the few following *Brethren* and *Lodges*, viz.

Marquis of CAERNARVON the Right Worſhipful GRAND MASTER.

—DUke of MONTAGU,
   Duke of RICHMOND,
—*Earl* of INCHIQUIN, } Former
—*Earl* of LOUDOUN, } Grand
—*Earl* of DARNLEY, } Maſters
—GEORGE PAYNE, Eſq;
—*Rev. Dr.* DESAGULIERS,
—MARTIN FOLKES, Eſq;
—WILL. COWPER, Eſq; } Former
—NATHANIEL BLAKER- } Deputy
   BY, Eſq; } Grand
—THOMAS BATSON, Coun } Maſters.
   ſellor at Law,
—Sir ROBERT LAWLEY, }
   Baronet,
—WILLIAM GRÆME, } Former
   M. D. } Grand
—MARTIN CLARE, A. M. } Wardens
   and F. R. S.
—Mr. JACOB LAMBALL,
   Carpenter.
—Hon. Charles Stanhope, Eſq;
—Hon Edward Montagu, Eſq;
—Capt. Robert Maynard.
—Sir Hugh Mac Brite, Baronet, of
   the antient Lodge of *Killwining.*
—Sir John de Lauge, *Maſter* of the
   Fountain-Lodge on *Snow-hill.*
—*Daniel Hopkins,*
—*Humphrey Primate,* }
—*Richard Bowyer,* } Eſqs;
—*Benjamin Taylor,*
—Mr. *Thomas Deſaguliers.*
—Mr. *William Goſton.*
—Mr. *John Glaſs.*
—Mr. *John Banks.*
—Capt. *Thomas Burgeſs.*
—Mr. *Samuel Greer*
—Mr. *Pat. Ramſay,* Chirurgeon.

—JOHN WARD, Eſq; D. Grand Maſter.
—Lord GEORGE GRAHAM, } *Grand*
—*Capt* AND. ROBINSON, } Wardens.
—Mr. *John Revis* the Secretary.
—Edward Hody, M. D.
—Richard Rawlinſon, L. L. D.
—James Ruck Junior,
—Fotherby Baker,
—Samuel Barrington, } Eſqs;
—John Jeſſe,
—Thomas Jeffreys,
—Mr. Benjamin Gaſcoyn, Wine-
   Merchant.
—Mr Henry Prude, Apothecary.
—Mr. George Monkman, Attorney.
—Mr. Nath. Adams, Optician.
—Mr. James Coſtin, Attorney.
—Mr. Samuel Lowman, Merchant,
   a preſent *Steward.*
—Mr. George Garret.
—Mr. *Lewis Philip Boitard.*
—Mr. *Charles Hoar,* }
—Mr. *William Renwick,* } Attornies.
—Mr. *John Maddock,*
—Mr. *William Dodd,* } Vintners.
—Mr. *Richard Skikelthorp,*
—Mr. *James Aſtley,* Punch-maker.
—Mr. *Triſtram Chambers,* Upholder.
—Mr. *Daniel Delander,* Watch-maker.
—Mr. *John Baker,* Carpenter
—Mr. *Eraſmus King,* Mathematician.
—Mr. *John Pine* the Engraver.
—Mr. *J. Siſſon* the Inſtrument-maker.
—Mr. *William Stephenſon* the Glover.
—Mr. *Thomas Aris* the Printer.
—Meſſieurs *Ward* and *Chandler,* Book-
   ſellers, at *London, York* and *Scarborough.*

Former Stewards.

LODGES.

LODGES.

THE Steward's *Lodge.*
KING's-Arms in the *Strand.*
--Forrest's *Coffee-house.*
---Ditto the Old Lodge.
--Fountain on *Snow-hill.*
---Swan and Rummer in *Finch-Lane.*
--Queen's-Head in Great *Queen-street.*
---Mount in *Grovenor-street.*
--Mourning-Bush near *Aldersgate.*
---King's-Arms in New *Bond-street.*
--King's Arms in *Wild street.*
---King's-Arms in *Piccadilly.*
--Fountain near the *Royal-Exchange.*
--Gordon's *Punch-house* in the *Strand*
--La Guerre in St. *Martin's Lane.*
--Hoop and Gryffin in *Leadenhall-street.*
--Berry's *Coffee house* in *Bridges-street.*
---Key and Garter in *Pall-Mall.*
--Royal Standard in *Leicester-Square.*
---Black Posts in *Maiden-Lane.*
--Vineyard in St. *James's Park.*
---Sun in *Holbourn.*
---Anchor and Crown near the *Seven-Dials.*
---Gun in *Jermyn-street.*
---Gun at *Billingsgate.*
---Globe in *Fleet-street.*
---Globe in *Old Jewry.*
---Bacchus in *Bloomsbury-Market.*

---Turk's Head in *Greek-street, Soho.*
---Bell and Dragon near *Golden-Square.*
---Bell in *Nicholas-Lane.*
---Half-Moon in *Cheapside.*
---Queen's-Head in *Knaves-Acre.*
---Shakespear's-Head in *Marleborough-street.*
---Horn in New *Palace Yard.*
---Crown in *Fleet-Market.*
--Crown in *Smithfield.*
---Three Tons on *Snow-hill.*
--Three Tons in *Smithfield.*
---Three Tons in *Newgate-street.*
---Braund's-Head in New *Bond-street.*
--Checquer at *Charing-Cross.*
---Antwerp near the *Royal-Exchange.*
---Star and Garter in St. *Martin's-Lane.*
---Bear in the *Strand.*
---Fountain in *Katharine-street.*
---Castle in *Drury-Lane.*
---Cameron's *Coffee-house* in *Berry-street*
---Katharine-Wheel in *Windmill-street.*
---Rainbow in *York-Buildings.*
--Daniel's *Coffee-house, Temple-Bar.*
--Queen's-Head in the *Old-Bailey.*
--King's-Head in St. *John's street.*
--Sun in *Fleet-street.*
--Sun in St. *Paul's Church-Yard.*
---Rummer in *Queen-street, Cheapside.*

N. B. An Impression in *Folio* of the *Grand Master's* Sword of *State* (formerly the *Sword* of Gustavus Adolphus King of *Sweden,* and next of Bernard Duke of *Sax-Weimar,* with their Names on the *Blade*) which was presented to the *Fraternity* by our former *Grand Master* THOMAS HOWARD *Duke of* Norfolk, richly adorn'd at the *Hilt* with Corinthian *Columns* of Massy Silver, and on the *Scabbard* with the *Arms* of Norfolk in Silver, the *Masons Arms,* and some Hieroglyphics, &c. (perform'd by Brother *George Moody* the *Sword-bearer*) all explain'd, illuminated and embellish'd, is to be sold by Brother John Pine the Engraver, in *Old Bond-street* near *Piccadilly.* Where also may be had

The small *Engraven List* of the *Lodges,* renew'd annually with their Removals.

F I N I S.

Corrigenda.

Page Line
8   32. for 𝕰𝕽𝕬𝕹𝕯 read 𝕲𝕽𝕬𝕹𝕯.
16   22. for A. C. read B. C.
25   10. After the Word *Cubits*, make
         a Comma.
27. In the Margin, Line 7. for *thn* read *the*
29   21. for *Treos* read *Theos*.
36   29. for Wars *ended* read Wars *began*.
43   28. for CORACALLA read CARA-
         CALLA.
46   9. for *Cousuls* read *Consuls*.
Ditto 18. *After* MAURICUS read *who*
         murder'd.
48   22. for *in St. Miniate* read *of St.*
         Miniate.
58   26. Instead of *did not at All depart*
         read *did not All depart*.
59   8, for *ruind* read *ruin'd*.
61   30. for ETHELBERT read KENRED.
75   17. for 1445. read 1443.
77   4. After CADWAN the First, delete
         the Comma.
85. In the 2d Column of the Margin
         at the End, after the Word
         Interview, instead of a
         Punctum make a *Comma*.
108 16. for *mostly richly* read *most richly*.

110 2. for Capt. *Joseph Elliot*
         Mr. *Jacob Lamball*,
      read Mr. *Jacob Lamball* ⎱
         Capt. *Joseph Elliot*. ⎰
118. In the Margin, Line 1. for 1723
         read 1724.
125. In the Margin, instead of
      5. Mr. *William Hopkins*, read
      5. Mr. *William Serjeant*.
and for 7. Mr. *Gerard Hatley*, read
      7. *James Chambers*, Esq;
132. 3. for CAERMARTHEN read
         CAERNARVON.
Ditto in the Margin, for *Gentlemen* read
         Esquires.
134. In the Margin read,
      9. *Robert Wright*, Esq;
137. In the Margin read,
      9. Mr. *Peter Leige*.
139 in the Margin read
      9. *Henry Higden*, Esq;
      12. *Harry Leigh* Esq;
200. The Reference at the End, instead of
      5. *They*, read 4. *But*.
Accurate Reader, pray correct these
with your Pen, or any others you find.

Just Published,

By CÆSAR WARD and RICHARD CHANDLER, Bookfellers at the *Ship* juft without *Temple-Bar, London*, and fold alfo at their Shops in *Coney-Street* YORK and at SCARBOROUGH SPAW,

I. A General Dictionary Hiftorical and Critical, including That of the celebrated MONS. BAYLE. The whole containing the Hiftory of the moft *Illuftrious Perfons* of all Ages and Nations. In Ten Volumes Folio. Price 15 *l*

II. A New Abridgment and Critical Review of all the State Trials and Proceedings for *High-Treafon*, from the Reign of King *Richard* II. to the Year 1737. By Mr. *Salmon*. In One Vol. Folio. Price 1 *l*. 10 *s*.

III. The VOCAL MISCELLANY, a Collection of above 800 *celebrated Songs*, many of which were *never* before printed, with the Names of the Tunes prefixed to each Song. In Two Pocket Volumes. Price 6 *s*.
N. B. *Either Volume may be had alone.* Price 3 *s*.

IV. The *Beauties of the Englifh Stage*. Confifting of all the celebrated *Paffages, Soliloquies, Similies, Defcriptions*, and other Poetical Beauties in the ENGLISH PLAYS Ancient and Modern, continued down to the prefent Time. Digefted under proper Heads in Alphabetical Order, with the Names of the Plays and their feveral Authors referr'd to. In Two Pocket Volumes. Price 5 *s*.

Puriffima mella ftipant. VIRG.

V. *Les Amufemens de Spa*; or, the Gallantries of the SPAW in GERMANY. Intermix'd with many entertaining Hiftories of the *principal Perfons*, reforting thither. Adorn'd with thirteen curious Copper Plates of the Fountains, Walks, Avenues, &*c*. In Two Pocket Volumes. Price 6 *s*. with Cuts, or 5 *s*. without.

VI. MAGNA BRITANNIA ANTIQUA ET NOVA; or, a New Survey of *Great Britain*; wherein, to the Topographical Account given by Mr. *Cambden*, and the late Editors of his *Britannia*, is added a *more large Hiftory*, not only of the *Cities, Boroughs, Towns* and *Parifhes* mentioned by them, but alfo of many other Places of Note and Antiquity fince difcovered; with the Pedigrees of *all our Noble Families* and Gentry, &*c*. In 6 Vols. Quarto, compleat. Price 3 *l*.

Of the faid WARD *and* CHANDLER *Bookfellers, as above-mentioned, Gentlemen may be fupply'd with great Variety of Books in all Sciences at the loweft Prices. Who alfo give* Ready Money *for any Library or Parcel of Books.*

CPSIA information can be obtained at www.ICGtesting.com
Printed in the USA
BVOW06s1325110215

387314BV00002B/19/P